Contemporary British Musicals

Contemporary British Musicals

'Out of the Darkness'

Edited by
Clare Chandler and Gus Gowland

methuen | drama
LONDON • NEW YORK • OXFORD • NEW DELHI • SYDNEY

METHUEN DRAMA
Bloomsbury Publishing Plc
50 Bedford Square, London, WC1B 3DP, UK
1385 Broadway, New York, NY 10018, USA
29 Earlsfort Terrace, Dublin 2, Ireland

BLOOMSBURY, METHUEN DRAMA and the Methuen Drama logo are trademarks of Bloomsbury Publishing Plc

First published in Great Britain 2024

Copyright © Clare Chandler, Gus Gowland, and Contributors, 2024

The authors have asserted their right under the Copyright, Designs and Patents Act, 1988, to be identified as authors of this work.

Cover design and illustration by Holly Capper

All rights reserved. No part of this publication may be reproduced or transmitted in any form or by any means, electronic or mechanical, including photocopying, recording, or any information storage or retrieval system, without prior permission in writing from the publishers.

Bloomsbury Publishing Plc does not have any control over, or responsibility for, any third-party websites referred to or in this book. All internet addresses given in this book were correct at the time of going to press. The author and publisher regret any inconvenience caused if addresses have changed or sites have ceased to exist, but can accept no responsibility for any such changes.

A catalogue record for this book is available from the British Library.

A catalog record for this book is available from the Library of Congress.

ISBN: HB: 978-1-3502-6805-0
PB: 978-1-3502-6803-6
ePDF: 978-1-3502-6804-3
eBook: 978-1-3502-6807-4

Typeset by Deanta Global Publishing Services, Chennai, India
Printed and bound in Great Britain

To find out more about our authors and books visit www.bloomsbury.com and sign up for our newsletters.

Contents

List of Illustrations — vii
List of Contributors — viii
Foreword *Kate Marlais* — xi
Foreword *Tim Sutton* — xiii

Introduction — 1

1 Bros abroad: Masculinities in transition and homosocial bonding in Dougal Irvine's *Departure Lounge* Broderick Chow — 13

   Dougal Irvine interview — 29

2 'The smell of rebellion' and 'The stench of revolt': The carnivalesque dramaturgy of *Matilda the Musical* from page to stage Stephanie Lim — 33

   Ellen Kane interview — 49

3 'Glitching' of gender and temporality in *Lift* (2013) Jozey Grae — 53

   Perfect Pitch interview – Andy Barnes, Wendy Barnes — 63

4 *Bend It Like Beckham: The Musical:* Embodying British identities Kelsey Blair — 67

   Preeya Kalidas interview — 83

5 *Flowers for Mrs Harris:* Covid-19, women's work and the musical's 'some kind of bliss' Sarah K. Whitfield — 87

   Rachel Wagstaff and Richard Taylor interview — 99

6 'You're him and he is you': Identification with the disabled 'freak' in *The Grinning Man* (2016) Ellen Armstrong — 105

   Toby Olié interview — 121

7 'Something precious you don't simply give away': Intersections of love and queer expression in *Everybody's Talking About Jamie* Hannah Thuraisingam Robbins — 125

   Rob Hastie interview — 137

8 'One of a kind, no category': Coding race, gender and excess in *SIX*
   Aviva Neff, PhD — 141

   Josh Bird interview — 154

9 *My ~~Left~~/Right Foot the Musical* *Judith Drake* — 157

   Noisemaker interview — 172

10 'As if gathered in a verbatim fashion': The (mis)use of documentary markers in Chris Bush and Matt Winkworth's *The Assassination of Katie Hopkins* (2018) *Cyrielle Garson* — 177

   Lucy Osborne interview: Designer *The Assassination of Katie Hopkins* — 190

Conclusion — 195

Index — 199

Illustrations

1	*Standing at the Sky's Edge*	6
2	Original cast of *Departure Lounge*	15
3	*The Grinning Man*, 2017 revival cast	111
4	*My ~~Left~~/Right Foot the Musical* (2019), National Theatre Scotland	161
5	*Mayflies*	198

Contributors

Clare Chandler is a musical theatre practitioner and researcher. As a lecturer, Clare has worked at the Liverpool Institute for Performing Arts, Edge Hill University and the University of Wolverhampton. She is currently a senior lecturer in Musical Theatre at the University of Lincoln, UK. Clare's research interests include the impact of technology on the development of contemporary musical theatre, feminism and musical theatre, and pedagogical practice and performer training. She directed the national premiere of *Angry Birds the Musical* by Dougal Irvine in 2018. Clare is currently studying for a PhD at Lancaster University.

Favourite British musical: Changes weekly, currently *Operation Mincemeat*

Favourite British musical song: 'Change of Plan' *A Mother's Song*

Gus Gowland is an award-winning musical theatre writer and composer (*Mayflies* – York Theatre Royal, *Pieces of String* – The Stage Debut Award 2018) and is also Post-Graduate Musical Theatre Co-ordinator at Leeds Conservatoire. Gus has previously worked at the University of Lincoln, University Centre Shrewsbury and University of Wolverhampton, all UK, where he obtained his PhD in 2020. His research interests include LGBTQ+ representation in musical theatre and contemporary British musical theatre.

Favourite British musical: *Les Misérables*

Favourite British musical song: 'When I Grow Up' *Matilda*

Broderick D. V. Chow is Reader and Director of Learning, Teaching and Inclusion at the Royal Central School of Speech and Drama. His research investigates sport, fitness, physical culture in relation to masculinities. He is the author of the forthcoming book *Muscle Works*.

Favourite British musical: *London Road*

Favourite British musical song: 'Gethsemane' *Jesus Christ Superstar*

Stephanie Lim is a scholar, educator and dramaturg. She holds her PhD in Drama and Theatre from the University of California, Irvine, and master's in English from California State University, Northridge. Her research interests include musical theatre, Deaf and disability studies, and American popular culture.

Favourite British musical: *Chess*

Favourite British musical song: 'Out of the Darkness (A Place Where We Belong)' *Everybody's Talking About Jamie*

Jozey Grae is a performer and writer with a passion for blowing up the gender binary. As an artist, they have performed, written and composed for children's theatre and for their own theatre company (Flickbook Theatre). Jozey has served as a freelance advisor on gender inclusivity for certain events and currently performs regularly at a popular theme park, while also teaching on contemporary musicals at the University of Wolverhampton.

Favourite British musical: *SIX*

Favourite British musical song: 'The Sex Talk' *The Phase*

Kelsey Blair is Assistant Professor in the Department of English at Concordia University in Montreal, Canada. She is a theatre, performance and cultural studies scholar, a university teacher, an author and a freelance writer.

Favourite British musical: *Les Misérables*

Favourite British musical song: 'Don't Cry for Me Argentina' *Evita*

Sarah K. Whitfield is a dramaturg, music and theatre researcher and academic. She has worked as dramaturg on a variety of musicals and queer theatre. She uses digital humanities research to challenge established narratives, focusing on uncovering the work that under-represented and minoritized figures do and have done in the arts.

Favourite British musical: *The Diary of a Nobody*

Favourite British musical song: 'Go Slow Johnny' Kneehigh's production of *Brief Encounter*.

Ellen Armstrong is a theatre PhD candidate at the Guildford School of Acting. She has published and presented on accessible theatre pedagogy, disability representation in theatre, and British Sign Language interpreted performance, with these areas informing her work as a dramaturg and accessibility consultant on new musical theatre writing and production.

Favourite British musical: *That Day We Sang*

Favourite British musical song: 'Same But Different' *Islander*

Hannah Thuraisingam Robbins is Associate Professor of Popular Music and Director of Black Studies at the University of Nottingham. They specialize in representations of race, gender, and queerness in the British and American musical.

Favourite British musical: *The Phantom of the Opera* or *SIX*

Favourite British musical song: 'Pure Imagination' *Charlie and The Chocolate Factory*

Aviva Helena Neff is the Director of Youth & Community Learning at Columbus College of Art & Design and an adjunct faculty member with Otterbein University Department of Theatre and Dance. An honours graduate of Goldsmiths College (MA, Applied Theatre), Dr Neff enjoys working in devised theatre and theatre for social change with participants aged from 1 to 100. She is an ensemble member with Teatro Travieso, which premiered her solo performance, *Blood, Earth, Water*, in 2021, written as part of a practice-as-research PhD at the Ohio State University. Dr Neff has recently published works on mediatized race and identity, mixed-Black women in Reconstruction-era New Orleans, and inclusive theatre pedagogy. Dr Neff is very fortunate to serve as a freelance intimacy coordinator and director within the incredible theatre community in Columbus.

Favourite British musical: *Oliver!*

Favourite British musical song: 'Food, Glorious Food' *Oliver!*

Judith Drake is a disabled PhD candidate in European Theatre at the University of Edinburgh focusing on Scottish disability theatre. She has established an archive for Birds of Paradise Theatre Company and was part of the creative team for their award-winning co-production with NTS of *My Left/Right Foot the Musical* (2018–19).

Favourite British musical: *Les Misérables*

Favourite British musical song: 'One Day More' *Les Misérables*

Cyrielle Garson is Lecturer in Contemporary Anglophone Theatre at Avignon University and a member of the ICTT (cultural identity, texts and theatricality) research team. She has published widely on British verbatim theatre including a 2021 monograph on the subject entitled *Beyond Documentary Realism: Aesthetic Transgressions in British Verbatim Theatre*.

Favourite British musical: *London Road*

Favourite British musical song: 'One Day More' *Les Misérables*

Foreword

KATE MARLAIS

It is an exciting time to be a writer of musicals in this country.

The reason I write musicals? I would say it is because they allow me to create a world removed from my own reality. While musicals will almost certainly include elements of familiarity, for me, a musical offers the key to a fantastical portal where music and words are woven together with an artist's thread. These heightened worlds allow us to explore our collective sense of wonder. And the exploration of something so intangibly vast leads us back to where we are with ourselves; we find comprehension in uncertainty because that is so often where meaning lies.

The British musical is on the threshold of a renaissance. Even though there is still a long road of equilibrium, representation, investment and opportunity yet to be travelled, an excitement remains keenly felt among our small, but tenacious, writing community. No one person may have the answer to the challenges still faced by writers and creators of British musical theatre, but collectively we hold tightly to one another and push forward with our common desire to articulate our place in the world. The reason I write musicals may be to create worlds in search for meaning. But those worlds are all the more resonant because they are grounded within community.

When writing musicals, I'm fuelled by a propensity against being constrained by the 'known', or what has come before. The world of a musical itself has endless possibilities. In the last few years, I see more and more writers seeking to break down the (un)conscious barriers that have been laid for us, not by us. Truly exciting genre-melding pieces of work are emerging, as writers explore the most distinct way to tell their stories; naturally then, demoded delineations are becoming breached on all fronts. The richer the needed diversity in British musicals will be as a result.

Right now, the world whirls and rocks in an uncertain place. We try to find ways to make sense of it. Artists often articulate uncertainty incredibly well. Sometimes this emerges as a blurred classification of their creation – a kind of search of meaning across borders, perhaps? Take, for example, the hotly debated topics: 'Is it a musical?' and 'Is it a play with songs?'

Whatever you believe makes a 'musical', or even a 'good musical', musicals are changing. How we value them is changing. How we watch them is changing. Who makes them, performs them and houses them is changing. Therefore, how we write musicals must change. The stories we tell must change. The language, the unhealthy tropes and the awareness must change. The truths addressed, the questions asked, and the ideas sounded out must change. As a result, their audience will change. We will see a more representative auditorium. And musicals will speak louder and further.

As we continue to re-navigate and re-interrogate, and we look at the landscape of British musicals, we find that musicals (and their creators) are starting to look and sound rather different to what has come before.

It is, of course, important to say that Broadway has always led the way by far in terms of output. Thus, perhaps the musicals they have produced had the chance to be more diverse. With more platforms on which shows could exist came more opportunities – to try things, to fail, to learn, to go again. Faith (by which I mean a belief in, and trust of, the artists driving the project) and funding breed freedom (for said artist – both artistically and mentally). Likewise, freedom breeds faith and funding for new things. The cycle continues.

Have British musicals truly moved as far forward as they might've done if they'd had the same number of opportunities to try, fail, learn, to go again? I'd suggest not. I'm sure this book will go some way to offering a combination of factors as to why. But the things that my mind keeps returning to are indeed fear, faith and funding.

Even though many wonderful works have emerged over the years, until very recently, really there were only a few main avenues through which a musical seemed to be able to emerge. After a while, these avenues inevitably start to become too saturated. The only way to continue forward is to break off and form separate paths; we must go round, off-piste and explore the unknown. Uncertain paths aren't the easiest, but they are, with certainty, the most interesting, evocative and enriching. Especially with the rapid rise of digital and social media, we can now create and promote differently, and have easy access to see what is happening in the world outside of our own borders. Musicals are more accessible than ever, bringing in new audiences with new demand for vital and original stories, proper representation, and fresh sounds, visuals and ideas.

We may not be entirely conscious of it yet, but I feel that we are at the start of creating a fresh, infinite tapestry of musical theatre. We are on that journey around the edges. Weaving around bends, learning-curves and corners, missteps and discoveries. And the really exciting thing is that nobody can predict their own destination because there are infinite possibilities of where each writer could take this journey. Just as a musical might not reveal exactly what it is saying until the very end (both in the process of writing and telling it), we must collectively trust that we know individually and instinctively the most interesting route to take, as we respond to and absorb the world around us. Because the uncertainty of an unknown destination is what will keep this art form truly alive. So musicals can continue to inspire, in the truest sense.

I hope that we all carry on moving forward, all unknowing, all uncertain, but brave and collectively fused in this sense of belonging to something. A movement in time. A re-routing of art and a re-rooting of ambition.

Kate Marlais, composer, February 2023

Foreword

TIM SUTTON

Musical theatre's an American art form,
American? no, that can't be
What about Gilbert and Sullivan?
And more crucially – what about me?

So says writer Susannah Pearse, pushing back against Leonard Bernstein's provocation. Her song encapsulates the paradox faced by all non-American musical writers. Rodgers and Hart, Bernstein and Stephen Sondheim (in his way) all paid tribute to the groundbreaking work of Gilbert and Sullivan. But by the 1930s and 1940s, it was the Great American Songbook which held sway, and Noël Coward was in the thrall of Cole Porter.

Andrew Lloyd Webber and Tim Rice, the undisputed titans of the 1970s and 1980s British Musical, studiously avoided American subjects (though not American music). Instead, they looked to the Old and New Testaments, and to the history of a South American dictator and his mistress.

But since the Cameron Mackintosh-produced megamusical swept the globe in the 1980s, America has pushed back with the massive hits *Wicked*, *Hairspray*, *The Book of Mormon*, *Hamilton*, not to mention smaller-scale critical darlings such as *Fun Home*, *Hadestown* and *Caroline, or Change*.

If you are a lover of musicals, you'll remember the first time the drug entered your bloodstream. For me it was the film version of *Singin' in the Rain*, shown on BBC One on New Year's Eve. Here was a complete world which was gregarious, historical, hysterical and romantic, with song and dance to make your heart sing. It made complete sense to me, and I wanted to watch more of them, be in them, and eventually to write them.

I became an addict, a convert, a zealot. I wanted to make people think, cry and laugh as they watched a show that has fallen from my brain and heart onto the page and stage. One starts (at the very beginning) with ardour and idealism. These, plus a good dose of good fortune, will armour you against the inevitable knockbacks, confidence bombs and reversals you encounter. You continue because you know that making musical theatre is the only sensible thing. What else is a person to do – get a job?

It's a lucky writer, however, who never experiences disappointment or disillusionment. Suddenly the wider world is indifferent and cynical, the press is snobbish, musicals are out of date and out of touch, and the best have already been written. They sound like they're from another era. Why should we even bother?

Well, idealism needs a side order of realism. Musicals are HARD. Hard to conceive, to write, and to produce. You need time, talent and tenacity, and you probably need to get at least one out of your system before you're even approaching good. You need a certain monomania, tempered with the wisdom to recognise a good suggestion. More than anything you need a team of people who will be supportive but also challenging – the collective mind that knocks the corners of a piece until it finds its best form – 'abrasion', as the great Stephen Sondheim called it. If it takes a village to raise a child, it takes a brains trust to raise a musical.

The hard knocks are all part of the deal: writers need shaping and challenging just as much as their shows. It's a warm and fuzzy feeling to spend time at a salon of new songs, or a music theatre conference, or a showcase, to break bread with like-minded authors who believe passionately in the art form. Then, we stumble out of our happy bubble into the horrible cold shock of the real world, filled with people who have never heard of Dave Malloy. A relative of mine once described my profession as a niche of a niche of a niche. Surely, I thought. it's not *that* many niches.

And yet there is good news for writers of British musical theatre. Since the 1980s tastes and producing models have changed. The blockbuster has slackened its grip, and aspiration of scale has been challenged by aspiration of outlook. In 1990, a handful of British writers clustered around Sondheim's personality and pedagogy, specifically in his role as the first visiting Professor of the Cameron Mackintosh Chair of Contemporary Theatre at the University of Oxford.

The thirteen students who attended these classes went on to form the Mercury Workshop, the first musical theatre collective of its kind. This growing community diversified in the subsequent decades, eventually becoming Mercury Musical Developments. In the intervening time, UK writers have sought to find a modern language for musicals. Composers and lyricists are being welcomed from the worlds of street poetry, hip-hop, gig and verbatim theatre. Two musicals – *Matilda* and *London Road* – emerged from the subsidised sector. They couldn't have been more different from one another, yet both were a cause for renewed optimism in the British musical (Tim Minchin is from Northampton, in case you're wondering).

At the same time, a new generation of independent producers are championing the form. Producers such Katy Lipson, Adam Lenson, Perfect Pitch and Kenny Wax are all nurturing new work in their own way. Artistic Directors are making serious commitments to the development of the form, and some of the best new shows now come from our regional theatres.

Since the turn of the century I have seen a true deepening of ability and aesthetic from creators of new British musicals. They now attend vocational workshops and university courses to study their craft. They access and study a huge volume of work online, and collaborate with colleagues all over the world. Their desire to tell stories through song and dance seems stronger than ever. In the light of this, I couldn't be happier to welcome this new collection of essays on the current state and status of the British musical. The American art form has been scrutinized from every angle, but study of its British equivalent has been relatively neglected until now. I hope you find these reflections stimulating, provocative, and ultimately encouraging. We have a lot to sing about.

Tim Sutton, composer and lyricist, February 2023

Introduction

The British musical is dead. Long live the British musical!

At the start of the 2010s the contemporary British musical was in a state of despair. A string of high-profile failures, including Boublil and Schönberg's *Marguerite* in 2009, left newspapers jokingly pondering how to solve a problem like the West End musical[1] while solemnly announcing its demise.[2] This was not a new phenomenon – a decade prior, the *New York Times* had declared the 'living death'[3] of the British musical with the ill-conceived Cliff Richard vehicle *Heathcliff* (1996). For Grace Barnes 'the British musical had largely reverted to being a faded photocopy of its now more innovative Broadway counterpart'[4] with creativity stifled as creators were, according to Andrew Lloyd Webber, repeatedly 'trying out work and getting it wrong'.[5] With no apparent means of turning the tide, British musicals appeared to have 'ground to a halt'.[6]

Over the last decade, the British musical landscape has undergone a remarkable transformation, marked by a flourishing of creativity and success. This turnaround can be attributed in part to the shift in Arts Council England funding, which began including musical theatre in 2011, and the tireless efforts of organizations like Perfect Pitch, Musical Theatre Network and Mercury Musical Developments. In recent years, the British musical has seen significant developments and breakthroughs, ushering in a new era of optimism. With smash hits like *SIX* achieving global success, *Matilda the Musical* dominating cinemas and a slew of British productions, including *Standing at the Sky's Edge*, *Operation Mincemeat*, *The Great British Bake Off Musical* and *Sylvia*, being performed across London, the British musical appears to be experiencing something of a renaissance.

According to Miranda Lundskaer-Nielsen, British musicals are often relegated to mere footnotes[7] in the history of musical theatre, further highlighting the dominance of the Broadway musical. Writing in 2016 Gordon, Taylor and Jubin highlighted the 'paucity of critical texts'[8] exploring the British musical. In the years that have followed there has been growing interest in the historiography of British musical theatre.[9] However, there is a continued lack of critical engagement with contemporary industry practices and aesthetics. This book seeks to fill that gap by exploring the aesthetics of contemporary British musicals and situating them within their wider industry context.

Despite common polemics that portray the British musical as an outdated and inferior form, forever overshadowed by its US American counterpart, the truth is far more complex. While some may attempt to reduce the British musical to tired stereotypes, the reality is that it is far more diverse than the narrow label suggests. Josh Bird, digital producer of *SIX* and a musical theatre writer, acknowledges that 'we're really good at it when we get it right',[10] and it is crucial to recognize the successes of the British musical and further develop its legacy. As this book illustrates, the British musical has undergone significant developments and transformations in recent years, showcasing its ability to innovate and entertain audiences worldwide.

As Sean Mayes and Sarah K. Whitfield highlight, 'British musical theatre is not confined to a limited number of theatres in a few streets of London's West End'.[11] This book sets out to demonstrate the remarkable breadth of the British musical theatre scene, featuring case studies of musicals that have originated from an array of places across Great Britain; Sheffield, Mold, Glasgow, Chichester, Bristol, Stratford and London. From these varied locations emerge ten distinct musicals that weave together to create a vivid and multifaceted portrait of the contemporary British musical theatre landscape at the end of the decade. Through this rich and heterogeneous collection of musicals, we want to showcase the boundless stylistic originality and creative energy that characterizes the current state of British musical theatre.

We're British, don't you know?

In the post-Brexit landscape, the question of national identity has become more complicated, and using national identity to define cultural works has become increasingly political. To paraphrase Florian Scheding; while a musical might have the potential to sound a nation into being, the nation is not a necessary condition of a musical.[12] Nevertheless, it's important to highlight the musicals being produced across the UK and recognize their broader impact. By doing so, we're not attempting to erect aural borders[13] but, rather, to initiate a dialogue that, as Scott Gilmour observes, has been lacking in this particular field where 'sometimes it's like everyone's in their own little microcosm'.[14]

As the UK moves forward in this era of uncertainty, it is more important than ever to recognize and embrace the contributions that the British musical has made to the cultural landscape, both at home and abroad. Our use of the term British in this book is not intended to be prescriptive or exclusive. Rather, we have employed it as a shorthand for the works produced within the geographic confines of England, Scotland and Wales; within Great Britain. We acknowledge that this definition is not perfect as it leaves out important voices and perspectives from Northern Ireland (considered part of the UK but not part of Great Britain).

Rethinking the dominance of the Broadway musical

In scholarship, the pervasive influence of Broadway musicals is being challenged[15] to redress the paucity of global attention given to non-anglophone musicals. Indeed, as David Savran astutely observes, the definition of a musical is 'contested, contingent, and unstable'.[16] The musical is a distinctly US American art form, its evolution intertwined with US American history and widely documented as such by scholars. Mayes highlights that the 'history of musical theatre is a complex one, and many of us know it as an unchallenged tale largely written by a private club of white men',[17] a narrative many are working to deconstruct.

As the rhizomatic nature of musical theatre is revealed and its single-origin story, centred around the Great White Way, is beginning to be unpicked, there is a growing recognition that 'musical theatre is no longer the exclusive property of players in the West'.[18] In this context the need to highlight and explore musical theatre form and practice beyond Broadway is all the more important.

Challenging the dominance of the Broadway musical and its stylistic features will take time. The overwhelming focus on the Broadway musical in musical theatre scholarship has unintentionally led to the homogenization of musical theatre aesthetics; these are 'a set of implicit norms rarely articulated because [they are] tacitly understood'.[19] The British musical, on the other hand, has struggled to establish a clear identity and presence on the global stage. Designer Lucy Osborne ponders, 'we know what [a Broadway musical] is, don't we? So why don't we know what a British musical is?'[20] For too long, the British musical has been reduced to a handful of limited perspectives, whether it be the singular focus on London's West End, the domination of one composer in Andrew Lloyd Webber or nostalgia for the so-called 'British Invasion' of the 1980s. The Broadway–West End binary is constantly articulated by scholars in an attempt to delineate the two forms. Ellen Kane, associate choreographer, observes British musicals are 'always thought of as poor relatives'[21] to their US American cousins. Such comparisons only serve to reinforce the narrow view of musical theatre as a genre with only two epicentres: Broadway and the West End. This oversimplification fails to recognize the more complex and dynamic global and transatlantic cultural networks that shape and influence musical theatre around the world.

Laura MacDonald argues that the constant need to establish the British musical in relation to its American counterpart reveals 'the enduring presence and significance of American musical theatre to London and the West End in particular'[22]. This is not a new perspective; at the height of the so-called British Invasion, Trevor Nunn accepted his Tony award for *Cats* commenting that 'in England we dream of New York'.[23] US critic Robert Brustein bitingly observed, 'it was not the British who had conquered New York but Broadway that had totally debauched the British',[24] perhaps foreshadowing the decades of attempts to replicate Broadway musicals in the UK and the financially driven development of the West End as an incubation space for Broadway musicals.

In order to broaden the debate and support the genre's continuing development, it was important for us to situate academic engagement with these shows alongside industry interviews. Our aim was to avoid any separation of industry and academic practice and highlight intersections between the two fields through a hybrid approach. We found it fascinating how these interviews and critical analyses have intersected, highlighting the importance of this approach in understanding and appreciating contemporary British musical theatre.

What even is a British musical?

The question of how to define a British musical has been a recurring challenge for us. Our interviews with writers, directors and industry professionals have revealed the elusive and subjective nature of this inquiry. Is the nationality of the creators the defining factor? Or does the origin of the production, or even the content and themes of the musical, play a role? The reality is that any of these factors could potentially make a production a *British* musical, but none of them are definitive. To define a British musical by clarifying what it is not – a product of the American Broadway system who claim ownership of the art form – continues to reinforce the dominance of that musical theatre form within the discourse.

Instead of imposing exclusionary definitions that often make problematic assumptions about what or who counts, we deliberately refuse to define the British musical as a singular entity or nation-building cultural product. Instead, we have curated a collection of musicals that either come out of British funding structures or self-identify as British. The explorations and discussions within this book serve as a starting point, aiming to address the lack of engagement with the British musical and inspire further discourse. Our selection of shows is not intended to be canonical, and this book is by no means a definitive text. It would be almost impossible to cover the full range of contemporary British musicals in a single volume, just as it is the case with contemporary British plays.

What is clear is the musical is the UK's most popular theatrical form.[25] The cognitive dissonance at work then in casting the form as dead, as seeing it in a state of terminal decline, while at the same time proclaiming it as the potential saviour of the West End, suggests something is going on here. What is the actual state of the form in the UK? Despite initial assumptions that the British musical may have been in decline, the past decade has proven to be a period of vibrant creativity and growth across the genre. In fact, there were more British musicals produced than we anticipated, with a significant spike in new productions in the year 2018. For reasons that we cannot fully explain, this particular year saw the emergence of a number of key shows that brought a fresh perspective and new energy to the British musical landscape.

To better understand this explosion of British musical theatre over the past decade, we commissioned a forthcoming dataset[26] which tracks the production of musicals in the UK from 2010 to 2020. Analysis from this data challenges the dominant narrative that British musicals came to a standstill or stagnated, instead pointing to the scattered nature of the musical in the UK. The musical is not dead but rather dispersed, and the importance of regional production to the ecosystem of the musical has been poorly understood.

The process of forming the dataset reveals one of the most significant problems facing the musical in the UK, the lack of consistent data and archiving of near contemporary work in ways which make it available for future productions, revivals, teaching or scholarly enquiring; the authors note, 'the contemporary musical might not be dead, but it is in danger of disappearing'. We worked with a theatre historian to conduct this process, who noted the need to use many multiple primary sources to find information about musicals from no longer than thirteen years ago, drawing on blogs, listings, and archived theatre pages to point towards a complete dataset.[27] It is telling that it is easier to access information about a production from 1912 than 2012. This is not necessarily a problem about digital preservation or performance documentation but, rather, a symptom of the lack of recognition around the scale and significance of British musical theatre. It is, as Whitfield and Chandler note, a 'failure of our cultural imagination to see the musical as a serious theatrical form, a presentism which in turn perpetuates and reinforces established cultural hierarchies within the UK and beyond that centres London and pays little attention to the wider systems of production'.[28]

From the barricades to the bank

The relationship between commercial and subsidized theatre in the UK is historically complex. Musical theatre, often driven by commercial interests, 'is always – and unpredictably – overdetermined by economic relations and interests'.[29] The success of megamusicals in the 1980s, which made fortunes for producers Lloyd Webber and Cameron Mackintosh, can be seen as a reflection of 'Thatcherism in action'.[30] These shows, with their global franchises and merchandise, exemplified the excesses of neoliberalism.

However, it is worth noting the troubled relationship between subsidized and commercial theatre in musical theatre production. The Royal Shakespeare Company (RSC), profitably co-produced *Les Misérables*, making around £25 million in royalties from the show prior to the West End closure of the original production in 2019.[31] As funding for the arts continues to be squeezed, an act viewed by some as 'cultural vandalism',[32] subsidized theatres are increasingly seeking to emulate the RSC's success, and the debate over what should and should not be funded remains a significant issue (it took over sixty years for musical theatre to be recognized by the Arts Council England) (Figure 1).

We love you Sheffield will you marry us?

As scholars begin to question the dominance of Broadway in the study of US American musical theatre, it's equally vital to expand the scope beyond the West End when examining British musical theatre. It is crucial to delve deeper and investigate the success stories emerging elsewhere. Sheffield Theatres under the stewardship of Daniel Evans (2009–16) and Rob Hastie (interviewed later in the book) have quietly established themselves as a leading player in the development of new musicals in the UK. The success of Sheffield Theatres in the development of new musicals can be seen in the inclusion of two of their productions, *Everybody's Talking About Jamie* and *Flowers for Mrs Harris*, as case studies in this book. The company has achieved critical and commercial acclaim, with six productions originating from Sheffield being performed on stages worldwide in 2023.[33]

The success achieved by a city that is so removed from London, and one traditionally associated with industrial rather than cultural output, demands attention. Evans has stated that he started from the desire to create 'a sense of ownership and emotional investment'[34] from Sheffield audiences when he began his tenure at Sheffield Theatres. His legacy has been expanded by Hastie, who has capitalized on 'the power of the locally generated story'[35] to solidify the theatres' reputation. The achievements are even more impressive when you consider that 'Sheffield only gets £9 per head of the population in investment for the culture sector, compared to £33 for Manchester'.[36]

As Dougal Irvine notes, regional theatres can be 'where a lot of writers will earn their bread and butter',[37] and investing in musical theatre writers can pay off for the theatre if the right mindset is adopted. Sheffield Theatres' success is a prime example of this, as they took a brave approach eschewing the traditional regional theatre model of staging classic plays helmed by big names. Instead, they focused on 'ensemble-led, new pieces of work that require an audience to take a kind of leap of faith when they buy their ticket'.[38] This approach has paid off, with local audiences getting the opportunity to be part of shows that have gone on to transfer to Broadway and the West End.

It's clear that theatres outside of the traditional cultural hubs of London and New York can be a fertile ground for new talent and innovative productions. However, continuing to use these benchmarks of success perpetuates geographical hierarchies, reinforcing restrictive approaches as producers and theatres strive to create the next big thing and replicate previous successes. During discussions with the creators of the musicals featured in this book, it was fascinating to discover that many of the 'successful' shows were initially intended for a limited run but ended up exceeding expectations.

Herein appears one of the biggest differences between the approach to musicals in US American and Great Britain, longevity and legacy. As Noisemaker's Scott Gilmour and Claire McKenzie, who have worked in both contexts, note, in the United States 'one of the things that feels very different is that you're always having a conversation about the *next* production, or the *next* version of the show, or the *next* iteration of it'.[39] While the success of Sheffield, 'in a culture of if things transfer they are deemed a success',[40] might suggest a more Americanized approach to musical development, Evans and Hastie emphasize that their central focus is to 'make it for Sheffield'[41] – an approach that has repeatedly proven successful.

Clare Chandler

Figure 1 *Standing at the Sky's Edge*, National Theatre 2023. Credit: Helen Murray/ArenaPAL.

Chapter overview

As scholars and enthusiasts of musical theatre, it is our goal to contribute to a better understanding of the British musical by exploring ten case studies from the past decade. By examining the themes, subjects and innovations of these productions, we aim to showcase the range and diversity of the British musical and to highlight its significant contributions to the broader musical theatre landscape. It is our hope that this book will serve as a valuable resource for anyone interested in the past, present and future of the British musical.

Broderick Chow begins the book considering Dougal Irvine's early noughties musical *Departure Lounge* (2010) and exploring masculinities in transition. Chow explores the changing attitudes towards homosexuality discussing how Irvine's compositional choices, such as his use of the acoustic indie rock sound, make homosociality musically audible in the musical.

In Chapter 2 Stephanie Lim questions the progressive positioning of *Matilda the Musical* (2011), which challenges traditional perceptions of women and children. Lim focuses on the representation of the infamous Miss Trunchball and the complicated gender politics within the show. She argues that while the show features strong and intelligent female characters, the portrayal of Miss Trunchball reinforces negative stereotypes about women, and the use of a male actor to play the role further muddies the show's message about gender and female empowerment.

Jozey Grae offers a new perspective on Craig Adam's *Lift* (2013) by examining the show's moments of glitch and potential for gender expansive and non-binary character readings. The chapter explores non-binary space in British musical theatre by drawing on autoethnographic research and Queer Theory. Grae focuses on the French Teacher and the Ballet Dancer, arguing that the disruptions and disorientations within the musical allow for alternative interpretations of gender and identity.

Kelsey Blair examines *Bend It Like Beckham: The Musical* (2015) in Chapter 4, focusing on its portrayal of British multiculturalism at the turn of the twenty-first century. Blair analyses how the musical employs football, Bhangra dance and musical theatre conventions to explore the complexities of identity and multiple cultural experiences. The chapter highlights the ways in which *Bend It Like Beckham* offers nuanced representations of diverse identities and cultural signifiers.

Sarah K. Whitfield moves us to a more recent moment as she considers the 'bliss' of musical theatre screenings, recounting her own experience watching *Flowers for Mrs Harris* (2016) during the Covid-19 lockdown. She engages with the idea of feminist possibility in the musical and the ways that its showcasing of women's stories, friendship and joy were reflected in its digital legacy.

In Chapter 6, Ellen Armstrong uses *The Grinning Man* (2016) in order to discuss the tradition of the freak show within musical theatre, and ask how disability can and should be represented on stage. Armstrong takes particular note of the leading character of Grinpayne and the way puppetry is used to depict his physical difference.

Hannah Thuraisingam Robbins explores queer love and potential in *Everybody's Talking About Jamie* (2017) in Chapter 7. The chapter focuses on the characterization of Ray and Pritti Pasha and considers what the musical might offer to audiences of colour. Robbins uses their own lived experience to explore the role of the 'Aunty', drawing parallels between this role within the Caribbean communities they grew up with and South Asian communities.

Chapter 8 brings us to 2018 as Aviva Neff considers casting practices in *SIX*. Neff examines how the show acts as a reflection of the era in which it emerged, speaking to the rise of 'Beyoncé feminism' and the influence of social media on entertainment and political activism.

In Chapter 9 Judith Drake takes us to Scotland and the Birds of Paradise and National Theatre Scotland co-production *My Left/Right Foot the Musical* (2018). Drake considers how the musical uses disability simulation to raise questions and subvert conventions of disability representation, to create an inclusive musical

The final chapter in the collection addresses the recent aesthetic evolutions within the British verbatim musical genre. Here Cyrielle Garson considers the faux-verbatim musical's use of documentary markers in the post-truth era of fake news and conspiracy theories.

Notes

1. Alistair Smith, 'How Do You Solve a Problem Like the West End Musical?', *The Guardian*, 22 September 2011, Accessed 7 April 2023, https://www.theguardian.com/stage/theatreblog/2011/sep/22/musical-betty-blue-eyes-closure.
2. Matt Wolf, 'Marguerite and the Death of the West End Musical', *The Guardian*, 29 August 2008, Accessed 7 April 2023, https://www.theguardian.com/stage/theatreblog/2008/aug/29/margueriteandthedeathofth.
3. Sheridan Morley, 'Heathcliff, Go Back to the Moors', *The New York Times*, 19 February 1997, Accessed 7 April 2023, https://www.nytimes.com/1997/02/19/style/IHT-heathcliff-go-back-to-the-moors.html.
4. Grace Barnes, *National Identity and the British Musical: From Blood Brothers to Cinderella* (London: Bloomsbury, 2022), 9.
5. Lord Andrew Lloyd Webber cited in 'Andrew Lloyd Webber Becomes First Composer to Have Four Broadway Shows at once since Rodgers and Hammerstein', *The Telegraph*, 10 February 2017, Accessed 7 April 2023, https://www.telegraph.co.uk/news/2017/02/10/andrew-lloyd-webber-becomes-first-composer-have-four-broadway/.
6. Craig Hepworth, 'Why God, Why: The Death of The British Musical', *Whats on Stage*, 21 January 2010, Accessed 7 April 2023, https://www.whatsonstage.com/blackpool-theatre/news/why-god-why-the-death-of-the-british-musical_14636.html.
7. Miranda Lundskaer-Nielsen, 'The Long Road to Recognition: New Musical Theatre Development in Britain', *Studies in Musical Theatre* 7, no. 2 (2013): 158.
8. Gordon et al., *British Musical Theatre Since 1950* (London: Methuen 213, 2016).
9. See the work of Sarah K. Whitfield, Sean Mayes, Olaf Jubin, Robert Gordon, Millie Taylor, Grace Barnes, Ethan Mordden, Miranda Lundskaer-Nielsen.
10. Josh Bird, interview with the authors, 27 July 2022.
11. Sean Mayes and Sarah K. Whitfield, 'Introduction', in *An Inconvenient Black History of British Musical Theatre 1900–1950* (London: Methuen Drama, 2022), 5.
12. Florian Scheding, 'Introduction "Who Is British Music?" Placing Migrants in National Music History', *Twentieth-Century Music* 15, no. 1 (2018): 440.

13. Josh Kun, 'The Aural Border', *Theatre Journal* 52, no. 1 (2000): 1–21.
14. Scott Gilmour, interview with the authors, 8 September 2022.
15. We would encourage you to seek out the work of Hyewon Kim, Emilio Estevez, Sir Anril Pineda Tiatco, Jiyoon Jung, Sanne Thierens, Alejandro Postigo, Leesi Patrick, Laura MacDonald and others who have broadened the scope of musical theatre scholarship drawing attention to the musical's global reach.
16. David Savran, 'Musical Theatre Mobilities: Around the World in Eighty Years', in *The Routledge Companion to Musical Theatre*, ed. Laura MacDonald et al. (London: Routledge, 2023), 10.
17. Sean Mayes, 'Preface', in *An Inconvenient Black History of British Musical Theatre 1900–1950* (London: Methuen Drama, 2022), xvi.
18. Kim Varhola, 'Introduction: Scenes from a Showbiz Couple's Travelodge', in *The Routledge Companion to Musical Theatre*, ed. Laura MacDonald et al. (London: Routledge, 2023), 378.
19. Derek Miller, 'Five, Six, Seven, Eight: Broadway by the Numbers' (draft 2023) 5, Accessed 7 April 2023, https://www.visualizingbroadway.com/broadway/miller_broadway-by-the-numbers_draft-2023-01-23.pdf.
20. Lucy Osborne, interview with the authors, 14 December 2022.
21. Ellen Kane, interview with the authors, 26 July 2022.
22. Laura MacDonald, 'To Remind You of My Love: London's Love Affair with The American Musical', *Comparative Drama* 56, no. 1&2 (2022): 100.
23. Trevor Nunn cited in *State of the Nation*, ed. Micheal Billington (London: Faber & Faber, 2007), 289.
24. Robert Brustein cited in Billington, *State of the Nation*, 289.
25. In the nineteen years since its creation the publicly voted What's on Stage Best Regional Production has gone to a musical fifteen times, and 'Theatre and the West End in the United Kingdom (UK)' from *Statista* states, according to their data, 'Musicals are the most popular form of theatre' in the UK, Accessed 7 April 2023, https://www.statista.com/topics/3689/theatre-and-the-west-end-in-the-united-kingdom-uk/#topicOverview.
26. Sarah K. Whitfield and Clare Chandler, *Understanding British Musical Theatre: Drawing on the Data 2010–2020* (forthcoming).
27. Musical Theatre Network began their listings page in 2017, https://musicaltheatrenetwork.com/listings/.
28. Whitfield and Chandler, *British Musical Theatre by Numbers 2010–2020*.
29. David Savran, 'Toward a Historiography of the Popular', *Theatre Survey* 45, no. 2 (2004): 213.
30. Billington, *State of the Nation*, 284.
31. Matthew Hemley, 'RSC Begins Crunch Talks with Cameron Mackintosh over *Les Misérables* Royalties', *The Stage*, 16 January 2019, Accessed 7 April 2023, https://www.thestage.co.uk/news/rsc-begins-crunch-talks-with-cameron-mackintosh-over-les-miserables-royalties.
32. Juliet Stephenson cited in 'Arts Funding Cuts "Cultural Vandalism", says Juliet Stevenson, at DCMS Protest', *The Guardian*, 22 November 2022, Accessed 7 April 2023, https://www.theguardian.com/culture/2022/nov/22/arts-council-england-cuts-are-cultural-vandalism-says-juliet-stevenson.
33. *The Good Person of Szechwan* (Crucible Theatre, Sheffield), *Wildfire Road* (Playhouse, Sheffield), *Life of Pi* (Gerald Schoenfeld Theatre, New York), *Accidental Death of an Anarchist* (Lyric Hammersmith Theatre, London), *Standing at the Sky's Edge* (National Theatre, London), *Birds & Bees* (School tour, Sheffield).

34. Daniel Evans cited in 'Daniel Evans: My Sheffield Highlights' by Ben Hewis, *What's on Stage*, 25 July 2016, Accessed 7 April 2023, https://www.whatsonstage.com/chichester-theatre/news/daniel-evans-interview-sheffield-chichester_41358.html.
35. Rob Hastie, interview with the authors, 17 October 2022.
36. YP Comment, 'Standing at The Sky's Edge Success Underlines Sheffield's Cultural Potential', *The Yorkshire Post*, 1 March 2023, Accessed 7 April 2023, https://www.yorkshirepost.co.uk/business/standing-at-the-skys-edge-success-underlines-sheffields-cultural-potential-the-yorkshire-post-says-4046926.
37. Dougal Irvine, interview with the authors, 22 July 2022.
38. Rob Hastie, interview with the authors, 17 October 2022.
39. Scott Gilmour, interview with the authors, 8 September 2022.
40. Daniel Evans cited in 'Daniel Evans: "If We Can Imagine It We Should Be Able to Depict It"', *WhatsOnStage*, 26 January 2015, Accessed 7 April 2023, https://www.whatsonstage.com/london-theatre/news/daniel-evans-interview_36990.html.
41. Daniel Evans cited in 'Daniel Evans: "If We Can Imagine It We Should Be Able to Depict It"'.

Works Cited

Bannister, Rosie (2015), 'Daniel Evans: "If We Can Imagine It We Should Be Able to Depict It"', *WhatsOnStage*, 26 January (accessed 7 April 2023).

Barnes, Grace (2022), *National Identity and the British Musical: From Blood Brothers to Cinderella*. London: Bloomsbury.

Billington, Michael (2007), *State of the Nation*. London: Faber & Faber.

Bird, Josh (2022), Interview with the authors, 27 July.

Furness, Hannah (2017), 'Andrew Lloyd Webber Becomes First Composer to Have Four Broadway Shows at Once Since Rodgers and Hammerstein', *The Telegraph*, 10 February (accessed 7 April 2023).

Gilmour, Scott (2022), Interview with the authors, 8 September.

Gordon, Robert, et al. (2016), *British Musical Theatre Since 1950*. London: Methuen.

Hastie, Rob (2022), Interview with the authors, 17 October.

Hemley, Matthew (2019), 'RSC Begins Crunch Talks with Cameron Mackintosh over *Les Misérables* Royalties', *The Stage*, 16 January (accessed 7 April 2023).

Hepworth, Craig (2010), 'Why God, Why: The Death of The British Musical', *WhatsOnStage*, 21 January (accessed 7 April 2023).

Hewis, Ben (2016), 'Daniel Evans: My Sheffield Highlights', *What'sOnStage*, 25 July (accessed 7 April 2023).

Irvine, Dougal (2022), Interview with the authors, 22 July.

Kane, Ellen (2022), Interview with the authors, 26 July.

Khomami, Nadia (2022), 'Arts Funding Cuts "Cultural Vandalism", Says Juliet Stevenson, at DCMS Protest', *The Guardian*, 22 November (accessed 7 April 2023).

Kun, Josh (2000), 'The Aural Border', *Theatre Journal*, 52 (1): 1–21.

Lundskaer-Nielsen, Miranda (2013), 'The Long Road to Recognition: New Musical Theatre Development in Britain', *Studies in Musical Theatre*, 7 (2): 158.

MacDonald, Laura (2022), 'To Remind You of My Love: London's Love Affair with The American Musical', *Comparative Drama*, 56 (1&2): 93–124.

Mayes, Sean (2022), 'Preface', in Sean Mayes and Sarah K. Whitfield (eds), *An Inconvenient Black History of British Musical Theatre 1900–1950*, xiv–xvii. London: Methuen Drama.

Mayes, Sean and Sarah K. Whitfield (2022), 'Introduction', in Sean Mayes and Sarah K. Whitfield (eds), *An Inconvenient Black History of British Musical Theatre 1900–1950*, 1–14. London: Methuen Drama.

Miller, Derek (2023), 'Five, Six, Seven, Eight: Broadway by the Numbers', draft, 5 (accessed 7 April 2023).

Morley, Sheridan (1997), 'Heathcliff, Go Back to the Moors', *The New York Times*, 19 February (accessed 7 April 2023).

Osborne, Lucy (2022), Interview with the authors, 14 December.

Savran, David (2004), 'Toward a Historiography of the Popular', *Theatre Survey*, 45 (2): 211–17.

Savran, David (2023), 'Musical Theatre Mobilities: Around the World in Eighty Years', in Laura MacDonald et al. (eds), *The Routledge Companion to Musical Theatre*, 9–24. London: Routledge.

Scheding, Florian (2018), 'Introduction: "Who Is British Music?" Placing Migrants in National Music History', *Twentieth-Century Music*, 15 (1): 439–92.

Smith, Alistair (2011), 'How Do You Solve a Problem Like the West End Musical?', *The Guardian*, 22 September (accessed 7 April 2023).

Statistica Research Department. 'Theatre and the West End in the United Kingdom', *Statistica*, https://www.statista.com/topics/3689/theatre-and-the-west-end-in-the-united-kingdom-uk/ (accessed 7 April 2023).

Varhola, Kim (2023), 'Introduction: Scenes from a Showbiz Couple's Travelodge', in Laura MacDonald et al. (eds), *The Routledge Companion to Musical Theatre*, 377–82. London: Routledge.

Whitfield, Sarah K. and Clare Chandler (forthcoming), *Understanding British Musical Theatre: Drawing on the Data 2010–2020*.

Whitfield, Sarah K. and Clare Chandler (forthcoming), *British Musical Theatre by Numbers 2010–2020*.

Wolf, Matt (2008), 'Marguerite and the Death of the West End Musical', *The Guardian*, 29 August (accessed 7 April 2023).

YP Comment (2023), 'Standing at The Sky's Edge Success Underlines Sheffield's Cultural Potential', *The Yorkshire Post*, 1 March.

1 Bros abroad

Masculinities in transition and homosocial bonding in Dougal Irvine's *Departure Lounge*

BRODERICK CHOW

In the opening number of Dougal Irvine's *Departure Lounge*, four eighteen-year-old boys sing the following couplet:

We'd like to shag your daughter
That's what your daughter's for [. . .][1]

Departure Lounge was first produced in 2008. The musical concerns four eighteen-year-old boys trapped by delays in an airport departure lounge after a week-long lad's holiday in Malaga, Spain. The lads reminisce about their booze-filled holiday (much of which they cannot remember clearly), have their friendships tested (often in relation to women they desire), make self-discoveries and think about how their lives and relationships will change as they move on to university. Throughout, they are visited by the spectral presence of Sophie, an idealized and all-knowing figure of femininity described in the dramatis personae as '18-20 yrs. Cute slapper'. At least initially, the boys perform with a theatrical bravado that seems to parody what popular discourse in 2021 would call 'toxic' masculinity. Despite this sense of parody, in light of contemporary movements since 2008 towards equity and social justice (Black Lives Matter, #MeToo, StopAsianHate) and the re-examination of masculinities they have prompted, the lines make for a jarring opening.

This historical disorientation is something Dougal Irvine is aware of too. Sitting down to speak to me on a Zoom call, Irvine notes: '[I wondered] if all these changes in the landscape [*of contemporary society*], were they suddenly going to kill the show? Should we even allow characters to do this? And to get a laugh from it as well?'[2] He notes that the multiple rewrites of the book and libretto between its first draft in 2004 and its final version in 2011 were 'perhaps reflecting the moment that we're in . . . a different society'.[3] The musical – a young, early piece of work by the writer – thus represents both a period of transition in both Irvine's consciousness and social consciousness as such. Due to its minimal staging requirements and small cast, *Departure Lounge* remains an extremely popular piece today, especially among amateur dramatic groups and fringe performances. However, as Irvine playfully suggests, 'I don't know if I could watch it myself now. [. . .] I'm a dad now, and I'm not sure I could forgive my eighteen-year-old self for being that rude.'[4]

This chapter explores the disjuncture between this early musical exploration of masculinities in transition (in which white, cisgender, heterosexual masculinity is presented as what performance theorist Peggy Phelan would call 'unmarked') and the present-day vantage point that enables a consideration of their identities as identities.[5] By historicizing *Departure Lounge* we can see the social and political forces that construct the lads' 'transitory' white English masculinity. While at first glance *Departure Lounge* seems to be a boisterous critique/celebration of toxic masculinity, what it actually depicts – through music, lyric and narrative – is masculinity *itself* in transition, a subject befitting its liminal setting. I first outline the musical's narrative and theatrical conceit, situating it in the context of the popularity of the 'package holiday' and the scripted behaviour expected and experienced by young British men ('lads on tour'). In the second section I explore key frameworks in masculinities studies, specifically Raewyn Connell's framework of 'hegemonic masculinity' (and other extensions of this concept in sociology) and Eve Kosofsky Sedgwick's literary analysis of homosociality, that enable an understanding of the characters social positioning. I analyse how homosociality is made musically audible and undone in Irvine's compositional choices – especially his choice of an acoustic indie rock sound and use of canon. The final section explores *Departure Lounge* in light of changing attitudes towards homosexuality. Finally, in a coda, I consider Irvine's final script before retiring to become a full-time teacher, the straight play *Memoirs of an Asian Football Casual* (2018). Between *Departure Lounge* and *Memoirs* Irvine's work outlines a fast-moving period of transition in British social history.

The Narrative: *Benidorm* meets *Rashomon*

Departure Lounge is a young piece, both in the ages of its characters and the fact that it was the first piece of musical theatre writing from Irvine, at the time a young musical theatre actor performing in the UK revival of *Miss Saigon*. The first draft was completed in 2004, and the score reflects Irvine's love for guitar-based British pop, which had not been seen on musical theatre stages at the time. Irvine notes that inspiration for the piece came when he himself was waiting at a European airport. He saw a group of young Danish men across the departure lounge and thought, despite the differences in nationality and language, 'those guys are me and my friends.' The encounter brought back memories of his own lads' holiday at eighteen.

From the 1970s onwards, the 'package holiday' to destinations in Southern Spain and the Balearic Islands developed on the increasing affordability of airfare and were targeted at British holidaymakers. All-inclusive holidays generated large tourist-dependent local economies and became associated with bad behaviour. Sociologist Daniel Briggs argues that the package holiday constitutes a type of script for a British masculine rite of passage marked by 'deviant' and 'risky' behaviours (binge-drinking, unprotected sex, drug-use) for the potential reward of 'social status'.[6] This script is 'ideologically constructed for them by marketing companies, corporations, travel operators and flight companies and the media'.[7] The package holiday script of excessive consumption and 'living large' comes at a heavy cost: far from being restorative, Briggs's informants (a crew of working-class young men from a UK coastal town) experienced that returning home from holiday reinforced feelings of their everyday lives as depressing and mundane.[8]

Irvine's narrative establishes and then deconstructs the script of the package holiday. The entirety of the show takes place in the aftermath of the holiday, as JB, the group's self-declared leader, Jordan, the handsome ladies' man discovering his sexuality, daredevil Pete, and subordinate Ross, recount stories of the holiday. In a review for *British Theatre Guide*, Matt Boothman writes, 'The best bits of Dougal Irvine's new musical call to mind a sort of booze-hazy *Rashomon*: the natural disparities between the four lads' perspectives are compounded by alcohol-induced memory distortion.'[9] Irvine shows in real time the holiday come-down and self-reflexive evaluation of these young men's lives elaborated in Briggs's research. The fixed identities and social positions of the lads quickly established in the opening number 'Brits on Tour' (e.g. Ross sings: *I'm Roland Blarg, but please don't call me that / I think Ross is cooler, or do I sound a twat?*' demonstrating his self-doubt and group positioning in a single couplet) are challenged by varying accounts of 'Thursday Night', betrayal, coming out and moving on to university.

The dramatic action of *Departure Lounge* is primarily static and based in dialogue. There are three main dynamics of conflict, transition and resolution within the group of lads that the musical explores: Ross and Pete; JB and Ross; and Jordan and self. All three are facilitated by the presence of Sophie, the only female figure (though not precisely a 'character' as she is a mercurial and shifting presence) onstage (Figure 2). Ross, the most nervous and subordinated of the group, has fallen for Sophie during the holiday, expressing his feelings in a ballad ('Sophie') reminiscent of the songwriting of Gary Barlow. Unbeknownst to Ross, but known to Jordan, Pete has slept with Sophie, leading to the two lads falling out. Meanwhile, JB and Ross – the oldest friends in the group – are also growing apart. JB's sense of self relies on Ross being a loyal, yet subordinated friend, while Ross is moving on and growing tired of this relational dynamic. This is primarily explored in 'Do You Know What I Think of You?', an interesting and beautiful number that begins as a homosocial love song but goes

Figure 2 Original cast of *Departure Lounge*. Credit: Courtesy of Wendy Barnes.

on to reveal the asymmetrical nature of the friendship. Finally, Jordan struggles (briefly) with his sexuality in 'Secret (Part Two)', eventually coming out as gay to his friends in the final scene of the musical. The guys are surprised ('JB: You don't like girls?!! You've pulled half of Spain this week!') but extremely accepting and even happy for him.

Sophie appears variously as object of desire, a 'magical' feminine figure, a menacing 'monstrous' feminine figure ('Your family'd barely notice if you disappeared a whole week would they? Your butler'd be the only one who'd miss you') and even a taunting maternal figure ('You miss your Mummy don't you Pete? You wonder if she ever held you close. If you ever sucked on her titty'). The various figurations of Sophie are directed at the lads' self-discovery, passage into manhood and eventual reification of the homosocial group, echoing Sedgwick's articulation of homosociality that I go on to explore herein. Her purpose is established in 'Female', the second number of the musical and the only moment in which Sophie sings:

> Let me take control I'll set you free-male
> This slapper's in your soul can't you – see male?

The presence of Sophie is part of a wider structure of male homosocial bonding that Sedgwick, citing Gayle Rubin, calls the 'male traffic in women'.[10] Although the role features one spectacular number and several interesting 'trickster' scenes, Sophie's interiority is left unexplored until the conclusion of the musical, when the 'real' Sophie comes onstage and is shown to be profoundly unbothered by her time with the boys, reframing their deep emotional investment. Prior to this, her role primarily serves the primacy of hetero-patriarchal relations. However, unlike (for example) David Mamet's *Speed-the-Plow*, where the role of the single-named 'Karen' serves the same function, in *Departure Lounge* Irvine's spectral, non-realist use of the female figure and the unique dramaturgy of the musical theatre form opens this masculinist formation to both critique and reinforcement. Next, I explore some of the key frameworks in masculinity studies that help us understand this dual positioning.

'Hegemonic' masculinities and homosocial bonding

A 2022 audience saturated in online discourse might describe the boys' behaviours, language, jokes and attitudes as evidence of 'toxic masculinity', a term that has been problematized by multiple scholars.[11] As Michael Salter notes, the term was coined as part of the mythopoetic men's movement of the 1980s, a movement of (mostly white, mostly straight) men's only wilderness retreats and drum circles, which aimed at asserting an authentic and protective 'warrior' masculinity in contrast to a violent, bullying and sexist 'toxic' masculinity.[12] The mythopoetic men's movement was itself anti-feminist and aimed at reinforcing traditional gender binaries because it argued that toxic masculinity arose as a result of the 'feminization' of boys through second-wave feminism.[13] However, there is no denying the term's massive scholarly and popular appeal. As Carol Harrington notes, 'its appeal lies in its ability to summon a recognizable character type', even if its usage is frequently vague or undefined.[14] For Andrea Waling, it is precisely the tendency to see masculinity as a set of 'types' that is the problem, since this leaves the structural critique of the gender binary unexplored.[15]

The term rarely appeared before 2015, and then took off in usage in 2016 due in part, no doubt, to the election of Donald Trump as president of the United States and the resurgence of populist politics across the globe.[16] As the first draft of *Departure Lounge* was written in 2004, a full twelve years earlier, we can safely assume that the term was not in circulation at the time. In a sense, it is to the musical's benefit that it does not engage with this form of typological analysis. Instead of simply critiquing a 'character type', Irvine's script explores how such behaviours manifest in a structure of relations. Thus, the musical might be said to be an exploration of 'hegemonic', rather than toxic, masculinity.

Though the terms are often used interchangeably, hegemonic masculinity is not the same as toxic masculinity. It was developed in the work of sociologist Raewyn Connell based on empirical study of young men in Australia.[17] Connell argues that masculinity is less 'what men are' and more 'what men do', a set of practices determined by other social relations, including relations with women, class, race, sexuality, power and so on.[18] The encounter between relations of power, production and desire with bodies we read as 'men' and those we read as 'women' produces the structure of 'hegemonic masculinity', a set of practices and behaviours that occupies the hegemonic or leading 'position in a given pattern of gender relations.'[19] Despite often being misinterpreted by many as such, Connell maintains that hegemonic masculinity is not a character type.[20] Instead, it describes the 'currently accepted' hierarchy that positions a certain set of characteristics at the top, with other forms of masculinities playing subordinate and complicit roles.[21] The form of masculinity that occupies a hegemonic position is always in transition.[22] So, although JB, Jordan, Pete and Ross can be seen as character types (Alpha male, soft heart-throb, wild man and insecure nerd), another way of analysing the musical is to focus on the dynamics between them and how their masculinities form through their relationships with each other.

We see this particularly in the relationship between JB and Ross. From the start, it is clear that JB occupies the hegemonic position in the group. His first sung line declares it: '*I'm James Bartholomew Watson, my friends call me JB [. . .] They're all top lads and they all look up to me.*' His class position and distinction from the other boys are clearly marked (he is 'upper middle middle upper class'), and there are references to his wealthy, but distant, father and the fact that JB has paid for the other lads to go on holiday. JB is also casually misogynistic ('You'll get loads of skirt at Oxford,' he tells Ross, 'Sophisticated totty, quote 'em a sonnet and you'll be up to your nuts in guts') and racist.[23] The other lads occupy what Connell calls 'subordinated' positions around him.[24] This does not mean, necessarily, that JB is a bully or leads the group through force or violence. Rather, Pete, Jordan and Ross evidence a 'complicit masculinity'; accruing the 'benefits of patriarchy without enacting a strong version of masculine dominance'.[25]

I would argue that *Departure Lounge* is more sophisticated than many sociological misinterpretations of hegemonic masculinity, because it recognizes the fluidity of how patriarchy is organized and the 'agency of subordinated and marginalized groups'.[26] Throughout the piece, Pete, Ross and Jordan struggle against JB's hegemony, while JB himself seems to suffer from having to occupy the hegemonic position. Even more than the narrative, Irvine emphasizes these masculine dynamics in the musical score. We see this perhaps best in JB and Ross's duet, 'Do You Know What I Think of You?'.

The song appears about halfway into the show, at the first point when Ross and JB are alone together onstage. There is an immediate tonal shift when the group reduces from four to two, with JB and Ross becoming introspective. Their musings about the transition from A-Levels to university is interrupted by another fantasmatic appearance by Sophie. In a flashback of sorts, JB confronts her, warning her not to 'mess him [Ross] around', because 'Ross is one of the guys.' The 'memory' of Sophie suddenly becomes menacing:

> **Sophie**   Your family'd barely notice if you disappeared a whole week would they? Your butler'd be the only one who'd miss you. [. . .] What would your Dad do JB? Would he like me? Bit of working class. I'm a slapper really aren't I?

After confronting JB about his deepest insecurity, that is, his distant relationship with his father and his lack of a supportive family structure, it becomes clear that JB relies emotionally on his bond with Ross. His sung lyrics in 'Do You Know What I Think of You?' give voice to what he cannot speak aloud:

> **JB**   *Do you know what I think of you*
> *You've been my best mate since key stage two*
> *While I'm around you'll never feel fear*

Yet, while the song, which is in the style of an acoustic pop ballad, is structurally equivalent to the musical theatre love duet, when Ross begins to sing, it is clear that the homosocial bond is asymmetrical.

> **Ross**   *Do you know what I think of you I've felt like this for a year or two*
> *I'm sitting here wishing you'd disappear*

The duet continues in this manner, with JB expressing his love for his friend, and Ross singing of 'how much [he's] grown', away from JB. In this way, the song is exemplary of the musical's nuanced treatment of hegemonic masculinity. While JB's hegemony is maintained by his various forms of structural advantage, in particular his class position, it is also undercut by his insecurity and the fact that his leadership of the group is not emotionally fulfilling. In this sense, *Departure Lounge* illustrates the feminist argument that patriarchy harms men. As bell hooks writes, 'patriarchy demands of all males that they engage in acts of psychic self-mutilation, that they kill off the emotional parts of themselves.'[27] This emotional discontinuity enables the subordinated masculinities represented by his friends (e.g. working class, queer, non-dominant) to assert their agency. Irvine's vocal composition makes this audible.

Martin Sutton's classic essay 'Patterns of Meaning in the Musical', observes that the discontinuity between sung and spoken voice in the musical gives musicals their particular symbolic power.[28] That is, the meaning of the musical can be found in the disjuncture of the numbers, whose expansive freedom represents the 'Id', and the book, whose realist presentation represents 'inhibition and repression.'[29] The narrative is the reality principle that 'surrounds, regulates and keeps in check the voluptuous, non-realist excesses of the number', the unruly Id of the musical.[30] This psychoanalytic dynamic is clearly played out in 'Do You Know What I Think of You?', which enables JB and Ross to give voice to emotions and affects that cannot be permitted within the social organization of their friendship group and which the other cannot, at least diegetically, hear. One might see the spoken lines at the end of the song reasserting the status quo: '*JB:* Alright Rosco? / *ROSS:* Yeah mate.'

More important than even the lyrical discontinuity that makes plain JB and Ross's contrasting objectives is Irvine's vocal composition. The fact that Irvine composed *Departure Lounge* for guitar enables a complex exploration of emotional dynamics: the chord structure is typically pop, but the voicings are very specific (and very difficult to recreate on a keyboard). For example, the second chord of the opening riff is 'Amaj7(add 9th omit3rd) over F#', while the pre-chorus uses the guitar's unique property of building and accreting small tonal changes to its advantage: 'C#m / C#m7/8 / C#m7/A# / F# / F#m7(add11) / Bsus7 / B7 / B7sus2 / B7'. Over this chord structure the melody is built around long, held riffs on open vowels, sung in harmonies that shift from major to minor, allowing the voices to snake around each other in sometimes dissonant and other times consonant ways. Like the work of Jonathan Larson and Lin-Manuel Miranda, *Departure Lounge* recruits pop composition to musical theatre storytelling. In this case, the pop-rock sensibility is drawn from a particularly British genre of boy band, which includes acts such as McFly, Busted, The Wanted, Blue, and, above all, Take That. Irvine notes the influence of this pop form on his writing and his desire to bring this sound, which had not to that point been heard in musical theatre, to the British stage.[31] 'Do You Know What I Think of You?' could even be a template for Robbie Williams and Gary Barlow's reunion single 'Shame' (2010). In the video for that song – a homosocial ballad that expressing regret – Williams and Barlow consciously play on the aesthetics and narratives of Ang Lee's filmic adaptation of Annie E. Proulx's novella *Brokeback Mountain*, a knowing wink to the homoerotics of boy bands and male duets.

By referencing homosocial spaces in popular music (rock bands, boy bands), Irvine breaks with other conventions of representing homosociality in musical theatre. Unlike female duets, which Stacy Wolf argues are quite ubiquitous in musical theatre, male duets are much more rare.[32] When they appear, they often represent competitive homosocial dynamics. In her book *Between Men*, Sedgwick described a kind of 'erotic triangle' in which the bonding (desire) between two men was practiced through their relation to a woman (or women).[33] In Sedgwick's argument, homosocial desire upholds patriarchy through a system in which women become a kind of currency men use to improve their ranking on the masculine social scale. Sociologist Michael Flood's work with young men confirms Sedgwick's literary analysis (evidence of cultural works' ability to script social patterns as much as vice versa); he argues that young men's heterosexual relations are organized by their homosocial ones.[34] This kind of triangle is common in many male duets in musical theatre, such as 'Pore Jud is Daid' (*Oklahoma!*), 'Pretty Women' (*Sweeney Todd*), 'Agony' (*Into the Woods*) all the way to Georges Bizet's *The Pearl Fisher*'s duet 'Au fond du temple saint', sung by Nadir and Zurga, who are in love with the same woman.

Unlike these other duets, 'Do You Know What I Think of You?' is not about the homosocial triangle but homosocial desire *as such*, which sets *Departure Lounge* apart from the narrative conventions of traditional musical comedies where the formation of the heterosexual couple is the ultimate goal. Musical theatre scholar Stacy Wolf argues that 'a musical's heterosexual story takes place in a world consisting of two clearly delineated homosocial communities. The actual scenes, songs and dances focus on the heterosexual couple's lack of compatibility and on their better fit within their respective homosocial spheres, which are represented through singly gendered chorus numbers, trios, and duets'.[35] In Wolf's queer reading, these singly gendered numbers represent queer spaces within the overwhelmingly heteronormative narrative. In *Departure Lounge*, however the sole female figure Sophie does not represent the hoped-for heterosexual union, but a disruptive element in the homosocial world of the lads. In this way, the show as a whole might be seen as a complex and even critical exploration of hegemonic masculinity and homosocial dynamics in action.

Historicizing *Departure Lounge* through 'inclusive' masculinity

The dynamics of hegemonic masculinity and homosociality explored in *Departure Lounge* are, if not universal, at least cross-culturally recognizable. Other aspects of the piece are extremely 'British', representing a specific period of political and social change in British history. When Irvine began writing *Departure Lounge* at twenty-four, he 'hadn't seen [himself] represented in musical theatre, neither the characters nor the sound'.[36] Theatre itself seemed 'too rich, too sophisticated, too highbrow', and throughout Irvine's career he has pushed back against theatre's inaccessibility in terms of both cost and content. Paraphrasing Henry David Thoreau, he says, theatre 'doesn't really capture the unfiltered experience of the masses leading their lives of quiet desperation'.[37] When *Departure Lounge* premiered, it became casually known as '*The Inbetweeners: The Musical*' and brought in new audiences to the theatre who might not otherwise go, who were drawn to the recognizable and ordinary lives the musical portrays.

But 'ordinary' is always relative. With distance we might recognize this ordinariness as historically specific and worthy of analysis. The year *Departure Lounge* appeared at Southwark's Waterloo East Theatre, 2010, also marked the beginning of an ongoing period of governmental austerity and social precarity, inaugurated by the election of the coalitional government of the Conservative Party and Liberal Democrats. Within a year, the transition to university that the lads play out in the story would become an exceedingly fraught period in most young people's lives as universities' teaching grant was cut and tuition fees were raised to £9,000 per year. Universities became reliant on student numbers for fiscal sustainability; effectively marketizing education, while simultaneously producing young graduates as indebted subjects. Meanwhile, other aspects of social welfare and services were slashed by the Conservatives and racism and xenophobia grew exponentially, in line with the government's 'Hostile Environment' policy. In 2022, after Brexit and two years of the ongoing Covid-19 pandemic, with what is now being called the 'cost-of-living' crisis, the Brits Abroad trip in *Departure Lounge* seems like a privilege, and the period of transition to university weightier than might have been intended by the young Irvine. This distance makes *Departure Lounge*'s class antagonisms, between JB and the other boys, much more resonant.

Another social antagonism whose terrain has shifted enormously since the original production of *Departure Lounge* is homophobia and the acceptance of LGBT+ people. In 2007, the American sociologist C. J. Pascoe argued that homophobia and heterosexism were constitutive elements of the gendered hierarchy among young people.[38] In Pascoe's ethnographic analysis of an anonymous US high school, the 'f-slur'[39] was ubiquitous among her interlocutors but was not necessarily associated with sexual identity as such. Rather, it was used as a gendered insult, symbolizing the failure of masculinity. 'Penetrated men,' she writes, 'symbolize a masculinity devoid of power, which, in its contradiction, threatens both psychic and social chaos'.[40] Homophobic abuse – verbal and physical – polices this potential chaos and regulates the gender order.

Initially, Irvine seems to simply represent homophobic adolescent culture, which can be quite uncomfortable for audiences in 2022. Within five lines of the opening of the piece, JB says, 'This delay is extremely gay,' cueing the opening number, 'Brits on Tour', where the boys harmonize:

JB	*That's so gay . . .*
Ross	*That's so gay . . .*
Pete	*That's so gay . . .*
Jordan	*That's so gay . . .*

While it is not an open term of abuse like the 'f-slur', the use of 'gay' as an insult to mean something generically negative has been argued to be part of the wider homophobic culture among young people.[41] However, by the time we see Jordan start to struggle with his sexuality, it is clear that the motivation of the musical is not to represent/reproduce homophobia. Rather, like other aspects of hegemonic masculinity, *Departure Lounge* charts the larger social shifts around homosexuality and homophobia among young men.

The mid-show ensemble number, 'Why Do We Say Gay?' explores the nuances of young men's relationship to homosexuality and inclusion. As Jordan questions the use of the term, 'the stage becomes a classroom', and the other boys explain that in comparison to other insults, gay is 'original' and 'wholesome', 'euphoric' and 'symbolic', 'erotic' and 'psychotic.' What it isn't (intended to be) is homophobic:

[*mid-song dialogue*]
JB   Look Jordan, I hear what you're saying, but we're not homophobic.
Pete   No way man, I love gay people. Not like that.
Ross   Apparently one in five people are gay. Some say more like one in four . . .

The three straight friends adhere to the common argument that 'gay' as an insult does not actually have anything to do with sexuality. Instead, they sing, it is a way to signify their in-group homosocial bond:

Pete/JB/Ross	*What we like to hear is a rousing cheer*
All	*That makes us feel like we're the only ones*
Pete/JB/Ross	*Coz we really are the best of chums*
All	*Yes we really are the best of chums*

The number ends with a fugue-like canon with JB, Ross and Pete singing contrapuntal melodies on the word 'gay'. Eventually, Jordan himself joins in, his melody rising above the rest on a sustained falsetto A above tenor high C, perhaps signalling his eventual revelation of his own queer identity.

The group's non-homophobia is confirmed when Jordan comes out to them in the show's final moments. While surprised, JB, Ross and Pete accept Jordan's sexuality quickly, with JB even declaring, 'It looks like we're gonna have to find a new word to insult each other.' This rapid and uncontroversial acceptance reflects what some sociologists have called

'Inclusive Masculinity' – a shift towards inclusion, especially towards non-hetero sexual identities, in young men in the post-industrial West. Inclusive masculinity was elaborated by Eric Anderson in 2009. Based on qualitative research with young men of university age, Anderson suggests that homophobia and 'homohysteria' (the fear of being labelled gay) has declined, enabling young straight men to engage in behaviours, such as expressing physical affection, that might have previously threatened their sense of masculinity.[42] Further to Anderson's research, sociologist Mark McCormack has argued that inclusive masculinity explains how the pejorative usage of 'gay' should be seen as context specific and dependent on intention.[43] Like the characters in *Departure Lounge*, McCormack's adolescent male interlocutors 'judged the phrases as acceptable because they knew the person who was saying them' and understood the usage within their group as non-homophobic.[44] Inclusive masculinity has been challenged for its sample bias: Anderson's original theory was based on a study of only thirty-five young, white, middle-class men in the UK, making the generalizability of the *theory* questionable.[45] However, Anderson's work can be understood as more descriptive than analytical, not producing a theory of masculinity but describing a social group – precisely the same social group that *Departure Lounge* depicts. Therefore, a fun musical number like 'Why Do We Say Gay?' can also be considered a realist depiction of a transition in the nature of masculinity in Britain.

However, the lads' inclusive, non-homophobic attitudes do not necessarily demonstrate a utopian impulse either. Firstly, although the lads may understand their in-group use of 'gay' as non-homophobic, the audience is not part of their in-group. Thus, the song and other lines in the play uncomfortably play with homophobia for comedic purposes (see, for instance, the lyrics where the straight boys shout synonyms for 'gay', all of which refer in a puerile way, to anal sex). More importantly, though, the acceptance of queer difference by dominant heterosexist culture does little to undo the systems that uphold this structural advantage. As Anderson and McCormack admit, inclusive masculinity does not challenge heterosexism, even if it indicates that homophobia may be declining in certain spheres. 'Inclusive' masculinity, for both our boys and Anderson and McCormack's interlocutors, may be more inclusive of non-hegemonic, subordinated masculinities, but it is not necessarily more inclusive of women and non-binary people. The boys' attitudes to women do not evolve in the same way. Thus, their inclusive group might be representative of the kinds of behaviours that Pascoe and Bridges have documented in their work on 'hybrid masculinities', wherein young (white, heterosexual) men flirt and play with behaviours associated with homosexuality, sometimes in a comic way, to disavow or 'symbolically distance' themselves from hegemonic masculinity while at the same time not challenging gender binaries or systems of power, and perhaps even reifying them.[46]

The queer spectre haunting the group is Jordan and the desire he is never given the opportunity to express. With his soaring vocal lines, sensitivity and moral clarity, Jordan emerges as the most sympathetic figure among the boys. In a late 'I wish' moment, he says, 'I'm one of the guys but I'm more than that. I'm an individual and I gotta realise it.' He then goes on to express his desire ('I was looking at that Spanish Garda in his uniform and I just . . .') before this is policed violently by JB ('Stop right there. Stop. Now. Stop. Jesus! Fuck!'). Jordan's queerness is absorbed within the collective without actually threatening or destabilizing the social order. One wonders, what would happen if Jordan were to give voice, even to sing, his desire?

Coda: Whiteness and masculinities in *Memoirs of an Asian Football Casual*

Throughout this chapter, I have explored how Irvine's writing and vocal composition captures a historical point of transition for young men, during a period in which social, political and economic forces were opening eyes around the world to racism, misogyny, homophobia, transphobia, class antagonisms, ableism and other forms of marginalization and discrimination. The fact that the subject of this musical – horny, obnoxious and badly behaving young men – seems to jar with 2020s sensibilities captures that transition itself. What might easily be dismissed, in the post #MeToo era, as simple representation of hegemonic masculinity actually contains its own internal critique via Irvine's compositional choices. At the same time, I have also demonstrated that one of the show's more progressive or inclusive themes, the boys' attitude to homosexuality, while marking a transitional moment for masculinity, does not necessarily challenge the status quo.

However, there is a 'white elephant' in the room, which is the unmarked whiteness of our lead characters. In his interview, Irvine stated that he had not considered the ethnicity or race of the characters, which is not mentioned in the libretto. Yet, the social milieu of the boys makes it difficult not to consider them, if not racially 'white', then in some way aligned to 'whiteness', which is to say, the form of structural and systemic advantage aligned to white people. This is demonstrated in subtle ways, though never addressed directly. For example, in the number 'Thursday Night', the characters adopt a version of Multicultural London English (MLE) to rap the verses. While you might imagine Black or non-white actors also doing this, the 'gag' hinges on the distance between the MLE they put on to their own accents. The genre of music on which the score is based, furthermore, is primarily associated with young white men. However, whiteness is perhaps most present in the fact that it is *not* present. While *Departure Lounge* is very clear in its exploration of gender, class and sexuality, race is never vocalized (except in one or two casually racist jokes by JB). As Richard Dyer suggests, 'the sense of whites as non-raced is most evident in the absence of habitual speech and writing of white people in the West'.[47] This invisibility, or unmarkedness, of race within the musical thus aligns with the wider 'invisibility of whiteness as a racial position in white (which is to say dominant) discourse'.[48] Whiteness also becomes present when we consider the casting of the piece. While mixed-race actor Liam Tamne played Jordan in the London production and is featured on the cast recording, an all-Black or all-Asian cast of *Departure Lounge* would signify very differently, since one would assume a group of four Black or Asian lads might encounter at the very least some unwanted staring in the overwhelmingly white culture of British holidaymakers to Spain.[49]

Dougal Irvine would address this absence directly in what would be his last play before retiring from the theatre to take up a career in teaching, *Memoirs of an Asian Football Casual* (2018). Based on Riaz Khan's autobiographical book, *Memoirs*, like *Departure Lounge*, also tells the story of masculinity. *Memoirs* is not a musical, but it is a hugely theatrical piece of dramatic writing that uses direct address and meta-commentary. The narrative is a picaresque, starting with Khan's family's history of immigration (from Afghanistan to Pakistan to Leicester), his upbringing in a Pathan Muslim household and the racism he encountered from white kids and skinheads on the streets of Leicester, to his eventual initiation into the Leicester City Football Club's gang of hooligans, the Baby Squad. Irvine gives context to racial conflict in Britain in the 1980s (the stage directions at the top of Scene Five read: *Voice over/clips: National Front march in Leicester. Government refusing to condemn them. Support for the far right in high places*).[50] Against this backdrop and the values of his strict parents against which he was beginning to rebel, the multi-racial gang of hooligans, or 'casuals', became a place where Khan could explore his identity. Eventually, he becomes conflicted with the violence of the scene. He drifts away after witnessing the horror of the Hillsborough Disaster of 1989, in which ninety-six people died and 766 people were injured in a fatal crush at Hillsborough Stadium.

The similarities between Irvine's first and last pieces for the theatre are striking: both are representations of highly homosocial environments that feature young men acting out obnoxious, albeit socially decriminalized,[51] behaviour during an extremely transitory period in their lives. Both pieces brought also new audiences into the theatre in a manner truthful to Irvine's motivation to make theatre more accessible. However, in *Memoirs*, Irvine's maturity as a writer is demonstrated by his command of Riaz Khan's voice. In contrast to the four boys in *Departure Lounge*, Riaz is given the stage to articulate the multiple versions of himself. The play features only two actors: one playing Riaz and the other playing his brother, Suf. Nearly every scene features the refrain, 'Who am I?' This starts as a way of introducing the carousel of characters Riaz and Suf will play, from people in their lives to far-right British politician Enoch Powell. However, the device is also a way of marking Riaz's personal transitions: 'Who am I? I am me aged fifteen. I am playing football on Rushy Mead estate with Suf and some boys my age.'[52] The final scene of the play shows Riaz in the present (i.e. 2018):

> Who am I? I am me, aged forty-three. I have a wife and four children. I have a degree from De Montford University where I am employed as a lecturer. I am a practising Muslim who loves wearing Fila, Stone Island and Adidas Gazelles. I work with the British council, advising them on tackling extremism within the Islamic community. Recently, I've seen the rise again of the far right; I've seen them recruiting in football grounds, preaching hate, blaming the immigrant for society's problems. I approach far-right leaders on the street, confront them face to face. I listen; I do not judge, I seek to understand. Because of my background as a hooligan they will talk to me.[53]

While the identities of our *Departure Lounge* lads, who occupy the position of the default subject of Western society, goes 'unmarked', *Memoirs* portrays a lad who is marked as different from the outset, and who must find his place in a society not ordered for his flourishing. Thus, Riaz cannot help but articulate these internal and social conflicts (in his very witty, dynamic voice). *Departure Lounge* might therefore be seen as an early, youthful exploration of Irvine's authorial concerns with masculinity that were realized more fully, or in a different way, in *Memoirs*. Between the first and 'last' pieces, Irvine grapples with what it means to be a man in Britain, along its many intersections.

Notes

1. Dougal Irvine, *Departure Lounge* (unpublished libretto), 2010. All lyrics quoted have been drawn from the revised libretto. The author would like to thank Dougal Irvine for kindly providing a libretto and the cast recording, which features Steven Webb, Chris Fountain, Liam Tamne,

Jack Shalloo and Verity Rushworth. I would like to thank him for his generosity in sitting down (online) for an interview and answering questions via email.
2. Dougal Irvine, 'Interview with' Broderick Chow, conducted online on Zoom, 2 October 2021.
3. Irvine, 'Interview with'.
4. Irvine, 'Interview with'.
5. Peggy Phelan, *Unmarked: The Politics of Performance* (London: Routledge, 1996).
6. Daniel Briggs, 'Capitalismo Extremo, Ideology and Ibiza: A New Perspective of Youth Deviance and Risk on Holiday', *Papers from the British Criminology Conference, British Society of Criminology* 13 (2013): 33–50 (34).
7. Briggs, 'Capitalismo Extremo', 34.
8. Briggs, 'Capitalismo Extremo', 46–7.
9. Matt Boothman, 'Departure Lounge', *British Theatre Guide*, n.d. (2010), https://www.britishtheatreguide.info/reviews/departurelounge-rev.
10. Eve Kosofsky Sedgwick, *Between Men: English Literature and Male Homosocial Desire* (New York: Columbia University Press, 1985), 16.
11. See Carol Harrington, 'What Is "Toxic Masculinity" and Why Does It Matter?', *Men and Masculinities* 20, no. 10 (2021): 1–8; Andrea Waling, 'Problematising "Toxic" and "Healthy" Masculinity for Addressing Gender Inequalities', *Australian Feminist Studies* (2019), doi:10.1080/08164649.2019.1679021.
12. Michael Salter, 'The Problem with a Fight against "Toxic Masculinity"', *The Atlantic*, 27 February 2019, https://www.theatlantic.com/health/archive/2019/02/toxic-masculinity-history/583411/.
13. Salter, 'The Problem with a Fight against "Toxic Masculinity"'.
14. Harrington, 'What is "Toxic Masculinity"', 6.
15. Waling, 'Problematising', 2.
16. Harrington, 'What is "Toxic Masculinity"', 2.
17. Raewyn Connell, *Masculinities*, 2nd edn (Berkeley: University of California Press, 2005).
18. Connell, *Masculinities*, 73–5.
19. Connell, *Masculinities*, 76.
20. Connell, *Masculinities*, 76.
21. Connell, *Masculinities*, 77.
22. Connell, *Masculinities*, 76.
23. Referring to a replica matador sword he has bought as a souvenir, JB says, '(Japanese accent) Ah, bendy plastic, come from Taiwan' (8). The discontinuity between the stage direction and the line is almost certainly intended to make JB the butt of the joke.
24. Connell, *Masculinities*.
25. Raewyn Connell and James W. Messerschmidt, 'Hegemonic Masculinity: Rethinking the Concept', *Gender & Society* 19, no. 6 (2005): 829–59 (832).
26. Connell and Messerschmidt, 'Hegemonic Masculinity', 847.
27. bell hooks, *The Will to Change: Men, Masculinity and Love* (New York: Washington Square Press, 2004), 66.
28. Martin Sutton, 'Patterns of Meaning in the Musical', in *Genre: The Musical*, ed. Rick Altman (London: BFI, 1981), 190–6 (191).
29. Sutton, 'Patterns of Meaning', 191.
30. Sutton, 'Patterns of Meaning', 191.
31. Irvine, 'Interview with'.

32. Stacy Wolf, '"We'll Always Be Bosom Buddies": Female Duets and the Queering of Broadway Musical Theater', *GLQ: A Journal of Lesbian and Gay Studies* 12, no. 3 (2006): 351–76 (352).
33. Sedgwick, *Between Men*.
34. Michael Flood, 'Men, Sex, and Homosociality: How Bonds between Men Shape Their Sexual Relations with Women', *Men and Masculinities* 10, no. 3 (2007): 339–59.
35. Wolf, '"We'll Always Be Bosom Buddies"', 353.
36. Irvine, 'Interview with'.
37. Irvine, 'Interview with'.
38. C. J. Pascoe, *Dude, You're a Fag: Masculinity and Sexuality in High School,* 2nd edn (Durham: Duke University Press, 2007[2011]).
39. Note that Pascoe's book and journal articles liberally cite the 'f-slur' in full, even in the titles themselves. In my citational practice, I represent the slur in full when referring to Pascoe's titles in the footnotes, but choose not to in the body of the text itself.
40. C. J. Pascoe, '"Dude, You're a Fag": Adolescent Masculinity and the Fag Discourse', *Sexualities* 8 (2005): 329–46 (329).
41. See Hannah Kiribige and Luke Tryl, *Tackling Homophobic Language* (London: Stonewall Education Guides, 2015).
42. Eric Anderson, *Inclusive Masculinity: The Changing Nature of Masculinities* (London: Routledge, 2009).
43. Mark McCormack, 'Maybe "That's So Gay" is Actually Ok for Young People to Say', *The Conversation*, 4 July 2014, https://theconversation.com/maybe-thats-so-gay-is-actually-ok-for-young-people-to-say-28687.
44. Eric Anderson and Mark McCormack, 'Inclusive Masculinity Theory: Overview, Reflection and Refinement', *Journal of Gender Studies* 27, no. 5 (2018): 547–61 (553). Of course, like any microaggression, the intent of the speaker does not mitigate the impact on marginalized persons.
45. Nicola Ingram and Richard Waller, 'Degrees of Masculinity: Working and Middle-Class Undergraduate Students' Constructions of Masculine Identities', in *Debating Modern Masculinities: Change, Continuity, Crisis?*, ed. Steven Roberts (London: Palgrave Macmillan, 2014), 35–51.
46. Tristan Bridges and C. J. Pascoe, 'Hybrid Masculinities: New Directions in the Sociology of Men and Masculinities', *Sociology Compass* 8, no. 3 (2014): 246–58 (246).
47. Richard Dyer, 'The Matter of Whiteness', in *White Privilege: Essential Readings on the Other Side of Racism*, 5th edn, ed. Paula Rothenberg (New York: Worth Publishers, 2015), 9–14.
48. Dyer, 'The Matter of Whiteness', 11.
49. Anette Pankratz, 'Fifty Shades of White: Benidorm and the Joys of All-Inclusiveness', in *The Intersections of Whitness*, ed. Evangelia Kindinger and Mark Schmitt (London: Routledge, 2019).
50. Dougal Irvine, *Memoirs of an Asian Football Casual* (unpublished playscript provided by the author).
51. Jill D. Weinberg, *Consensual Violence: Sex, Sports, and the Politics of Injury* (Berkeley: University of California Press, 2016), 23.
52. Irvine, *Memoirs*, 12.
53. Irvine, *Memoirs*, 62.

Works Cited

Anderson, Eric (2009), *Inclusive Masculinity: The Changing Nature of Masculinities*. London: Routledge.

Anderson, Eric and Mark McCormack (2018), 'Inclusive Masculinity Theory: Overview, Reflection and Refinement', *Journal of Gender Studies*, 27 (5): 547–61.

Boothman, Matt (2010), 'Departure Lounge', *British Theatre Guide*, https://www.britishtheatreguide.info/reviews/departurelounge-rev.

Bridges, Tristan and C. J. Pascoe (2014), 'Hybrid Masculinities: New Directions in the Sociology of Men and Masculinities', *Sociology Compass*, 8 (3): 246–58.

Briggs, Daniel (2013), 'Capitalismo Extremo, Ideology and Ibiza: A New Perspective of Youth Deviance and Risk on Holiday', *Papers from the British Criminology Conference, British Society of Criminology*, 13: 33–50.

Connell, Raewyn (2005), *Masculinities*, 2nd edn. Berkeley: University of California Press.

Connell, Raewyn and James W. Messerschmidt (2005), 'Hegemonic Masculinity: Rethinking the Concept', *Gender & Society*, 19 (6): 829–59.

Dyer, Richard (2015), 'The Matter of Whiteness', in Paula Rothenberg (ed.), *White Privilege: Essential Readings on the Other Side of Racism*, 5th edn, 9–14. New York: Worth Publishers.

Flood, Michael (2007), 'Men, Sex, and Homosociality: How Bonds Between Men Shape Their Sexual Relations with Women', *Men and Masculinities*, 10 (3): 339–59.

Harrington, Carol (2021), 'What Is "Toxic Masculinity" and Why Does it Matter?', *Men and Masculinities*, 20 (10): 1–8.

hooks, bell (2004), *The Will to Change: Men, Masculinity and Love*. New York: Washington Square Press.

Ingram, Nicola and Richard Waller (2014), 'Degrees of Masculinity: Working and Middle-Class Undergraduate Students' Constructions of Masculine Identities', in Steven Roberts (ed.), *Debating Modern Masculinities: Change, Continuity, Crisis?*, 35–51. London: Palgrave Macmillan.

Irvine, Dougal (2010), *Departure Lounge* (unpublished libretto).

Irvine, Dougal (2021), 'Interview with' Broderick Chow, conducted online on Zoom, 2 October.

Irvine, Dougal (2018), *Memoirs of an Asian Football Casual* (unpublished playscript provided by the author).

Kiribige, Hannah and Luke Tryl (2015), *Tackling Homophobic Language*. London: Stonewall Education Guides.

McCormack, Mark (2014), 'Maybe "That's So Gay" Is Actually Ok for Young People to Say', *The Conversation*, 4 July.

Pankratz, Anette (2019), 'Fifty Shades of White: Benidorm and the Joys of All-Inclusiveness', in Evangelia Kindinger and Mark Schmitt (eds), *The Intersections of Whiteness*, 200–18. London: Routledge.

Pascoe, C. J. (2005), '"Dude, You're a Fag": Adolescent Masculinity and the Fag Discourse', *Sexualities*, 8: 329–46.

Pascoe, C. J. ([2007] 2011). *Dude, You're a Fag: Masculinity and Sexuality in High School*, 2nd edn. Durham: Duke University Press.

Phelan, Peggy (1996). *Unmarked: The Politics of Performance*. London: Routledge.

Salter, Michael (2019), 'The Problem with a Fight Against "Toxic Masculinity"', *The Atlantic*, 27 February.

Sedgwick, Eve Kosofsky (1985), *Between Men: English Literature and Male Homosocial Desire*. New York: Columbia University Press.

Sedgwick, Eve Kosofsky (2015), *Between Men: English Literature and Male Homosocial Desire*. New York: Columbia University Press.
Sutton, Martin (1981), 'Patterns of Meaning in the Musical', in Rick Altman (ed.), *Genre: The Musical*, 190–6. London: BFI.
Waling, Andrea (2019), 'Problematising "Toxic" and "Healthy" Masculinity for Addressing Gender Inequalities', *Australian Feminist Studies*, doi:10.1080/08164649.2019.1679021.
Weinberg, Jill D. (2016), *Consensual Violence: Sex, Sports, and the Politics of Injury*. Berkeley: University of California Press.
Wolf, Stacy (2006), '"We'll Always Be Bosom Buddies": Female Duets and the Queering of Broadway Musical Theater', *GLQ: A Journal of Lesbian and Gay Studies*, 12 (3): 351–76.

Dougal Irvine interview

Writer *Departure Lounge*

What is your favourite British musical?

Our House

What's your favourite British musical theatre song?

All the songs from *Lift* by Craig Adams are beautiful but 'All About Her' is my favourite from the show.

What training did you do for your career?

I didn't set out to become a writer, it was more of an evolution. I was working as an actor. And a couple of times during downtime between shows, or while I was on a long contract, I would write songs. Sometimes they were funny songs or parodies of songs I already knew. I never really intended to write for the theatre. I was always aware that I came from a place of relative ignorance in terms of craft so I was always doing my own research, watching YouTube videos and trying to learn how to shape a show.

I was coming back from a series of concerts in Sweden in 2004 and I saw four guys sitting in the departure lounge in Gothenburg airport and they just really reminded me of myself and my friends growing up. I couldn't understand what they were saying but I could just recognize the characters in the group. So I started writing that first scene for *Departure Lounge*. It started flowing out of me, and by the time the plane had landed I had the 'Brits on Tour' hook in my head.

Departure Lounge is the first musical we look at in the book – do you, or indeed did you, see this as a catalyst for British musical theatre?

That's a big question! I don't honestly know. It might be that there are writers who have seen the show who then go on to do other things. So there may be a ripple effect because of that. As a writer, I don't think I saw much of that ripple effect. I think I was too busy trying to make a living. People would tell me that they'd seen the show, or other shows it had influenced, which was brilliant. What people more often than not said to me was that they saw the guitar as a viable instrument for writing a show. At the time the piano very much dominated new musical theatre.

We would go into a theatre and the sound designer wouldn't have a clue how to make the show sound right. So, usually I worked very carefully with the sound designer to show them how to make the guitar sound. That's really the only thing that I saw as a writer in terms of what the show influenced. It really was a case of it got me some commissions and got me to the next job. I always thought that eventually I'd write *the show* that would have the big reach. *Departure Lounge* has probably had more productions than any other show I've written. I think that's just because it's cheap and easy to put on. You can put it on anywhere with four chairs, five actors and two guitars. So, that's it. Whether it caused change? I really don't know.

Being involved in Perfect Pitch was a key point. *Departure Lounge* was, I think, Perfect Pitch's second project. Andy and Wendy were part of a collection of people getting together at that time and trying to put shows on and I think that that movement definitely caused change. It got some people to come to showcases for new musical work who wouldn't normally. And *Departure Lounge* got to go to Edinburgh and New York because of the work of Perfect Pitch. So maybe the catalyst wasn't so much the show but rather the group of people who were part of it. At the time we were just doing it. It felt like a lot of people were scared of sharing their work. We just went for it. I remember talking at a lot of musical theatre conventions and people would say, what's your advice? And I would say just get it on. Get it on because you learn when an audience sees your work, you get that feedback, and you can feel how you move a group of people (real people not just industry people), nothing beats that.

You wrote the book, music and lyrics for *Departure Lounge*, can you talk a little bit about the process?

When I wrote the draft I didn't do a plan but I had in my head the types of songs I wanted within the show. Like it's a mixtape for somebody, and you want the fast number and you want the slow number and you want the company number and even sad numbers. So I knew I had to have those different types of songs in the show. And when I was thinking of the original story, those songs instinctively came to me. I learned to workshop and take feedback and rewrite and write music notation. I learned it all on that show. I knew I could write three minute songs but I didn't know if I could write scenes.

We took it to the Dirty Little Secrets Festival in 2005. Having it on and just seeing the audience fall about with laughter, showed me that it worked. And then it was a case of watching it in front of an audience, feeling the journey fresh each night and going, okay now let's try and tighten up the narrative. There isn't much narrative at the moment. It's a series of jokes, then they fall out with each other and then they get back on the plane. Then it was a case of tweaking the book to fit the songs because the songs always sort of worked. Initially, we didn't have Sophie at all. We only had four guys and then I thought well, I need a female voice, almost to act as an antagonist. So I put her in the show and that changed the dynamic of the show. She was brilliant. She was also able to be in the boys' memories which gave us insights to their character in a way that they couldn't reveal in front of each other.

And then in 2007, we got a chance to showcase *Departure Lounge* at the Arts Theatre. It was retitled *Unzipped* in case it didn't work. It was really rude. And we had people walking out. The show is pretty offensive in terms of its language and potentially could insult people from all walks of life and there were much ruder jokes in that version. And it was my first lesson to go hang on a second, I've really got a responsibility here. If I want people to care about these characters, I've got to sort the story out a bit more. And particularly it was that song 'Why Do We Say Gay?'. At the time, Jordan was gay in the show but we didn't know it as the audience and so you just saw a bunch of people making gay jokes and making fun of people, which is awful. It was actually when it finally went to Edinburgh in 2008 that I worked with the director, Christian Durham, and he really helped me fix that song. He said, 'I love the song. But as a gay man. I find it really offensive and I want to help you make it work in the show'. So having Jordan as the antagonist of the song, as a slightly awkward and inarticulate character meant that he had those sorts of things working against him and suddenly the song worked. It worked so much better because the audience were then free to laugh at the naivety of the boys.

So each time it was on in front of audiences, I was able to learn from it and see what worked and what didn't. When we came back from Edinburgh it was clear that Sophie needed to have a song as well, we needed to see a bit more about what she is. So during the 2009 New York run I wrote a song for Sophie. I wasn't really happy with the song, but it was too late to change it. I rewrote that song for the Chicago production, same moment, same device, but it just was a better song. Sophie's newer song ('Female') has the same hook as 'Brand New' on the cast album but it's more about gender stereotypes. So the show was still evolving and then after that point, I sort of figured I'd been working on it for six years, and I was working on other stuff by that point, so I just let it go. I've never been able to licence the show, I think because it's so rude so any licence requests have come via my agent – who calls it 'the show that keeps on giving'.

How do you feel about *Departure Lounge* now?

I have a funny relationship with the show. It's the first show I ever wrote. So I think it's definitely the least skilled and least crafted show I wrote. If I had to rank all the shows I've written it wouldn't make my top three, although I've got a real soft spot for it. Whenever I see it I'm reminded of that exuberance and energy. I'm not 100 per cent sure if it's still relevant in places. I don't think shows necessarily should be done again and again and again forever and reinterpreted if bits of them don't work. So if it becomes a dinosaur because of that reason, then that's ultimately a good thing because it's showing a not very nice part of culture.

Can you just talk a little bit more about what influence writing *Departure Lounge*, and the whole process of that, has had on the following work that you made?

I think my job musically with *Departure Lounge* was to get acoustic Britpop into a musical, which I hadn't seen before. And I was very comfortable writing in that idiom, because that was me growing up. As it was such a small studio show you could get away with a speedier delivery of lyric. As I started to write for larger spaces, I learned to elongate the sound a bit – elongate lyrics, elongate melody lines, use more repetition.

I always tried to move on as a writer. I always tried to do something I've not done before. And as soon as I'd written *Departure Lounge* I knew that that was as close to me and my background as I can get in terms of the voice of the characters, and the way they would speak – sort of English/Essex kind of sound and then that acoustic guitar sound. The seed of the writer I was going to grow to be is all there in *Departure Lounge*, but I was just trying to always move on in one aspect from it and grow in some form. Whether it was the sounds expanding or the melody lines expanding with the integration of book and lyrics, or just bringing in a new sound entirely and just filtering that through the system and seeing what came out. I never wanted to write a *Departure Lounge* sequel, but obviously I have an idea for it and it's all plotted out. But yeah, it's the time . . .

What advice would you give to aspiring writers?

There was a good piece of advice I think Hammerstein gave Sondheim about having a goal for each show that extends your craft in some ways. So each new show I wrote I focused on either learning a new thing, playing with a new limitation interval, researching a new piece of music or watching a different piece of theatre, and suddenly there was something that I would have to learn and grow and achieve myself as a writer in writing the show. Then, irrespective of what anybody thought of the show I could say it was a success because I've done this for myself on it.

2 'The smell of rebellion' and 'The stench of revolt'

The carnivalesque dramaturgy of *Matilda the Musical* from page to stage

STEPHANIE LIM

Bambinatum est maggitum – 'children are maggots', or so Miss Trunchbull's school motto goes in *Matilda the Musical* (2010). Generating an instant narrative payoff in the form of an underdog story, Trunchbull's disdain towards children is akin to other fictional principals like Professor Umbridge from the *Harry Potter* series, Miss Minchin from *A Little Princess*, Mr Brocklehurst of *Jane Eyre* or even *The Breakfast Club*'s Vice Principal Richard Vernon and *Buffy the Vampire Slayer*'s Principal Snyder. With a strong – though at times flawed – female heroine at its core,[1] *Matilda* is frequently viewed as a progressive work that challenges the traditional conventions of both children and female figures. *New York Times* theatre critic Ben Brantley declares the show is 'the most satisfying and subversive musical to come out of Britain' and 'an exhilarating tale of empowerment as told from the perspective of the most powerless group of all'.[2] Playwright and theatre scholar Kristin Perkins likewise asserts that '*Matilda* is subversive in how it presents revolution and girlhood', albeit with questionable and exploitative labour practices towards women and children.[3] *Matilda* stands out especially during a West End season that did not see many female heroines, winning a then-record seven Olivier Awards, including Best New Musical. On the surface, then, the musical presents an easy-to-understand message that encourages and celebrates the intellectual and imaginative capabilities of children. However, a deeper exploration of the musical uncovers a more complicated gender politics, one that seems to uphold the traditional social norms of the Western world and, perhaps, even the more regressive tendencies of the source material's author, Roald Dahl.

What type of social world and power structures does the show establish? Through whose perspective are the musical's rights and wrongs defined? While director Matthew Warchus suggests that audiences readily take away the musical's moral of 'putting the wrongs of the world to right',[4] Perkins points out that 'The much more compelling argument in critiquing Broadway as a neoliberal institution is not that audiences will leave with no change of heart, but that Broadway reproduces troubling power structures in the production of shows'.[5] I draw from Mikhail Bakhtin's theory of the *carnivalesque* to interrogate the musical's dramaturgy, which simultaneously manifests an upside-down world and emphasizes feminist attitudes.[6] At the same time, the show's carnivalesque drive reinforces traditional social roles, the binary (re)presentation of gendered traits, and the heteronormative family unit. Probing what societal structures are performed and perpetuated through *Matilda*, this chapter investigates the dramaturgical choices made in adapting the Dahl novel into a stage musical, including the show's treatment of female and child characters, the addition of music and the secondary 'Acrobat Story', and the frequent casting of men in the role of Miss Trunchbull, which follows pantomime lineage. Although many see the leading character's childness and femaleness as radical, *Matilda the Musical* ultimately maintains conventional social and gendered hierarchies.

'It's like Music': Roald Dahl in adaptation

Derived from Roald Dahl's beloved 1988 children's novel of the same name, *Matilda the Musical* follows the young titular character, a five-year-old girl of immeasurable talent and intelligence who is constantly ignored and bullied by her parents and Miss Trunchbull. Emboldened by the stories she reads, Matilda uses her imagination and wit (and a little bit of magic via telekinesis) to take control of her own life story. In a *BroadwayWorld* article, Danielle Ashley reflects on the popular trend of adapting children's books into Broadway musicals, specifically focusing on how 'Roald Dahl teaches life lessons to audiences in magical ways'.[7] With both real-life application and boundless imagination, Dahl's writing has easily translated to theatrical performance. As of this writing, five Dahl novels have been adapted for the musical stage: in addition to *Matilda*, this includes a 2008 opera version of *The Witches* (novel originally published in 1983) by Marcus Paus; Benj Pasek and Justin Paul's 2010 version of *James and the Giant Peach* (novel published in 1961); Marc Shaiman and Scott Wittman's 2013 musical adaptation of *Charlie and the Chocolate Factory* (1979), as well as an earlier, lesser known adaptation by Leslie Bricusse and Timothy Allen McDonald called *Roald Dahl's Willy Wonka*; and two adaptations of *Fantastic Mr Fox* (1970), including a 1998 opera by Tobias Picker and a 2016 adaptation by Sam Holcroft and Arthur Darvill. Twenty-two years after Dahl published *Matilda*, writer Dennis Kelly, composer Tim Minchin, and director Matthew Warchus teamed up to create the musical adaptation, with additional design provided by Rob Howell (set and costumes), Hugh Vanstone (lighting), Simon Baker (sound), Peter Darling (choreography) and Paul Kieve (illusions). Produced by the Royal Shakespeare Company, the musical debuted at Stratford-upon-Avon in 2010, played the West End, Broadway, Australia, Canada and New Zealand, and toured across the United States, the United Kingdom and Ireland.

Dahl's adaptability across stage and screen mediums is due, in part, to his entertaining, nonsensical and macabre writing style that continues to reach across generations. Cinema studies scholar Whitney Crothers Dilley explains that 'Dahl's stories, while written for children, are not "safe," or sanitized for children's tastes as dictated by adults – instead, real-world violence, adult dissension, anger, and strife, war, speculation, loneliness, and death are continuously intruding into his child protagonist's world'.[8] The dangerous and somewhat alarming content of Dahl's stories is nonetheless shrouded in the eccentric fantasy worlds and unfettered imagination of his young characters; as with fairy tales, Dahl's stories 'are complex narratives of wish fulfillment'[9] that teach readers – and viewers, in the case of stage productions – 'that a struggle against severe difficulties in life is unavoidable, is an intrinsic part of human existence – but that if one does not shy away, but steadfastly meets unexpected and often unjust hardships, one masters all obstacles and at the end emerges victorious'.[10] A work like *Matilda* allows adults to tap into their child-like natures – 'to see themselves in the adult-sized children, and perhaps celebrate their own choices not to grow up entirely'[11] – offering a visual feast and ostensibly universal ideology for theatremakers and audiences alike. Kelly similarly emphasizes that audiences, whatever age they may be, ally themselves with the show's children rather than its adults, insisting 'that anyone should be able to watch the show, but they should watch it – to some extent, they should watch it as a child. The idea was never to be childish, but we could be child-like. So when everyone watches it, hopefully they watch it as a kid'.[12] In this way, the positionality and identification of Dahl's readers and of the musical's audiences are framed through the relatability of the child protagonist.

In addition to Dahl's authorial panache, Dahl's very name triggers a nostalgia that is experienced by readers on a global scale, 'not only throughout Europe and the United States but in Brazil, Thailand, Japan, even – despite what is politely called his anti-Zionism – Israel'.[13] In *Roald Dahl: A Biography*, Jeremy Treglown asserts that 'between 1980 and 1990, over eleven million of his children's books were sold in paperback form – considerably more than the total number of children born there in the same period. By the end of his life, every third British child, on average, bought or was given a book by him each year'.[14] Creators like Darvill, Kelly and Minchin have also acknowledged their lifelong knowledge and love of Dahl's works in interviews.[15] Those same children who grew up reading his books, like myself, are now in their thirties, forties and fifties – and are also today's most avid content-creators and ticket-purchasers. In making Dahl's commercial attraction explicit, I draw particular attention to the fact that increased interest in adapting Dahl's work occurred primarily in the 2010s. In addition, while Dahl's writing and the resulting stage adaptations are *about* children, they are not necessarily only *for* children. Instead, the works stretch across large readerships and followings on both sides of the stage and screen.

Matilda, like Dahl's other titles, lends itself well to musical form because theatre proffers expansive possibilities to manifest the novel's fantasy or magical realism style. Laura MacDonald describes designer Howell's set as 'draw[ing] the audience into the playing space, inviting spectators to fill in the blanks in Matilda's world for themselves, rather than watch the kind of presentational and prescriptive performances on detailed, realistic sets expected in much musical theatre production'.[16] This push against the conventions of musical theatre is also echoed by the creative team, who found the novel's rebellious overtones particularly productive. Minchin explains in an interview with Australia's ABC News that he remained 'happily naïve'[17] to the formal rules of musical theatre and, in so doing, mirrored the show's spirit of naughtiness and rule-breaking. Kelly also admits to knowing 'nothing about musicals' but perceived 'moments in this story where a song would want to happen'.[18]

Kelly's sentiments about the novel's adaptability highlight two direct, though fleeting, references to music in the novel. The first occurs during a scene between Matilda and local librarian Mrs Phelps, who helps Matilda develop a penchant for reading: in response to Matilda's feelings about not being able to understand everything expressed in Hemingway, Phelps suggests to her, 'don't worry about the bits you can't understand. Sit back and allow the words to wash around you, like music'.[19] The second reference occurs three-quarters into the novel, after Matilda's caring teacher, Miss Honey, recites a poem by Dylan Thomas: 'Matilda, who had never before heard great romantic poetry spoken aloud, was profoundly moved. "It's like music," she whispered'.[20] The magic and musicality of writing and words translate well to literal music and to the structure of musical theatre, wherein characters are often understood to express their innermost thoughts and desires through song.

Plucky heroines and nasty boys: Dahl and the representation of women

Despite the popularity of and musicality found within his work, Dahl has not existed without scrutiny, recently prompting the family to issue a posthumous apology.[21] In her 2021 *Time* article, Megan McCluskey traces the anti-Semitism, racism and misogyny expressed throughout Dahl's lifetime and works.[22] Treglown describes Dahl as 'a war hero, a connoisseur, a philanthropist, a devoted family man who had to confront an appalling succession of tragedies. He was also . . . a fantasist, an anti-Semite, a bully, and a self-publicizing troublemaker'.[23] Writer Ruth Margolis interrogates Dahl's representation of women in particular, explaining how 'Many of Dahl's books include representation of women that can only be described as hateful. While plucky female heroes are present, irredeemably awful and physically repulsive women, like the aforementioned Miss Trunchbull, are more common. There are nasty, unattractive men and boys too, but the women seem to carry the brunt of it'.[24] Yet, Dahl's themes of empowerment cause others to take a Barthean approach, thereby avoiding any intent or meaning as derived from the author. Many scholars direct their attention to the creation of Matilda during the 1980s, when the social role of women had moved beyond domesticity to functioning outside of the home:

> Dahl foregrounded a female character with a high level of independence, intelligence and strength. Matilda is such a girl and much more; she is a role model that young girls can look up to. Unlike some other female characters in the book . . . she does not comply with (some extent still entrenched) gender stereotypes and schemas according to which a girl or a woman should be meek, submissive and weak.[25]

Vidović and Vidović's description of Matilda adds to Margolis's account of the character's 'pluckiness', which may appear more acceptable for a young child still exploring her own identity and place in the world; such an unruly nature may not be so tolerated in the case of older women – and is not, in the specific case of Miss Trunchbull, who has a similar rebelliousness against gender stereotypes. Marta Þórðardóttir acknowledges that Dahl's work presents women inconsistently but also concludes that *Matilda*'s characters teach young girls to 'see that there is no mold that they have to fit; instead, they can be who and what they want to be'.[26] Þórðardóttir goes on to explain the feminist undertones that exist, in that 'women can be heroes or villains, and they can even have more than one role'.[27]

Within *Matilda the Musical*, the lack of strong role models (among women specifically and adults in general) can be interpreted as more purposeful and fruitful than treacherous. On-stage, the absence of loving parents draws out the agency and determination of Matilda, who sings lines like 'Just because you find that life's not fair, it / doesn't mean that you just have to grin and bear it' and 'Nobody else is going to put it right for me, / Nobody but me is gonna change my story / Sometimes you have to be a little bit naughty'.[28] Off-stage, however, the show's seemingly progressive stance towards women and children is paradoxically controlled by an all-male creative team, with Perkins noting that 'The lack of female advisement in the creation of Matilda is startlingly retrograde in a musical that strives to be forward thinking'.[29] How much of the musical, then, is influenced by the male perspectives that surround the work, from its original author to the creative team? To what extent does the musical disrupt and/or preserve Dahl's problematic views? In light of these continued debates, I consider what changes are made in developing *Matilda* for the musical stage, and specifically whether the show attempts to 'correct' any of the ideological ambiguities that exist.

A world turned upside-down: The carnivalesque in *Matilda the Musical*

While the musical closely follows the subversive spirit of the original novel, the transition from page to stage induced several shifts, including the addition of music and a notable secondary story called the 'Acrobat Story', told by Matilda herself. In addition, the role of Miss Trunchbull is commonly played by markedly tall men, most with stocky builds, in almost all iterations of the musical. Of the limited scholarship that compares the musical to the book, Einat Natalie Palkovich's essay '"Put It Right": Matilda as Author in *Matilda the Musical*' closely analyses the changes implemented by Kelly for the stage, such as the reordering of the novel's scenes, which see Matilda playing pranks on her family before she attends her first day at Crunchem Hall.[30] Instead, Kelly 'plac[es] episodes in which Matilda suffers cruelty from her parents and headmistress alongside her more questionable actions against others, [balancing] out the drama so that it continues to present Matilda positively'.[31]

Borrowing from children's literature scholar John Stephens, I propose that *Matilda* is a *carnivalesque interrogative text*, wherein child characters 'interrogate the normal subject positions created for children within socially dominant ideological frames',[32] thereby accentuating the ideologies that operate within the text. In short – and as I have written elsewhere[33] – the carnivalesque is a world temporarily turned upside-down, during which 'an explicit rebellion against the social hierarchies and system of values in place' occurs. Bakhtin's 'Rabelaisian carnival' is a socially disruptive and celebratory period in which 'all who are highest are debased, all who are lowest are crowned'.[34] The notion of a subversive, yet transient, realm is key to both the carnivalesque framework and *Matilda*'s story arc, both in the novel and on stage, where Matilda can act with an air of anti-establishment but not in ways that completely overthrow the structural hierarchy of the classroom or home. In other words, *Matilda* functions as a story 'in which characters temporarily take over from figures of authority and often make mischief, but control their own worlds for a time'.[35] Literary scholar Kristen Guest similarly observes this contained disorder in the novel, wherein the depiction of Matilda as sensible and quiet operates as an 'integration of intellect with classically feminine attributes of quiet self-effacement' which 'makes clear that, on the outside at least, Matilda poses no threat to the existing social order'.[36] This same concept is echoed in the character of the meek and mild Miss Honey,[37] a point I will return to in more detail.

Matilda the Musical thrives in the upside-down realm temporarily established in Dahl's writing, in which adults are childish and children are adult-like. Madeline Spivey, for example, concentrates on the adultness of Matilda, who has the knowledge of an adult while inhabiting the body of a child. This hybridity acts as a means to explore constructed otherness versus genuine otherness, that is, adult constructions of childhood versus the innate development of a child. In looking at Matilda, one is prompted to ask several basic questions: what does it mean to be a child? What does it mean to be an adult? And what does it mean for each to relate to the other?[38]

This adult–child divide is the first of several social structures and ideologies interrogated in the show, as Matilda is surrounded with incompetent, brash and senseless adults at home and school. Moreover, the adult–child divide is further inflected linguistically: whereas Dahl utilizes the article 'the' (*the father*, *the Trunchbull*) sixty-three times in the novel, which 'remov[es] any hint of affection or familial solidarity'[39] and objectifies the adult characters, this linguistic feature is removed from the musical altogether. Instead, Kelly and Minchin's libretto accents twenty-nine instances of 'the Trunchbull', collapsing the novel's hostility towards adults into the musical's antagonism towards the character of Trunchbull specifically.

The costumes visually accentuate the adult–child divide as well, with adult characters in colourful, but vulgar, outfits, invigorating illustrator Quentin Blake's black and white drawings in the novel. Mr Wormwood (as a businessman) wears a lime-checkered suit; Mrs Wormwood (an aspiring dancer) wears a bright pink and purple dress with frills; and even Mrs Phelps is garbed in shades of greenish-blue, with big curly hair, a bandana and large beads adorning her neck and wrists. Howell describes his costumes for the Wormwoods as reflecting 'how horrific it must be for Matilda, who buries herself in books and words and proper stories, and she's surrounded by these sort of garish vulgarians', going on to explain that it gave him 'tremendous license to really ramp up the colors and get exaggerated silhouettes going'.[40] In sharp contrast to the visually loud adult costumes, the children are almost always in school uniforms of dark grey and white shades, except in the opening number, 'Miracle', for which the children wear various costumes that evoke superhero and princess characters. The neutral colours given to the children, on the one hand, conjure the respectable and strict school setting effortlessly. On the other hand, the colours also ground the children as being more natural, practical and level-headed than the adults – another nod to the carnivalesque.

Despite Dahl and the show's emphasis on a world turned upside-down, the additional story and the panto-influenced casting of Miss Trunchbull (arguably the two most prominent changes from page to stage) only temporarily subverts the social order of the musical's playworld. The secondary story, called the 'Acrobat Story', is told by Matilda to Mrs Phelps across four segments during the show. The story follows a couple – an acrobat and an escapologist[41] – who perform incredible feats together but desperately want a child. After they become pregnant, the acrobat's sister reminds them of their contract, forcing them to perform 'the trick'; the story ends in tragedy, with the acrobat suffering terrible injuries and living only long enough to have the child. Dramaturgically, the story conceives of Matilda as 'an active storyteller, the author of a love story which she relates episodically throughout the show and which is revealed, in the end, to be part history and part prophecy',[42] as the escapologist is later revealed to be Honey's father. In a sort of carnivalesque fashion, this act also reverses the traditional form of storytelling from parent to child. The show emphasizes this physically, as Matilda stands on an adult-sized chair while Mrs Phelps, as her captive audience, occupies a child-sized chair. Although Matilda's narration gives the character a layer of agency, she nonetheless maintains social hierarchies through the narrative, in particular emphasizing gender roles. The 'Acrobat Story' reveals Matilda's longing for loving parents, but it also maintains a heteronormative family unit. It is also the female acrobat who performs the ultimate sacrifice for her child, as the circus performance is entitled 'The Burning Woman Hurling through the Air with Dynamite in Her Hair over Sharks and Spiky Objects, Caught by the Man Locked in the Cage'.[43] Whether deliberately or not, Matilda's storytelling is imbued with traditional social hierarchies.

Panto traditions and monstrous masculinities: Miss Trunchbull as drag villain

Miss Trunchbull, perhaps the most exaggerated of all characters in *Matilda*, is the most conspicuous social inversion on stage, conceived as a hypermasculine woman. Whereas Dahl describes her in animalistic terms ('enraged rhinoceros',[44] 'snorting';[45] 'bloodthirsty follower of stag-hounds';[46] 'hippopotamus'[47]) and militaristic ('stormtrooper';[48] 'tank';[49] 'marched'[50]), the musical's creative team's decision to cast a sizeable man in the role adds a visual layer of masculinity and stresses the character's monstrousness. Miss Trunchbull, in both book and stage form, is an Olympic hammer thrower, such that one would expect large muscles and vast strength compared to the small children. On stage, Trunchbull's upturned presentation is even more pronounced, as the character is most often cast with male performers.[51] Unlike in John Kander and Fred Ebb's *Chicago* (1975), where Mary Sunshine passes for a woman until the end of the show, and whose first name in the Playbill is typically abbreviated, *Matilda* makes minimal effort to hide the gender identity of the actor. The role is performed 'with no noticeable eyeshadow, mascara, or lipstick, and there isn't even a serious attempt to cover up five o'clock shadow which peaks through some of the publicity images . . . The only physical marker of femaleness is an amply padded bosom, but when combined with huge shoulder pads, the silhouette is far from feminine'.[52] Dahl's written descriptions of Trunchbull emphasize her athleticism and muscularity – depicting her as unconventionally female with a bull-neck, big shoulders, thick arms, sinewy wrists and powerful legs[53] – but he does not construct her through explicitly male terms, except when a student refers to her as 'sir'[54] and when an older student named Hortensia describes her as 'the Prince of Darkness'.[55] Therefore, the musical's intentional rendering of Trunchbull as perceptibly male generates a carnivalesque caricature that functions one step beyond Dahl's original creation.

Casting men as Trunchbull also borrows directly from the British tradition of pantomime, or panto, 'a theatrical spectacle that involves cross-dressing and role playing' which 'can be termed queer because its diegetic world is one of inversion where gender categories and sexual identities are disturbed'.[56] The pairing of panto and carnivalesque is a seemingly natural partnership in the case of *Matilda*, a way for the stage musical to easily accentuate Trunchbull's colossal size (physically) and status (socially) and to generate a space within which the young Matilda can subvert and overthrow her power. As a *panto dame*, the male performance of Miss Trunchbull can be likened to a drag performance of Lady Bracknell from *The Importance of Being Earnest*, or the always drag performance of Edna Turnblad from the more contemporary *Hairspray*. These characters are meant to be matronly figures, and rather than trying to hide the man (a kind of spectacle that is sometimes the goal of drag), the drag is utilized to highlight masculine characteristics for humorous effect (Coupland). The uninterest in hiding the man is truer of Miss Trunchbull than other panto dames.[57]

Trunchbull also corresponds with Martina Lipton's definition: 'The modern dame, like carnival's grotesque "unruly woman", is a man in female dress, and as such s/he is a site of anxiety that is dispelled through humour.'[58] Yet, the monstrous masculinity of Trunchbull – and audiences' clear positionality *against* her – is perhaps more line with what Simon Sladen calls the *drag villain* (a newer development within panto), 'an often glamorous and powerful female malevolent agent played by a man'[59] who also 'performs a narrative function [and] drives the plot'.[60] This distinction between dame and drag villain is productive here because Trunchbull, unlike Edna Turnblad, is framed as a Goliath to be defeated, not to be loved or accepted; as well, Trunchbull's strong disdain for children makes her an asexual female figure, unlike many dames. The anxiety generated through Trunchbull is not based on sexuality but, rather, on social and gendered ideologies.

Such a performance of Trunchbull as drag villain generates multiple layers of meaning, sometimes contradictory to each other. For some, this version of Trunchbull reinforces Matilda's feminism. Recalling her viewing of the show, Perkins ruminates:

> As an audience member, it takes on additional meaning to see Matilda not just fight against an oppressive schooling system, but fight against that system as embodied by a man. It takes on cultural meaning to see a man belittle the sweet-natured Miss Honey, to see a man mock children, to see a man try to squash the rumblings of revolt against his fascist regime. There is something particularly satisfying about seeing Matilda defeat Miss Trunchbull given the obvious presence of a man onstage. The visibility of the male actor in Miss Trunchbull then reinterprets Matilda's revolt as a feminist act.[61]

Perkins's account illustrates how the musical's depiction of Trunchbull is productive in terms of generating a clearer feminist approach, which is not as straightforward in the novel. That is to say, the musical uses the masculine as a shortcut to develop Matilda as a strong female character. Matilda is emphasized as *not* a boy, as the musical adds various instances of Mr Wormwood referring to her as a boy, up until the final scene. This gender emphasis gives Matilda particular femaleness, making her vanquishing of Trunchbull all the more a feminist act. In the same way, British-Iraqi performer Amrou Al-Kadhi describes how drag villains are 'truly loved; it is a role onto which audiences can exorcise all their social rage and prejudices, but ultimately escape them and renegotiate them'.[62] Trunchbull represents an aspect of society to be defeated, collapsing educational institutions, adults and men into a singular figure against which Matilda fights.

Undeniably, audiences are to disapprove of Trunchbull. The character is often performed to humorous effect: in one scene, Trunchbull calls Matilda a gangster; in another, Honey reports that Matilda is a genius, to which Trunchbull asserts that she can read too.[63] The show's comical treatment of Trunchbull is coupled with the portrayal of the Wormwood men as especially dim-witted. Matilda's older brother Michael speaks no more than one-word phrases during the show, and usually in repetition of what someone else has just said. Furthermore, Mr Wormwood is incapable of understanding Matilda's femaleness upon her birth, exclaiming, 'Oh my good lord! Where's his thingy?'.[64] In aligning Trunchbull with maleness, Kelly and Minchin generate both a more prominent revolt against authority, aggregating the adult characters – but especially male characters – together. This also elicits a parallel between the male-dominated spheres of the classroom and the home, underpinning the show's anti-establishment attitude. However, this also buttresses the notion that this society's authority figures are inherently male. In other words, in order to engender a feminist approach, the show establishes gender as a binary opposition in its traditional forms.

Some may also find a male-performed Trunchbull troubling, given that Trunchbull can also be read as a feminist character in her own right. This includes her aversion to children, the lack of a specified relationship or husband and her rejection of feminine stereotypes altogether. In this way, Kelly and Minchin's (re)construction of Trunchbull for the stage makes her more feminist than the titular character, perhaps even coded as lesbian. Yet, that Trunchbull is played by a man, and not subtly so, diminishes or even erases the character's feminist qualities and risks being interpreted as heightened male misogyny, especially in light of the all-male creatives.[65] Scholars like Guest argue that Dahl presents a range of women's possible trajectories: 'the "monstrous" Miss Trunchbull, who has assumed a life of action as a star athlete and working woman, and the narcissistic Mrs. Wormwood, who is figuratively entombed by the mass media images she embraces', as well as Miss Honey, 'a working woman who espouses a more forward-thinking view of women's potential and intelligence', but who is nonetheless shy, feeble, and – as her one of two solos indicates – 'pathetic'.[66] For Guest, these different caricatures 'indicate the disfiguring effects of the gendered scripts available to women in the late twentieth century'.[67] Thus, in separating Trunchbull from femaleness, the musical presents even less choices for females and for Matilda. Musically, the show also resists the type of queer feminism that Stacy Wolf elaborates on; whereas 'two women singing together in a duet, their voices intertwined and overlapping, their attention toward one another, can also signify as queer', there exist no duets between women in *Matilda*, except for a brief musical exchange between Matilda and Honey during 'When I Grow Up'.[68]

Most problematically, the ending of the show reinforces a traditional social hierarchy based on a particular type of woman. In both the novel and musical, the 'defeat' of Trunchbull prompts celebration, after Matilda and audiences discover that Trunchbull has actually murdered her brother – Honey's father, Magnus – and has taken over the family house, forcing Honey to live in a simple shed. In retaliation, during a class lesson led by Trunchbull, Matilda uses her telekinesis to write on the chalkboard as Magnus; Trunchbull, believing that Magnus has come back to avenge his death, is scared away, returning Honey's rightful inheritance to her. While in the book, Dahl appoints a Mr Trilby in Trunchbull's place, Kelly assigns Honey as new headmistress. This ending thus generates a number of implications in terms of the playworld's social hierarchy: first, Matilda's magical powers, even as she defeats Trunchbull, are cloaked in the fatherly figure and voice of Miss Honey's father, Magnus, such that the patriarchal order is resituated at the end of the story. Second, that Trunchbull is replaced by Honey can be read as rewarding the passive, submissive, and maternal female figure. After all, Honey plays no part in Trunchbull's overthrow. In addition, when it is revealed that Mr Wormwood has swindled the Russian Mafia, the Wormwood family must flee, leaving Matilda in a quandary; in the novel, Matilda comes up with the idea to live with Miss Honey, but in the musical, Miss Honey asks the Wormwoods to let Matilda stay with her. In this case, Honey volunteers as Matilda's caretaker, and Matilda merely substitutes one household for another at the end, maintaining the family unit. The male-dominated social order of the family is further demonstrated by the Wormwoods: Matilda's final 'goodbye' to the family is signified by shaking her father's hand, and Mrs Wormwood is mysteriously absent from Honey's negotiation to keep Matilda.

Revolting women and children: Conclusion

Notably, with the exception of British accents and slang (mostly, the use of 'telly'), there are no obvious markers of time or geography in the musical, blurring the show's historical context. It is therefore unclear whether the show's events take place in the 1980s, when the novel was published, or in the 2010s, when the musical debuted. Nevertheless, the shift of *Matilda* from Dahl's pages to the musical theatre stage takes on an important meaning. The show's subversive narrative impulse is, at least on the surface, seemingly obvious: the musical ends on a definitive celebratory note via the musical number, 'Revolting Children', during which the schoolchildren rejoice the downfall of the Trunchbull (the songs that follow are reprises of previous numbers), and we cheer when Matilda gets her happy ending. Through Kelly and Minchin's emphasis on Dahl's nonsensical world and the adult–child divide, the addition of the 'Acrobat Story' and the panto-inflected performance of Miss Trunchbull, *Matilda the Musical* calls attention to Western ideologies and rejects them, if only momentarily.

The significance of *Matilda* as a socially reflective text cannot be understated. Marking the book's thirtieth anniversary in 2018, a statue was erected in Great Missenden featuring Matilda facing Donald Trump – a modern-day rendering of who Matilda might be standing up to if she were around in 2018.[69] This use of Matilda as an empowered figure, facing one in a position of authority and who represents various social structures (patriarchal and financial, among others), demonstrates the powerful qualities the character has and which readers – both young and old – have latched onto. At the same time, such repurposing of Trunchbull as a menacing male figure may perpetuate a dismissal of or antagonism towards female characters that do not fit within socially defined roles. Soon after the Matilda–Trump statues were reported, Eva Wiseman of *The Guardian* also enthusiastically revisited *Matilda*, calling the current moment 'an age of women's rage'.[70] For Wiseman, characters like Matilda can and should be (re)claimed during 'a political moment when an increasing number of women have decided (or become too exhausted) to stop breathing through their rage, stop masking it with gentle listening faces and stop turning away. Instead, they're leaning into the fire – shouting, protesting, writing their anger on huge glittering signs and parading them through the streets'.[71] Seen in this way, Matilda embodies a global movement of female-driven influence and power, even if she is not a perfectly constructed heroine or feminist. *Matilda* remains one of only a handful of British-created musicals created in roughly the last decade to feature a subversive female character at its core, as well as adds to a small but expanding list of valuable, transgressive female voices within the musical theatre world at large – the growing 'smell of rebellion', as it were.

Notes

1. Because of Matilda's dubious actions, such as playing pranks on her parents, Charles Sarland offers a pessimistic view that Dahl's 'protagonists are heroines and heroes primarily because that is their plot role, not because there is anything in their psychological make-up that makes them inherently "heroic"' (37). See Madeline Spivey for more about the complicated construction of childhood in *Matilda*.
2. Ben Brantley, 'Children of the World, Unite!', *The New York Times*, 11 April 2013, https://www.nytimes.com/2013/04/12/theater/reviews/matilda-the-musical-at-shubert-theater.html (accessed 10 July 2021).
3. Kristin Perkins, '"If It's Not Right, You Have To Put It Right": The Play and Work of Children in Matilda the Musical', *AWE (A Woman's Experience)*, 5, no. 3 (2018): 3, https://scholarsarchive.byu.edu/awe/vol5/iss1/3/.
4. '"Making Matilda", Episode 3: Director Matthew Warchus on Bringing Dahl's "Colorful World" to Life', *YouTube*, uploaded by Broadwaycom, 27 March 2013, https://www.youtube.com/watch?v=IWyAA0exb8I.
5. Perkins, "If It's Not Right, You Have to Put It Right", 10.
6. Mikhail Bakhtin, *Rabelais and His World*, trans. Helene Iswolsky (Bloomington: Indiana University Press, 1984).
7. Danielle Ashley, 'Books to Broadway: Roald Dahl Teaches Life Lessons to Audiences in Magical Ways', *BroadwayWorld*, 29 April 2017, https://www.broadwayworld.com/article/Books-to-Broadway-Roald-Dahl-Teaches-Life-Lessons-to-Audiences-in-Magical-Ways-20170429 (accessed 11 July 2021).
8. Whitney Crothers Dilley, *The Cinema of Wes Anderson: Bringing Nostalgia to Life* (New York: Columbia University Press, 2017), 153.
9. Margaret Talbot, 'The Candy Man', *The New Yorker*, 4 July 2005, https://www.newyorker.com/magazine/2005/07/11/the-candy-man (accessed 10 July 2021).
10. Bruno Bettelheim, *The Uses of Enchantment: The Meaning and Importance of Fairy Tales*, e-book (New York: Vintage, 2011).
11. Laura MacDonald, '"Sometimes You Have to Make a Little Bit of Mischief": Matthew Warchus' Hybrid Approach to Musical Theatre Directing', *Studies in Musical Theatre* 6, no. 3 (2012): 358, doi:10.1386/smt.6.3.355_1.
12. '"Making Matilda", Episode 1: Librettist Dennis Kelly on Roald Dahl's Strong Heroine', *YouTube*, uploaded by Broadwaycom, 12 March 2013, https://www.youtube.com/watch?v=LKHP41Lejf4.
13. Jeremy Treglown, *Roald Dahl: A Biography*, e-book (Eugene: Harvest Books, 1995).
14. Treglown, *Roald Dahl: A Biography*.
15. See 'Fantastic Mr Fox Composer Arthur Darvill Talks Music and Songs!', *YouTube*, uploaded by NSTheatres, 22 November 2016, https://www.youtube.com/watch?v=COJKkyxYupU; '"Making Matilda", Episode 1'; and 'The Matilda the Musical Story', *Tim Minchin*, May 2021, https://www.timminchin.com/matilda/ (accessed 11 July 2021).
16. MacDonald, '"Sometimes You Have to Make a Little Bit of Mischief"', 358.

17. 'Tim Minchin on Writing the Music to Matilda by Roald Dahl', *YouTube*, uploaded by ABC News (Australia), 14 October 2014, https://www.youtube.com/watch?v=ClrN5YogqYI.
18. '"Making Matilda", Episode 1'.
19. Roald Dahl, *Matilda* (London: Puffin Books, 1988), 19.
20. Dahl, *Matilda*, 185.
21. 'Apology for Antisemitic Comments Made by Roald Dahl', *Roald Dahl*, n.d., https://www.roalddahl.com/global/rdsc-and-family-notice (accessed 10 July 2021).
22. Megan McCluskey, 'What to Know About Children's Author Roald Dahl's Controversial Legacy', *TIME*, 18 March 2021, https://time.com/5937507/roald-dahl-anti-semitism/ (accessed 11 July 2021).
23. Treglown, *Roald Dahl: A Biography*.
24. Ruth Margolis, 'Are My Favorite Childhood Books Teaching Bad Things to My Kids?', *The Week*, 25 February 2020, https://theweek.com/articles/895971/are-favorite-childhood-books-teaching-bad-things-kids (accessed 10 July 2021). Readers commonly point to *The Witches* (1983) as being one of Dahl's more explicitly misogynistic work, as the text repeatedly draws connections between witches and women.
25. Ester Vidović and Silvia Vidović, 'Gender Issues in Roald Dahl's Novel *Matilda*', in *Engendering Difference: Sexism, Power and Politics*, ed. M. Gadpaille, V. K. Horvat, and V. Kennedy (Newcastle upon Tyne: Cambridge Scholars Publisher, 2018), 228.
26. Marta Þórðardóttir, '*The Tiniest Mite Packs the Mightiest Sting*': Interpretations of Feminism in the Works of Roald Dahl (University of Iceland, Bachelor's thesis, 2019), 20.
27. Þórðardóttir, '*The Tiniest Mite Packs the Mightiest Sting*', 20.
28. Dennis Kelly and Tim Minchin, *Matilda the Musical* (New York: Music Theatre International, 2018), 12–13.
29. Perkins, "If It's Not Right, You Have to Put It Right", 10.
30. Einat Natalie Palkovich, '"Put it Right": Matilda as Author in *Matilda the Musical*', *Children's Literature in Education* 50, no. 2 (2019): 210–22.
31. Palkovich, '"Put it Right"', 218.
32. John Stephens, *Language and Ideology in Children's Fiction* (London: Longman, 1992), 120.
33. Stephanie Lim, 'Good Intentions and (Un)Acceptable Laughter: How the Carnival Inverts Cross-Cultural Relationships in *The Book of Mormon*', in *Singing and Dancing to The Book of Mormon: Critical Essays on the Broadway Musical*, ed. M. E. Shaw and H. Welker (Lanham: Rowman & Littlefield Publishers, 2016), 4.
34. Bakhtin, *Rabelais and His World*, 383. As part of his theorization of the world turned upside-down, Bakhtin also draws attention to the grotesque body, which is depicted in excess and exaggeration. Comparable moments in *Matilda* that highlight the body in excess are Matilda's pranks on her father (turning his hair bright green, and also supergluing his hat to his head), as well as Trunchbull's punishments on children, including twirling Amanda Thripp by the pigtails, stretching Eric by the ears, and forcing Bruce Bogtrotter to consume a whole chocolate cake. The show emphasizes these scenes in dramatic and theatrical ways, and often through a musical number.
35. Lynley, 'The Carnivalesque in Children's Literature', *Slap Happy Larry*, 19 August 2015, https://www.slaphappylarry.com/the-carnivalesque-in-childrens-literature/ (accessed 10 July 2021).
36. Kristen Guest, 'The Good, the Bad, and the Ugly: Resistance and Complicity in Matilda', *Children's Literature Association Quarterly* 33, no. 3 (2008): 249.

37. Guest, 'The Good, the Bad, and the Ugly', 249.
38. Madeline Spivey, 'Roald Dahl and the Construction of Childhood: Writing the Child as Other', *The Oswald Review: An International Journal of Undergraduate Research and Criticism in the Discipline of English* 22, no. 1 (2020): 97.
39. Murray Knowles and Kirsten Malmkjaer, *Language and Control in Children's Literature* (Milton Park: Routledge, 1995), 135.
40. '"Making Matilda", Episode 4: Designers Rob Howell & Hugh Vanstone on Setting the Stage for "Matilda"', *YouTube*, uploaded by Broadwaycom, 27 March 2013, https://www.youtube.com/watch?v=t8rvoX-yl0g.
41. The Escapologist was changed to The Escape Artist for the US version.
42. Palkovich, '"Put it Right"', 212.
43. Kelly and Minchin, *Matilda the Musical*, 18.
44. Dahl, *Matilda*, 67.
45. Dahl, *Matilda*, 67.
46. Dahl, *Matilda*, 83.
47. Dahl, *Matilda*, 105.
48. Dahl, *Matilda*, 67.
49. Dahl, *Matilda*, 67.
50. Dahl, *Matilda*, 141.
51. MTI's character breakdown for Trunchbull notes that any gender can play the role. Exceptions to the male-dominated casting include the 2019 production at The Muny in St. Louis, Missouri, when Beth Malone stepped into the role of Trunchbull, after Will Swenson pulled out due to a scheduling conflict, and a 2022 Netflix adaptation of the musical, for which Emma Thompson has been cast as Trunchbull.
52. Perkins, "If It's Not Right, You Have to Put It Right", 5.
53. Dahl, *Matilda*, 83.
54. Dahl, *Matilda*, 116.
55. Dahl, *Matilda*, 109.
56. Martina Lipton, 'Principally Boys? Gender Dynamics and Casting Practices in Modern British Pantomime', *Contemporary Theatre Review* 18, no. 4 (2008): 471, doi:10.1080/10486800802379565.
57. Perkins, "If It's Not Right, You Have to Put It Right", 5.
58. Lipton, 'Principally Boys?', 473.
59. Simon Sladen, 'Wicked Queens of Pantoland', in *Drag Histories, Herstories and Hairstories: Drag in a Changing Scene*, vol. 2, ed. M. Edward and S. Farrier (London: Bloomsbury, 2021), 195.
60. Sladen, 'Wicked Queens of Pantoland', 201.
61. Perkins, "If It's Not Right, You Have to Put It Right", 6.
62. Sladen, 'Wicked Queens of Pantoland', 206.
63. Kelly and Minchin, *Matilda the Musical*, 26–7.
64. Kelly and Minchin, *Matilda the Musical*, 6.
65. Eliot Glenn argues that the male performance of Trunchbull generates transphobia, though this seems to be a stretch since the maleness of Trunchbull is for the audience a sort of inside joke or unspoken understanding about the performer and the performance of the character.
66. Guest, 'The Good, the Bad, and the Ugly', 247.

67. Guest, 'The Good, the Bad, and the Ugly', 247.
68. Stacy Wolf, *Changed for Good: A Feminist History of the Broadway Musical*, e-book (Oxford: Oxford Scholarship Online, 2011), 18, doi:10.1093/acprof:oso/9780195378238.003.0000.
69. Megan McCluskey, 'Matilda Statue Faces Down Trump to Celebrate 30th Anniversary of Beloved Roald Dahl Classic', *TIME*, 1 October 2018, https://time.com/5411413/matilda-statue-trump/ (accessed 11 July 2021).
70. Eva Wiseman, 'Revisiting Matilda in an Age of Women's Rage', *The Guardian*, 14 October 2018, https://www.theguardian.com/lifeandstyle/2018/oct/14/revisiting-matilda-in-an-age-of-womens-rage (accessed 11 July 2021).
71. Wiseman, 'Revisiting Matilda in an Age of Women's Rage'.

References

'Apology for Antisemitic Comments Made by Roald Dahl' (n.d.), *Roald Dahl*, https://www.roalddahl.com/global/rdsc-and-family-notice (accessed 10 July 2021).

Ashley, Danielle (2017), 'Books to Broadway: Roald Dahl Teaches Life Lessons to Audiences in Magical Ways', *BroadwayWorld*, 29 April, https://www.broadwayworld.com/article/Books-to-Broadway-Roald-Dahl-Teaches-Life-Lessons-to-Audiences-in-Magical-Ways-20170429 (accessed 11 July 2021).

Bakhtin, Mikhail (1984), *Rabelais and His World*, trans. Helene Iswolsky. Bloomington: Indiana University Press.

Bettelheim, Bruno (2011), *The Uses of Enchantment: The Meaning and Importance of Fairy Tales*, e-book. New York: Vintage.

Brantley, Ben (2013), 'Children of the World, Unite!', *The New York Times*, 11 April, https://www.nytimes.com/2013/04/12/theater/reviews/matilda-the-musical-at-shubert-theater.html (accessed 10 July 2021).

Dahl, Roald (1988), *Matilda*. London: Puffin Books.

Dilley, Whitney Crothers (2017), *The Cinema of Wes Anderson: Bringing Nostalgia to Life*. New York: Columbia University Press.

'Fantastic Mr Fox Composer Arthur Darvill Talks Music and Songs!' (2016), *YouTube*, uploaded by NSTheatres, 22 November, https://www.youtube.com/watch?v=COJKkyxYupU.

Guest, Kristen (2008), 'The Good, the Bad, and the Ugly: Resistance and Complicity in *Matilda*', *Children's Literature Association Quarterly*, 33 (3): 246–57.

Kelly, Dennis and Tim Minchin (2018), *Matilda the Musical*. New York: Music Theatre International.

Knowles, Murray and Kirsten Malmkjaer (1995), *Language and Control in Children's Literature*. Milton Park: Routledge.

Lim, Stephanie (2016), 'Good Intentions and (Un)Acceptable Laughter: How the Carnival Inverts Cross-Cultural Relationships in *The Book of Mormon*', in M. E. Shaw and H. Welker (eds), *Singing and Dancing to The Book of Mormon: Critical Essays on the Broadway Musical*, 3–15. Lanham: Rowman & Littlefield Publishers.

Lipton, Martina (2008), 'Principally Boys? Gender Dynamics and Casting Practices in Modern British Pantomime', *Contemporary Theatre Review*, 18 (4): 470–86, doi:10.1080/10486800802379565.

Lynley (2015), 'The Carnivalesque in Children's Literature', *Slap Happy Larry*, 19 August, https://www.slaphappylarry.com/the-carnivalesque-in-childrens-literature/ (accessed 10 July 2021).

MacDonald, Laura (2012), '"Sometimes You Have to Make a Little Bit of Mischief": Matthew Warchus' Hybrid Approach to Musical Theatre Directing', *Studies in Musical Theatre*, 6 (3): 355–62, doi:10.1386/smt.6.3.355_1.

'"Making Matilda", Episode 1: Librettist Dennis Kelly on Roald Dahl's Strong Heroine' (2013), *YouTube*, uploaded by Broadwaycom, 12 March, https://www.youtube.com/watch?v=LKHP41Lejf4.

'"Making Matilda", Episode 3: Director Matthew Warchus on Bringing Dahl's "Colorful World" to Life' (2013), *YouTube*, uploaded by Broadwaycom, 27 March, https://www.youtube.com/watch?v=IWyAA0exb8I.

'"Making Matilda", Episode 4: Designers Rob Howell & Hugh Vanstone on Setting the Stage for "Matilda"' (2013), *YouTube*, uploaded by Broadwaycom, 27 March, https://www.youtube.com/watch?v=t8rvoX-yl0g.

Margolis, Ruth (2020), 'Are My Favorite Childhood Books Teaching Bad Things to My Kids?', *The Week*, 25 February, https://theweek.com/articles/895971/are-favorite-childhood-books-teaching-bad-things-kids (accessed 10 July 2021).

McCluskey, Megan (2018), 'Matilda Statue Faces Down Trump to Celebrate 30th Anniversary of Beloved Roald Dahl Classic', *TIME*, 1 October, https://time.com/5411413/matilda-statue-trump/ (accessed 11 July 2021).

McCluskey, Megan (2021), 'What to Know About Children's Author Roald Dahl's Controversial Legacy', *TIME*, 18 March, https://time.com/5937507/roald-dahl-anti-semitism/ (accessed 11 July 2021).

Palkovich, Einat Natalie (2019), '"Put it Right": Matilda as Author in *Matilda the Musical*', *Children's Literature in Education*, 50 (2): 210–22.

Perkins, Kristin (2018), '"If It's Not Right, You Have To Put It Right": The Play and Work of Children in Matilda the Musical', *AWE (A Woman's Experience)*, 5 (3): 2–14, https://scholarsarchive.byu.edu/awe/vol5/iss1/3/.

Þórðardóttir, Marta (2019), *'The Tiniest Mite Packs the Mightiest Sting': Interpretations of Feminism in the Works of Roald Dahl*, University of Iceland, Bachelor's thesis.

Sarland, Charles (2005), 'Critical Tradition and Ideological Positioning', in P. Hunt (ed.), *Understanding Children's Literature: Key Essays from The Second Edition of The International Companion Encyclopedia of Children's Literature*, 2nd edn, 30–49. London; New York: Routledge.

Sladen, Simon (2021), 'Wicked Queens of Pantoland', in M. Edward and S. Farrier (eds), *Drag Histories, Herstories and Hairstories: Drag in a Changing Scene*, vol. 2, 195–209. London: Bloomsbury.

Spivey, Madeline (2020), 'Roald Dahl and the Construction of Childhood: Writing the Child as Other', *The Oswald Review: An International Journal of Undergraduate Research and Criticism in the Discipline of English*, 22 (1): 93–123.

Stephens, John (1992), *Language and Ideology in Children's Fiction*. London: Longman.

Talbot, Margaret (2005), 'The Candy Man', *The New Yorker*, 4 July, https://www.newyorker.com/magazine/2005/07/11/the-candy-man (accessed 10 July 2021).

'The Matilda the Musical Story' (2021), *Tim Minchin*, May, https://www.timminchin.com/matilda/ (accessed 11 July 2021).

'Tim Minchin on Writing the Music to Matilda by Roald Dahl' (2014), *YouTube*, uploaded by ABC News (Australia), 14 October, https://www.youtube.com/watch?v=ClrN5YogqYI.

Treglown, Jeremy (1995), *Roald Dahl: A Biography*, e-book. Eugene: Harvest Books.

Vidović, Ester and Silvia Vidović (2018), 'Gender Issues in Roald Dahl's Novel *Matilda*', in M. Gadpaille, V. K. Horvat, and V. Kennedy (eds), *Engendering Difference: Sexism, Power and Politics*, 219–29. Newcastle upon Tyne: Cambridge Scholars Publisher.

Wiseman, Eva (2018), 'Revisiting Matilda in an Age of Women's Rage', *The Guardian*, 14 October, https://www.theguardian.com/lifeandstyle/2018/oct/14/revisiting-matilda-in-an-age-of-womens-rage (accessed 11 July 2021).

Wolf, Stacy (2011), *Changed for Good: A Feminist History of the Broadway Musical*, e-book. Oxford: Oxford Scholarship Online, doi:10.1093/acprof:oso/9780195378238.003.0000.

Ellen Kane interview

Associate Choreographer *Matilda*, Choreographer *Matilda The Musical* (film)

What is your favourite British musical?

Matilda

What's your favourite British musical theatre song?

I actually have to say I love 'Quiet' from *Matilda*. I think it's a very small song which has a huge impact for lots of different reasons. And every time I hear it in the show, it still surprises me how much I get from listening to it.

How did you train for this career?

I started my training late. I grew up in Hackney and there wasn't really much cultural stuff going on there. But in the community hall across the road from where I lived, on a Friday night, this woman – incredible woman actually, her name was Pat – ran a dance club for 50p. (A bit like Billy Elliot!) And initially my friend used to go and I used to get really bored. So I joined too. I must have been about ten. So for a couple of years I sort of started going across the road doing a bit of that with her, and then eventually I started making up the dances there for them.

I stopped that when I went to secondary school, and then a touring group from Lewisham College came to my secondary school which ignited something in me and I just knew that that's where I wanted to go to college. I did A-Levels as well. So I did A-Levels in the evening and I did the foundation course during the day.

After two years I applied to Rambert, The Place, London Studio Centre. I got into those places, but I got offered a scholarship for London Studio Centre. I wanted to be a contemporary dancer, but I also wanted to do jazz and LSC offered that wider training. So I trained there for three years. And that was the start really.

I've had the biggest gift that I think anyone in this career could have had. I worked, as an associate, with Peter Darling.

I met him doing a show called *Billy Elliot*. And we became great, great friends. He was an actor initially and I was a dancer. By the time I met Pete I'd been in a contemporary dance company called Richard Alston Dance Company. I had just left that company and then met Pete who was looking for an associate for *Billy Elliot*. Richard's company was very balletic, so those two things connected quite well.

So I guess I learned musicals and choreography in musicals really from Peter who's probably the best choreographer I know. Sort of trained with him on the jobs from *Billy Elliot* until *Groundhog Day* where I was co-choreographer.

Do you see *Matilda* as a key British musical?

I do. Yeah. I think it changed musical theatre actually. It was a different presentation of a musical and it was an empowering story for children, women, for girls, humans! The show has a sense of uprising and there is this sort of anarchic rumbling inside this very seemingly small story. I think the effect that it had on the industry was completely justified in terms of what it did at that time.

You know, when we first made it, we made it up in Stratford-upon-Avon. And it was meant to be just a six-week Christmas show. We all decamped up to Stratford, made this Christmas show and then it opened to great reviews. Next we were told it was going to London, but it wasn't until it sort of swept the Olivier awards that I kind of went – Ah, okay, this show is going to be a big deal.

How would you describe your contribution to *Matilda*?

Well, I would say it's quite large. I'm still very connected to the show now. Peter is the choreographer on the show, and I am his associate. I was integral to the physical language of the show, the demonstration, the teaching of the show, how the show runs now in terms of the structure of recasting, how the teaching of the kids works. I'm up there today after I've left you because there's new kids going in, a new cast going in. My role as associate choreographer works differently to Peter's as choreographer but they coexist very comfortably.

It helps that I've worked with Peter for so long, on so many shows. We became known as a sort of little package really. But everybody has associates, you know, I've got associates now. And I think we've been really blessed in the fact that we've worked on some incredibly successful big shows. The longer they've run, and the further they stretch, the more established that associate role becomes, because it's so necessary. Like, you can't have shows running in different countries with one person, you have to double up.

Matilda has been without a doubt one of the most rewarding parts of my life. You know, watching, learning how to communicate with and get these extraordinary things from children has been such a thing that I'm very, very proud of. But when you're in it, its actually exhausting, like you'd never really believe. We had three teams of kids. And if you can imagine, to get that many kids secure in a whole show like that, you're working from ten in the morning till nine at night, and that's with nine- and ten-year-olds. It's sort of relentless. We were not asking them to do 'kid' choreography, they're doing extraordinary stuff. So when we were building the show I was just focused on getting to the end.

How would you define what an associate choreographer is?

It's different from an assistant choreographer. An assistant I would say is someone who is not necessarily integral to the creative conceptual building of the piece, the movement language of the piece. An assistant is someone who you basically say, 'I need you to learn this, this and this', they learn it, they teach it, that's what they do, and very well. Whereas an associate, I've got two associates who work with me now, one of them is a more physical representation for me because I'm nearly fifty so I don't really dance full out all the time. And the other is a more conceptual and creative sounding board for me. And I would say anybody else is an assistant. My associates are the fundamental people that are in a room that I know I can build anything with.

Is there anything different about *Matilda* in terms of how it was rehearsed?

I've been fortunate enough to have done quite a lot of kids shows and the film obviously had like 200 plus kids in it. So there's a lot of navigation and negotiation with kids. You have to be very mindful of how you work. When you schedule things, how to get the best out of them. You know, it's a longer process. It's a much more protracted way of getting to the end result. Because they just simply cannot absorb in the same way that adults do. So there's a very structured approach, which hopefully allows everybody to get what they need, while protecting and safeguarding the kids. You are working a decent amount of time, enough to get them strong enough, to get them familiar, to get them where they need to be yet not pushing them past breaking. You don't want to get to a place where they're saturated. It's a fine balance. So it's quite different.

How do you feel about *Matilda*?

I'm super grateful for it. You know, it's just so crazy. At the point that *Matilda* came up, I was in Chicago. I was putting *Billy Elliot* on for Pete out there. And Pete came out to Chicago and just said, 'Look, you know, Matthew's (Warchus) got this Christmas show at the RSC. I don't know if you fancy it, but you know, I'd love you to do it'. It was subsidized theatre so it wasn't for financial gain. And I was like, you know what, I really want to do a new show with you. I love Roald Dahl. I'm gonna do it and I just did it and I did it for every right reason. I've never expected the story that has grown from that decision, all the things that have come from it. And for that I will be universally grateful. It has changed my life. And then now with the film I've had the most incredible time. So yeah, I think it's a fucking great story. It teaches so many great things that I believe in over and over.

Has the experience of working on *Matilda* shaped by the work that you've done since?

I wouldn't say *Matilda* has done that. I would say that Peter has done that. I can't speak highly enough of the gift that he has. I'm very fortunate to have connected to another human being in such a way that I totally understand everything he's talking about, and vice versa. I just felt like I was constantly absorbing and learning and watching and understanding and so it was like an apprenticeship of dreams. Now it's more like a co-creative thing because of course, once you've absorbed and processed and learned you then start to formulate yourself over the many years and then you begin to formulate together as opposed to just absorbing. Initially I didn't know anything about musicals, I just knew about contemporary dance so it took a long time to learn but I feel I've graduated now!

Billy was also another one of those really key monumental, amazing pieces of work. When I first met Pete I was very highbrow about the world of musical theatre. I wasn't interested in musicals, I was like why are you singing about a cup of tea? And why are you dancing shiny shiny out front? Peter showed me that you can do musicals in a way where everything has a reason. Another way. And I really thrive on that.

Are you still working in musical theatre?

Yes. I'm proud of all the shows I did with Pete, because they're all so different. I'm really proud of a show I did with director Nikolai Foster, a new version of *West Side Story*. I was quite afraid of it because obviously it's so iconic. But, I adored it, and I adored the company and I was really proud of that. I was also proud of *A Chorus Line* for different reasons. That's a really hard piece. And I felt like we made something which was so different. *Legally Blonde* at Regent's Park – we just flipped it on its head and I felt so proud of that company. I felt proud that we really set out and made a statement. We (Lucy Moss, the director, and I) stood by it and we did it and made work that made an impact. The company just rose to the challenge. So even though they are shorter runs and they may not be as heralded because the Curve doesn't qualify for the Oliviers etc . . . I feel the work was strong, the process was really healthy, and the companies felt proud of what we had made.

What advice would you give to aspiring choreographers?

Work with as many people as you can. It takes years unless you're super lucky. Be an assistant, be an associate, dance for different choreographers. Even if you want to choreograph yourself. Don't be above being the dancer that you were. Put yourself out there. Keep at it.

3 'Glitching' of gender and temporality in *Lift* (2013)
JOZEY GRAE

Introduction: The state of non-binary representation in the musical

Lift, written by Craig Adams and Ian Watson, premiered in London in 2013, and takes place during a fifty-four-second lift journey in Covent Garden station. The show delves into the lives of the eight characters sharing the lift; the two characters that are explicitly queer in the musical are the 'French Teacher' (who is a lesbian) and the 'Ballet Dancer' (who is a gay man). The presence of a gay and a lesbian character in *Lift* (2013) was, and still is, significant because the paucity of LGBTQ+ representation in general still exists today. However, the significance of *Lift* goes beyond that; these characters can also be read as resisting *chrononormativity* (heteronormative time) through both their queerness (*sexuality*) and through the dramaturgical structure of their narratives. Sarah Whitfield points out that '[q]ueer storytelling through the musical may explicitly resist chrononormativity (i.e., straight time), by unsettling the stasis and progress aspects of heteronormative productivity'.[1] *Lift* can be considered a contemporary concept musical. It is tied together by a central theme, which, in this instance, is a place; the lift at Covent Garden station. Around this, scenes play out in no particular order, showing us snippets of the multiple characters' lives. As with other concept musicals, such as Sondheim's *Company* (1970), there is no clear beginning, middle or end to any of the character's stories. We simply get an undefined insight into their lives; messy, disjointed, with no satisfying resolution. This resistance of a traditional heteronormative structure is key to opening up the potentiality of *Lift* as a work that provides unique opportunities for a gender non-binary reading.

> In order to make this chapter as accessible as possible, let us highlight a few key terms:
>
> **Gender:** As opposed to 'sex' (which refers to biology and chromosomes), gender is defined as a 'complex biopsychosocial construct'[2] relating to biological sex as well as internal identity, external expressions, experiences and roles within society.
>
> **Trans (transgender):** People who no longer identify with the sex they were assigned at birth. It is important to note that some people who identify as non-binary also identify as trans, whereas others do not.
>
> **Non-binary:** When applied to gender this refers to people whose gender identity/experience falls outside of the binary of male and/or female. There are other more specific identities under the non-binary umbrella such as *gender fluid*.

Gender fluid: A gender identity that falls under the non-binary umbrella. Defined as 'people [who] move between genders over time'.[3] This means that a gender-fluid person may sometimes feel male, sometimes female and sometimes in between or beyond those binaries. It is an identity that shifts and changes across time.

Queer: A complicated word with a complicated history. But we will focus on its usage herein. The aim of queer theory is, and has been, to question and challenge what is considered 'normal'. But, more specifically, the term is used to refer to genders and sexualities that fall outside of cisgender heteronormativity. Crucially, here, at times it is necessary to refer (without conflation) to queer *sexuality* and queer *gender* separately (this will be specified as such), but the term is also used more generally to refer to a resistance of cis-heteronormativity.

Note: The terms detailed here are those that are currently (in 2022) most widely used and accepted by scholars in the area and by the trans-inclusive LGBTQ+ community more generally. However, as the trans and non-binary movement is ongoing, terms can and do often change, so at the time of reading, these terms may have become outdated.

This chapter will create a non-binary space by drawing on the work of gender and sexuality theorists (as well as autoethnographic research elements) as a methodology for understanding this existing piece of musical theatre from a new perspective. Key feminist musical scholar, Stacy Wolf captures the reason that readings like this are so important: 'The pervasive nature of a media devoid of [queer] representation can lead spectators to see, hear, and experience musical theater differently, queerly.'[4] Queer people have long found ways to create space for themselves in art that does not canonically include them. In 2002, Wolf was revolutionary for her work to "determine how lesbians appear where none officially exist"[5] in certain musicals. I have found that the term *gender fluid* best describes my own gender identity. Though my sexuality and gender are minoritized, it is important to note that I still inhabit other privileges, as a white, non-disabled person. Something that has been key for me, as someone who experiences both my gender and sexuality as *fluid*, has been finding ways to insert my own experience and identity into art or pop culture that does not truthfully include those experiences or identities. This chapter is my way of doing this from an autoethnographic, academic perspective, building on the work of Stacy Wolf and crucially determining how non-binary people appear where none officially exist.

Non-binary gender identities transcend *chrononormativity* (or heteronormative time). They resist linear temporality and the goal expectations associated with it (what the character of the Ballet Dancer in *Lift* (2013) refers to as 'clichés'). Chrononormativity involves being able to 'narrate' life 'in a novelistic framework: as event-centred, goal-oriented, intentional and culminating in epiphanies or major transformations'.[6] The connection to musical theatre is evident; the genre favours a linear, goal-centred structure (the goal being a satisfying conclusion or end), usually involving heterosexual romance (a key aspect of chrononormativity). The purpose of this chapter is to unlock gender non-binary potentiality in an existing piece of British musical theatre. This kind of reading or reimagining of existing works of musical theatre is necessary and productive as a stopgap until there is some representation of non-binary gender identities in mainstream musical theatre. In 2019,

Equity drew attention to the fact that '[t]here is currently a lack of representation of the LGBT+ community in the arts in general, and of the trans community in particular'.[7] To highlight this paucity further, only two canonically gender non-binary characters have ever featured in a West End and/or Broadway musical, both since 2018. Musical theatre studies has only recently begun to address this. James Lovelock has drawn attention to the fact that previous musical theatre scholarship around gender and sexuality has been limited to binary categories and called for a 'move away from the binary of discussing "sexuality – both hetero- and homo"[8] – and to begin to consider bisexual, asexual, transgender and gender fluid identities'.[9]

The characters of the Ballet Dancer and the French Teacher will be examined as case studies in this chapter, in order to explore the idea that characters who do not function in heteronormative ways in musicals have non-binary potential. First, considering gender roles and cyber identity, the Ballet Dancer is read as occupying gender fluidity. Second, the French Teacher's number in the show – 'Lost in Translation' – provides a great analogy for the non-binary experience. Overall, the work of key non-binary gender and sexuality scholars, Meg-John Barker and Alex Iantaffi, will underpin the understanding of the wider context of non-binary gender in today's society and the importance of representation; alongside the work of Legacy Russell on *glitch*, as 'a fissure within which new possibilities of being and becoming manifest',[10] particularly in relation to cyber-identity. An autoethnographic approach based on my own experience with gender fluidity will also be key throughout. Finally, the concluding section argues that, through transformative readings like this, musical theatre academia can demonstrate the potential for movement and change within the space that past works of musical theatre offer and therefore improve their continued relevance. The chapter also concludes by acknowledging work that still needs to be done and by encouraging a look beyond the West End and Broadway, drawing attention to important emerging trans and non-binary musical theatre creatives.

A fugitive of the mainstream: Gender fluidity and the Ballet Dancer

The Ballet Dancer can be read as occupying non-binary space in several ways, first relating to a subversion of gender roles. The way the character is defined in cast lists (as 'Ballet Dancer') is significant in the first place, in that it may be read as gendered. Barker and Iantaffi point out that 'gender isn't isolated from the world around us',[11] in that while 'we can recognize flaws in the gender system . . . At the same time we grew up under that system and it is all around us all of the time'.[12] What that means is that people cannot control how other people read them; clothing, mannerisms and even job titles result in people making assumptions about someone's gender before they get a chance to explain it for themself. It is problematic and based on the rigid binary expectations of dominant western society, but it is likely that many people would read 'Ballet Dancer' in the cast list and assume a very different character than the one that appears. This can be seen as relating to the struggle of 'everyday misgendering'[13] for non-binary people; not only from a place of deliberate malice, but because heteronormative society has shaped the subconscious assumptions that people make and the ways in which they read other people's identities. As the show continues, it is revealed that the Ballet Dancer's name is Gabriel, but he is also known as Angel by his friends in London; these are also names which can be considered gender fluid.

Gabriel (the Ballet Dancer) makes an impact as a character that resists traditional gender expectations. Our introduction to him is with the lyrics: 'I was in a sauna being sucked off.'[14] First, this quite aggressive sexual language about transactional sex would certainly be perceived as masculine. Second, the lyric draws our attention to the fact that he has a penis, which in itself is a departure from the stereotypical image of a ballet dancer. Furthermore, he has a regional Newcastle accent which seems to position him as from a working-class background and has obvious parallels to the *one* other famous example of a male working-class ballet dancer in pop culture: *Billy Elliot* (2000). Gabriel is queer (*sexuality*), but we learn that his family and friends in his hometown are not aware of this as they would not approve; 'I do pretty much wherever it takes to appear as straight as possible up there, so I can come down here and dance about in tights without being disowned.'[15] This mirrors the lived experience of many queer people. He even reveals that he has a fiancée that he returns to in Newcastle to keep up the facade. However, he intends to reveal the truth of his identity to his family back at home in Newcastle, proclaiming, 'the king is dead, long live the queen'[16] in reference to himself. It is immediately clear how this could relate to the trans or non-binary experience, although Gabriel seems to say this in relation to his sexuality, as he is not trans. It could be argued that this is a conflation of queer *gender* and queer *sexuality* on the part of the writers or, more deliberately, the character. However, it is also possible to read this character through a, specifically, gender-fluid lens.

The Ballet Dancer can be read as gender fluid through his use of online personas, particularly when viewed through the lens of Legacy Russell's work on cyber identity in *Glitch Feminism* (2020). Partly as a result of receiving homophobic abuse, he pretends to be a woman in chat rooms, to attract the attention of straight men; 'My name is Sarah. Send. Lying about the size of my breasts. Lying about the fact that I have breasts.'[17] Russell writes of her relationship with the internet and argues that 'the skin of cyberidentity is uniquely queer.'[18] She describes her online personas over the years as integral to her exploration of her identity, particularly allowing her to break free from constraints of race and gender; the internet was similarly integral to my own exploration of self and gender. 'The construct of the gender binary is, and always has been, precarious . . . To exist within a binary system one must assume that our selves are unchangeable, that how we are read in the world must be chosen for us, rather than for us to define – and choose – for ourselves';[19] it is clear how this relates to what was pointed out earlier in this section, in relation to Barker's work on gender expression. However, what Russell explores, and what the character of the Ballet Dancer here occupies, is the idea that the internet and cyber identity allow the opportunity to *glitch* the binary, to *glitch* the way others perceive our identity, to explore the range of our own identity (including but not limited to gender) through the *glitch*; 'online, I sought to become a fugitive from the mainstream, unwilling to accept its limited definition of bodies like mine.'[20]

As the show progresses, the line becomes blurred between the online and away-from-keyboard versions of the character of the Ballet Dancer; this is particularly key in inviting a gender-fluid reading of the character. Of course, there are nuances to any experience or exploration of gender. First, unlike Russell, who describes herself as 'black, female-identifying, femme, queer',[21] the Ballet Dancer is a white, masculine-presenting male in his away-from-keyboard reality. Therefore, although he is queer, it is important to acknowledge his privilege when viewing him through the lens of Russell's work. Legacy Russell points out: 'I know that there are generations of folx now who have come of age or come into selfhood via the internet, and they've done this with no intention of being deceptive, but rather [are] truly invested in just trying to better understand what their range as human beings ought to be, and how to claim that,'[22] and the Ballet Dancer is not the only character to explore their range using online personas. The Ballet Dancer's online persona is played by another performer, and so literally occupies another *skin*, a young American woman. However, the online persona of the character (Bright Young Thing) he is engaging with online is *also* portrayed by another performer. This performer is also male, but allows him to express and explore a different side of his *male-ness*; therefore still *glitching* the way his gender is read by people around him in reality. Initially the female performer says all the lines that are 'typed' in the chat by the Ballet Dancer. However, as the musical progresses the 'typed' lines become shared between them; the two personas become more interchangeable, more fluid. This aspect of the show is particularly exciting for the ways in which gender and identity are played with.

The Ballet Dancer is one of multiple aspects of *Lift* that resist chrononormative structures and queer the traditional dramaturgy of the musical. He sings of wanting to get out of 'this space I'm in, this close confinement';[23] many of his lyrics refer to 'walls' that limit him. When viewed through the lens of Elizabeth Freeman's work on heteronormative temporality, we can understand these walls as a metaphor for the constructs of society and the difficulty queer people face in terms of simply existing within confines that often explicitly exclude their identities. Specifically the Ballet Dancer sings, 'I've gotta challenge what I see'.[24] Russell states: 'Through the digital, we make new worlds and dare to modify our own.'[25] Arguably, this is part of what he is doing when he explores his female self online. Also significantly, however, he sings: 'I've gotta push past this cliché driven life';[26] it seems that one of the things that this queer character feels constrained by is *chrononormativity*. The non-linear structure of *Lift* then becomes more impactful and integral; viewed through both Russell and Freeman's work it is resisting traditional heteronormative dramaturgy and modifying the structure of the musical to create a new world, both because of *and* on behalf of its queer characters.

Lost in translation: The French Teacher and the liminal experience

Lift further invites a non-binary reading through its relationship with language; after all language plays a part in constructing gender identity from both an internal and an external perspective. Meg-John Barker and Alex Iantaffi define *non-binary* as 'an umbrella term for all the gender expressions, identities, and experiences that fall outside of the binary gender system';[27] they go on to discuss examples of gender non-binary identities throughout history and across cultures. However, notably, this definition of *non-binary* was only added to the Oxford English Dictionary in 2018, as a result of the very recent non-binary movement. Diverse gender identities are seen by many to be a 'new trend'[28] as a result of this movement. In 1997, linguists Anna Livia and Kira Hall wrote on queer language: 'some linguists have also assumed that without its own denotative term, a concept must be lacking from a culture.'[29] However, my own experience with gender, along with Barker, Iantaffi and Lester's research, suggests that people have existed outside of the gender binary long before this term was popularized, or even recognized as an official definition in the dictionary. Non-binary musical theatre composer Éamon Boylan explains that their musical *Soft Butter* (2018) 'recalls the experience of growing up in a body (or identity) before having the language to express it';[30] this is something I strongly relate to in relation to my gender journey.

It is the French Teacher's sections, in particular, that can be read as exploring the liminal experience of growing up queer (or, specifically, non-binary) without having the language to express or explain it. In relation to this, it is important to return to the fact that *Lift* premiered in 2013, which predates the non-binary movement and certainly predates the term's incorporation into the Oxford English Dictionary in 2018. As such, it is not surprising that it is a musical that does not explicitly feature non-binary characters, or use the term. Strikingly, however, the musical's use of language in places is explicitly inclusive of identities outside of the gender binary. For example, in the opening number, the Busker sings, 'so, every morning there's a him, a her, a them looking for something';[31] a reference to the singular pronoun 'them', which is often the pronoun used by non-binary people in avoidance of binary gendered pronouns. The use of the singular 'they' 'dates back as far as the works of Chaucer and Shakespeare'[32] in the fourteenth and sixteenth centuries; however, the usage of this pronoun in relation to gender non-binary people is 'fairly recent',[33] coinciding with the recent non-binary movement which *Lift* precedes.

In a more abstract sense, the way language is explored through the character of the French Teacher can be read as occupying a non-binary space through the liminal experience of being 'Lost in Translation'. The concept of liminality refers to a state of ambiguity, of being in-between. In this song, she sings of being lost generally, in various places and concepts:

> Lost in translations of
> Lost in her phrasebook,
> Lost in her rucksack,
> Lost in her- mmmm-mm-mm
> Fuck, I'm lost.
> Lost in a cafe
> Lost in a picture
> Lost in a bookshop
> Lost in a footnote
> Lost in P.S.[34]

Although the character is singing this in relation to love and her feelings for her girlfriend, the liminal concept of being lost rings true with the experience of being non-binary. In their book, *Life Isn't Binary*, Barker and Iantaffi refer to the 'impact of invisibility'[35] in relation to the lack of bisexual representation. It is also true that today, and even more so in 2013, such invisibility was/is an issue for non-binary people; 'When our existence seems to be impossible in dominant culture it is challenging to imagine being in the world.'[36] The 'lack of belonging'[37] can make people feel lonely and *lost*. The list aspect of this chorus also delves into abstract language; it is impossible for a person to be literally lost in a footnote or phrasebook. The abstract metaphor here speaks to a feeling of liminality that relates to that idea (noted by Boylan and certainly felt by myself) of not having the literal language to express one's feelings or identity: of being 'lost in translation'.

The gendered nature of the French language amplifies the French Teacher's significance from a gender non-binary perspective, due to her job and the fact that it is Paris that her girlfriend has gone to. It is pointed out in Hall and Livia's book that 'French grammar, vocabulary, and morphosyntax place particular constraints on gay men and lesbians'.[38] This is due to the gendered aspects of the language; pronouns associated with differing objects or concepts are labelled as masculine or feminine. Therefore, it feels particularly significant that the first solo lyrics we hear from the French Teacher are: 'I was in the classroom doing pronouns.'[39] Head of the Montreal faction of Trans Trenderz (an all-trans music label), Kyng, has discussed their struggles with the French language as a non-binary person for whom it was their first language, in part because of the 'gendering [of] inanimate objects'.[40] However, 'how does the classification masculine/feminine function in language when an individual's sexuality does not conform to the general rules of heterosexual patriarchy that regulate grammar?'[41] Pastre looks at this in relation to sexualities (it is not surprising that a piece of work from 1997 may conflate sexuality with gender), but it can certainly be seen how this relates to non-binary gender identities as well. Through this lens, the French Teacher being 'lost in translation' is even more powerful when considering the ways in which the French language dematerializes the liminal experience of being non-binary. Especially because, as Kyng points outs: 'in French there's no (singular) *they*'[42] and therefore, there is no way for non-binary people to refer to themselves or each other without inventing a new term (which is much harder to integrate into society with speed).

Conclusion: A space to innovate

Meg-John Barker and Julia Scheele state that 'Queer theorists and post-structuralists would argue that there's never one "true" reading of any text – not even the one the author intended. Rather, there are always many possible readings, and the reader is implicated in the meanings that are (re)produced'[43]. This chapter has explored how the non-binary reader affects the meanings reproduced in *Lift* (2013), through both the application of academic theories and from an autoethnographic perspective. Non-binary people are especially under-represented in musical theatre practice and academia, and so this becomes especially important; 'as humans, we have both a desire – and indeed a neurobiological need – to belong, and to be mirrored.'[44] The work of Nimal Puwar in *Space Invaders: Race, Gender and Bodies out of Place* (2004) helps contextualize how we satisfy this need in relation to existing pieces of musical theatre: 'Space is not a fixed entity. "It moves and changes, depending on how it is used, what is done with and to it, and how open it is to even further changes"'.[45] Therefore, in order to allow the under-represented to see themselves mirrored and to improve the continued relevance of past works, musical theatre scholarship must treat said past works as being open to constant potential for movement and change and not as historical relics; resistant readings are just one form of this.

It is, however, important to note the problematic side of a resistant non-binary reading such as this. This chapter reads the gender identities and experiences of these characters from a white, western perspective, which offers only one intersectional view of gender; what is read as feminine or masculine differs across time, cultures and societies. Furthermore, reading aspects of a character as masculine or feminine (or male or female) imposes a binary in itself. In reality, non-binary gender identities and gender fluidity exist between and beyond those categorizations. Moreover, the fact is, openly non-binary characters are still grossly lacking in musical theatre. There has recently been a great deal of conversation around the importance of trans and non-binary representation in musical theatre; but still very little has been done to rectify the paucity, at least at commercial West End/Broadway level. West End and Broadway are widely viewed as the zeniths of musical theatre, but if we look beyond their constraints there is more promising work happening; there is an increase in emerging work that is created by gender non-binary artists and features non-binary characters.[46,47] Russell states that 'The glitch is for those selves joyfully immersed in the in-between, those who have travelled away from their assigned site of gendered origin. The ongoing presence of the glitch generates a welcome and protected space in which to innovate and experiment',[48] and I would propose that we learn from the addressed aspects of *Lift*, to strive to explore beyond the constraints of the heteronormative dramaturgy that dominates musical theatre; to endeavour to use the musical form to explore what it means to *glitch* the societal constructs that continue to limit and harm those whose identities fall outside of cisgender, white, heteronormativity.

Notes

1. Sarah K. Whitfield, 'Disrupting Heteronormative Temporality Through Queer Dramaturgies: Fun Home, Hadestown and A Strange Loop', *Arts* 9 (2), no. 69 (2020): 3.
2. Meg-John Barker and Alex Iantaffi, *Life Isn't Binary: On Being Both, Beyond and In-between* (London and Philadelphia: Jessica Kingsley Publishers, 2019), 58.
3. Meg-John Barker and Alex Iantaffi, *How to Understand Your Gender: A Practical Guide for Exploring Who You Are* (London and Philadelphia: Jessica Kingsley, 2018), 38.
4. Stacy Wolf, *A Problem Like Maria: Gender and Sexuality in the American Musical* (Ann Arbor: University of Michigan Press, 2002), 8.
5. Wolf, *A Problem Like Maria*, 4.
6. Elizabeth Freeman, *Time Binds: Queer Temporalities, Queer Histories* (Durham: Duke University Press, 2010), 4–5.
7. Equity, *Guidelines for Entertainment Professionals Working with LGBTQ+ Performers*, 2019, 3, viewed 20 February 2020, https://www.equity.org.uk/media/3465/equity_lgbt-casting-guide.pdf.
8. Millie Taylor and Dominic Symonds, Studying Musical Theatre: Theory and Practice (London: Palgrave Macmillan, 2014), 169.
9. James Lovelock, '"What About Love?" Claiming and Reclaiming LGBTQ+ Spaces', in *Reframing the Musical: Race, Culture, and Identity*, ed. Sarah Whitfield (London: Red Globe Press, 2019), 207.
10. Legacy Russell, *Glitch Feminism: A Manifesto* (London and New York: Verso, 2020), 29.
11. Barker and Iantaffi, *How to Understand Your Gender*, 198.
12. Meg-John Barker and Alex Iantaffi, *Life Isn't Binary: On Being Both, Beyond and In-between* (London and Philadelphia: Jessica Kingsley Publishers, 2019), 81.
13. Barker and Iantaffi, *Life Isn't Binary*, 65.
14. *Lift*. [Film]. Directed by Steven Paling. London: Digital Theatre, viewed 21 July 2021. Available from: Digital Theatre (2013).
15. *Lift*. [Film]. Directed by Steven Paling. London: Digital Theatre, viewed 21 July 2021. Available from: Digital Theatre (2013).
16. *Lift*. [Film]. Directed by Steven Paling. London: Digital Theatre, viewed 21 July 2021. Available from: Digital Theatre (2013).

17. *Lift*. [Film]. Directed by Steven Paling. London: Digital Theatre, viewed 21 July 2021. Available from: Digital Theatre (2013).
18. Russell, *Glitch Feminism*, 161.
19. Russell, *Glitch Feminism*, 6–7.
20. Russell, *Glitch Feminism*, 6.
21. Russell, *Glitch Feminism*, 4.
22. Sara Black McCulloch, 'Activating the Glitch: A Conversation with Legacy Russell', *Los Angeles Review of Books*, 2021, viewed 1 September 2021, https://lareviewofbooks.org/article/activating-the-glitch-a-conversation-with-legacy-russell/.
23. *Lift*. [Film]. Directed by Steven Paling. London: Digital Theatre, viewed 21 July 2021. Available from: Digital Theatre (2013).
24. *Lift*. [Film]. Directed by Steven Paling. London: Digital Theatre, viewed 21 July 2021. Available from: Digital Theatre (2013).
25. Russell, *Glitch Feminism*, 30.
26. *Lift*. [Film]. Directed by Steven Paling. London: Digital Theatre, viewed 21 July 2021. Available from: Digital Theatre (2013)
27. Barker and Iantaffi, *Life Isn't Binary*, 61.
28. CN Lester, *Trans Like Me: Conversations for All of Us* (New York: Seal Press, 2017), 150.
29. Anna Livia and Kira Hall, '"It's a Girl!": Bringing Performativity Back to Linguistics', in *Queerly Phrased: Language, Gender, and Sexuality,* ed. A. Livia and K. Hall (New York and Oxford: Oxford University Press, 1997), 10.
30. Stephi Wild, 'Soft Butter: A Trans Fantasia on Edible Themes Will Release Album Recording', *Broadway World*, 2019, viewed 1 July 2021.
31. *Lift*. [Film]. Directed by Steven Paling. London: Digital Theatre, viewed 21 July 2021. Available from: Digital Theatre (2013).
32. Barker and Iantaffi, *How to Understand Your Gender*, 32.
33. Barker and Iantaffi, *How to Understand Your Gender*, 33.
34. *Lift*. [Film]. Directed by Steven Paling. London: Digital Theatre, viewed 21 July 2021. Available from: Digital Theatre (2013).
35. Barker and Iantaffi, *Life Isn't Binary*, 23.
36. Barker and Iantaffi, *Life Isn't Binary*, 23.
37. Barker and Iantaffi, *Life Isn't Binary*, 23.
38. Geneviève Pastre, 'Linguistic Gender Play among French Gays and Lesbians', in *Queerly Phrased: Language, Gender, and Sexuality,* ed. A. Livia and K. Hall (New York and Oxford: Oxford University Press, 1997), 369.
39. *Lift*. [Film]. Directed by Steven Paling. London: Digital Theatre, viewed 21 July 2021. Available from: Digital Theatre (2013).
40. Max Jack-Monroe, '"They for Cool People": An Interview with Kyng', *Queer Language Evolution*, 2019, viewed 22 August 2021.
41. Pastre, 'Linguistic Gender Play among French Gays and Lesbians', 369.
42. Jack-Monroe, '"They for Cool People"'.
43. Meg-John Barker and Alex Iantaffi, *Queer: A Graphic History* (London: Icon Books Ltd, 2016), 102.
44. Barker and Iantaffi, *Life Isn't Binary*, 23.
45. Puwar, Nirmal, *Space Invaders: Race, Gender and Bodies out of Place*. Oxford: New York: Berg, 2004.

46. *The Phase* (by Meg McGrady and Zoe Morris) is a piece of musical theatre, written by non-binary artists and featuring non-binary characters, that is currently being developed in the UK.
47. True Voices Company celebrates and gives a platform to the voices of trans and non-binary musical theatre creatives in London, Chicago and New York through showcase and cabaret events.
48. Russell, *Glitch Feminism*, 30.

Works Cited

Barker, Meg-John and Alex Iantaffi (2018), *How to Understand Your Gender: A Practical Guide for Exploring Who You Are*. London and Philadelphia: Jessica Kingsley.

Barker, Meg-John and Alex Iantaffi (2019), *Life Isn't Binary: On Being Both, Beyond and In-between*. London and Philadelphia: Jessica Kingsley Publishers.

Barker, Meg-John and Jules Scheele (2016), *Queer: A Graphic History*. London: Icon Books Ltd.

Black McCulloch, Sara (2021), 'Activating the Glitch: A Conversation with Legacy Russell', *Los Angeles Review of Books*, viewed 1 September 2021, https://lareviewofbooks.org/article/activating-the-glitch-a-conversation-with-legacy-russell/.

Equity (2019), *Guidelines for Entertainment Professionals Working with LGBTQ+ Performers*, viewed 20 February 2020, https://www.equity.org.uk/media/3465/equity_lgbt-casting-guide.pdf.

Freeman, Elizabeth (2010), *Time Binds: Queer Temporalities, Queer Histories*. Durham: Duke University Press.

Global Musicals (2021), *Perfect Pitch*. Global Musicals, viewed 12 June 2021, https://globalmusicals.com/perfect-pitch/.

Jack-Monroe, Max (2019), '"They for Cool People": An Interview with Kyng', *Queer Language Evolution*, viewed 22 August 2021, https://queerlanguage.com/author/majac005/.

Lester, CN (2017), *Trans Like Me: Conversations for All of Us*. New York: Seal Press.

Lift. (2013). [Film]. Directed by Steven Paling. London: Digital Theatre, viewed 21 July 2021. Available from: Digital Theatre.

Livia, Anna and Kira Hall (1997), '"It's a Girl!": Bringing Performativity Back to Linguistics', in A. Livia and K. Hall (eds), *Queerly Phrased: Language, Gender, and Sexuality*, 3–18. New York and Oxford: Oxford University Press.

Lovelock, James (2019), 'What About Love?' Claiming and Reclaiming LGBTQ+ Spaces', in S. Whitfield (ed.), *Reframing the Musical: Race, Culture and Identity*, 187–209. London: Red Globe Press.

Lovelock, James (2022), *Telling Queer Stories: Producing New Musical Theatre with LGBTQ* Characters* [Webinar]. University of Wolverhampton, https://www.youtube.com/watch?v=kicuwpKB_j0 (accessed 4 February 2022).

Pastre, Geneviève (1997), 'Linguistic Gender Play Among French Gays and Lesbians', in A. Livia and K. Hall (ed.), *Queerly Phrased: Language, Gender, and Sexuality*, 369–79. New York and Oxford: Oxford University Press.

Puwar, Nirmal (2004), *Space Invaders: Race, Gender and Bodies Out of Place*. Oxford and New York: Berg.

Russell, Legacy (2020), *Glitch Feminism: A Manifesto*. London and New York: Verso.

Whitfield, Sarah K. (2020), 'Disrupting Heteronormative Temporality Through Queer Dramaturgies: Fun Home, Hadestown and A Strange Loop', *Arts*, 9 (2): 69, https://doi.org/10.3390/arts9020069.

Wild, Stephi (2019), 'Soft Butter: A Trans Fantasia on Edible Themes Will Release Album Recording', *Broadway World*, viewed 1 July 2021, https://www.broadwayworld.com/bwwmusic/article/SOFT-BUTTER-A-TRANS-FANTASIA-ON-EDIBLE-THEMES-Will-Release-Album-Recording-20190706.

Wolf, Stacy (2002), *A Problem Like Maria: Gender and Sexuality in the American Musical*. Ann Arbor: University of Michigan Press.

Perfect Pitch interview – Andy Barnes, Wendy Barnes

Producers/developers *Lift*

What is your favourite British musical?

Wendy *Les Misérables*

Andy *Starlight Express*

What's your favourite British musical theatre song?

Wendy 'One Day More' *Les Misérables*
Andy 'Bui Doi' *Miss Saigon*

What training did you do for your career?

Wendy I did a degree in performing arts at Middlesex Uni.

Andy My honest answer is, I trained in meeting people. I did go to Central and the course – in Creative Producing – gave me contacts and connections. But in terms of the skills that we apply to what we do – musically I still have very little authority other than as a consumer.

Wendy Both of us would say that our main training ground was from all the musicals that we saw and we loved and didn't love, from a very young age. I learnt a lot more from seeing things than I did in my training.

Do you, or did you, see *Lift* as a key moment for British musical theatre?

Andy I think we knew there was something different and progressive about it. I don't think either of us thought 'this is a game-changer'. I think we went 'there's something in this which is the way we want to go' and our commitment was to that.

Wendy And Craig's music. Craig sent through two songs and we invited him to our office and he sang the whole score to us, sat on the floor with his phone playing the backing tracks. We'd listened to a lot of shows by this point and I hadn't heard any music like that. That was really exciting to us.

Andy Craig's sound was so smart and so different but accessible. That's what made it worth fighting for.

Wendy We had been told since 2006 'there's no audience, this never goes well in this country'. So did it change the landscape of musicals? Probably not, but it definitely gave us the confidence that we knew what we were doing.

How would you describe your contribution to *Lift*?

Wendy Our ambition was always to develop the musicals for somebody to come along and pick them up and produce them. And when that wasn't really happening we thought we're going to have to set up a commercial producing company so that we can produce them because we seem to be doing that anyway. It was one of the first shows that we got a bit of funding for from Arts Council England. We were doing a showcase of 6 shows and we got funding to do further development to two of the shows, before we showcased them, to see if it made any difference. And we found categorically that it made a huge amount of difference. And that was the beginning of Perfect Pitch.

Andy Creatively, we were inputting constantly through this process: feedback, thoughts, marketing, workshops, everything. We didn't really get a lot of interest in the showcase because people were a bit like 'err, what's this?'.

Wendy But we discovered that the performers were 100 per cent in love with it, and that might have been my attraction to it. I recognized that these were songs you wanted to sing. The book wasn't quite working but everyone undeniably loved the score. We'd never made an album before but we thought, let's make an album of *Lift*.

Andy Jim Zalles, who wanted to be a producer, came to us and said what do I need to do to make this show happen? So I put a budget together that was something like £70k, fully assuming that he would not be able to do that and he said 'what do you think we'll get back?' and I said 'you should be prepared to lose 40 per cent'. He said but who is going to actually produce it? So we said 'ok'. Bearing in mind that that had never been our ambition with any of the shows that we were developing. We ended up doing 87 per cent box office, which meant that Jim lost very little money in the end.

Wendy The themes of *Lift* weren't widely out there. The score wasn't what you were used to. So when we got 87 per cent capacity that's the first time we felt like we were doing something right. And that there was a thirst for new writing.

Do you want to describe how being a musical theatre producer works?

Andy Ultimately, your job as a producer is to sell the show; to a venue, the artistic director, and then everybody who's going to back it and put money in. Our job is like a big ball of plasticine, and you shove a writer into it, and you shove a director into it, you shove a venue into it, and then you roll it along. There's no real direction – someone will stick a leg out and it'll go that way, and someone will stick an arm out and it'll go the other way.

Wendy When we started we just wanted to give opportunities to writers; make some good stuff, put it on a stage, hope people come and enjoy it. Now we want to change the audiences that are coming to musicals and we're looking to produce work that will help us do that. And that might change again in ten years. It changes how you work and think as a producer depending on what your aims are.

Andy Producers need to trust their creatives. But it goes both ways. We talk about the hill you die on. For example – trust me or not but the project happens that way, on that hill, or it doesn't happen. Likewise a writer should go, I'm going to die on the hill of not changing that bit because it's the essence of my writing, but it's all the other hills in between where you work out and navigate and trust each other on.

What was the rehearsal process for *Lift* like?

Wendy What worked for *Lift* was that the director had been part of the process for a long time leading up to it. Stephen Paling is Craig Adam's husband and he knew *Lift* inside out, he knew the vision for it, so we just knew that it was in safe hands.

Andy If they're the right person, we'll keep them on board throughout the whole thing. And I think that's part of our job – to identify if that person is the right person. Because to be fair, the writers don't always know. There can sometimes be friction, and that's sometimes a good thing.

How do you feel about *Lift* now?

Wendy *Lift* is very special to me. Maybe because I championed it, maybe because I felt it was a new voice of its time. And now every time someone sings one of the songs I feel proud of that, as if it was mine, I guess.

Andy I love it in a slightly different way to Wendy, but I'm very proud of it. We had a roster of ten shows, or whatever, back in the day. And that was mad and ad hoc, and we were eating beans on toast, because there was literally no money in it. But there was a wonderful adventure ahead of us to discover at that time, and *Lift* is a nostalgic reminder of that in a really positive way.

We had heard from a lot of people that there were no decent British writers, that the only good writing was happening in America, that nobody wants a British musical. Perfect Pitch came from the agreement that there wasn't enough material out there to put on. There were some good ideas, and some talent, but it all needed nurturing, developing. What *Lift* did was prove to us that the talent was there.

How do you think the work that you did on *Lift* has shaped what you've done since then?

Andy We knew that there were problems with the book, and if *Lift* were to happen upon us now, it would be a very different version that ended up on stage because we have much more confidence, and I think we're more skilled, in having those conversations. So I suppose that's definitely shaped how we work and how we move forward on other projects. We've made that resolution now to just be 100 per cent honest and deliver any difficult conversations with love and kindness, but not go against every sinew in our body if we're agreed.

Wendy It was *Lift* getting all the attention that started us thinking maybe we should licence these shows, and give them even more longevity. And that's all led to us now having our contract with Broadway Licensing. It was the first show that we workshopped rather than just put on. And it was our first album, and now we love an album!

Are you still working in musical theatre?

Andy 100 per cent we're still working in musicals. We're absorbed with the world of *SIX* at the moment and its octopus-like tentacles that seem to be spreading around the globe. All of which is allowing us to solidify and cement what we are passionate about doing in musicals, and with who, and how. What *SIX* has afforded us is the time and the focus to be able to make things happen in a way that we think will have a better contribution to the ecology of musicals in the long term.

What advice would you give aspiring writers or aspiring producers?

Andy Be humble, pick your battles, and work collaboratively.

Wendy If you want to write a new British musical or produce one, make sure you're seeing everything on the landscape at all levels. And when you want to send your work to a producer – make sure you send it to a producer who is working currently in a way that you want your show produced.

Andy And do your version of being a writer rather than what you think the expectation of being a writer is.

4 Bend It Like Beckham: The Musical
Embodying British identities

KELSEY BLAIR

Bend It Like Beckham: The Musical begins with a daydream. Over the speakers, a football announcer calls out sporting action, and it is revealed that the English national football team is playing a match against Germany.[1] The announcer divulges that David Beckham has recently scored the tying goal. The announcer wonders, 'Will Jess Bhamra be the striker to help England win its first World Cup since 1966?'[2] Before Jess – the musical's protagonist – can take a potentially game-winning penalty kick, the daydream is interrupted by her mother, Mrs Bhamra: 'Jesminder! How can you be dreaming of football when your sister is getting engaged tonight?'[3] The opening sequence sets up the central story arc and introduces two of the musical's distinctive features: an emphasis on multicultural British identity and the depiction of sporting action.

A stage-adaptation of the 2002 film, *Bend It Like Beckham* features music by Howard Goodall, lyrics by Charles Hart, and a book by Gurinder Chadha and Paul Mayeda Berges. As with the film, the musical depicts the story of Jess Bhamra, a teenage girl who comes from a traditional British South Asian family and loves football, despite her parents' disapproval. In the opening sequence, two iterations of the main character's name are spoken – a traditional Punjab name, Jesminder and a Western-inflected diminutive, Jess. The utterance of these two names begins to suggest the musical's interest in themes of identity and multiculturalism, the latter of which is noteworthy within the context of professional British musical theatre. In community and regional theatres, works by artists from ethnic minority communities – including British Black and British South Asian artists – have produced rich clusters of works including *Arawak Gold* (1998), *One Love* (2001), *Slamdunk* (2004), *The Harder They Come* (2006) and *Britain's Got Bhangra* (2010). As Millie Taylor notes, these and other productions provide 'an extraordinarily dynamic substrate in the community, regional and subsidized sectors'.[4] Importantly, however, works by artists from Britain's Black, Asian and minority ethnic communities have rarely been produced in the West End. To this end, after *Bombay Dreams* (2002), *Bend It Like Beckham* is the second British-developed West End musical where members of the core artistic team identified as British South Asian. Unlike *Bombay Dreams* – which was set in India and whose main characters were Indian – *Bend It Like Beckham* is set in London and features an explicitly multicultural story, with protagonists with various ethnic backgrounds as well as a diverse cast of ensemble players. As such, the musical was an important landmark for the presentation of elements of both British South Asian culture and British multiculturalism.

The presentation of cultures and multiculturalism is woven into the musical's sport theme. As with the film, the musical's title is a reference to English footballer David Beckham, who was known for his ability to seemingly 'bend', or curve, the ball around opponents. In featuring football as a thematic through-line, *Bend It Like Beckham* is in conversation with a small subset of professionally produced English-language plays and musicals about sports such as *Damn Yankees* (1955), *The Changing Room* (1976), *Sing Yer Heart Out for the Lads* (2003), *Take Me Out* (2003), *The Beautiful Game* (2008), *Bring It On: The Musical* (2011), *Rocky: The Musical* (2012), *Chariots of Fire* (2012) and *The Wolves* (2016). As is the case with these other works, the sporting theme facilitated the performance and presentation of sport-related skills, and while the musical did not feature the staging of an entire football match, actors enacted football skills such as kicking and heading a football. In combination with the musical's British South Asian and multicultural themes, the inclusion of sporting skills resulted in a unique mixture of physical and cultural styles including football, bhangra music and dance, traditional Punjab folk song and conventional Western musical theatre singing and dance. In this chapter, I explore the distinctive combination of physical and cultural influences and explore how the musical performs a late-twentieth-century multicultural ideal. Drawing from Diana Taylor's concept of the repertoire – a repository of embodied knowledges and memories akin to materials in an archive – I unpack the multi-layered knowledges and meanings activated by the performance of skills from football, bhangra dance and musical theatre. This analysis will show how *Bend It Like Beckham: The Musical* performs a turn-of-the-twenty-first-century version of British multiculturalism.

From screen to stage: British multiculturalism across time and mediums

Both the musical and the film depict the story of eighteen-year-old Jess Bhamra who lives with her parents – Mr and Mrs Bhamra – as well as her soon-to-be-married older sister Pinky. Jess adores football and idolizes David Beckham, but her parents disapprove of her passion. One day, Jess is spotted playing football with her best friend Tony by a young female player named Jules Paxton. Jules recruits Jess to play for the Harriers, who are coached by Joe, a young former player. Over the course of the musical, Jess must balance her sister's upcoming wedding alongside Harriers' training and games, and a love triangle between Jess, Jules and Joe. While some film critics questioned the formulaic elements of the romantic and sporting plots, many lauded the film's upbeat tone, themes of female empowerment, and cross-cultural negotiations,[5] and the movie was widely considered a surprise critical and financial success. Following its UK release, the film received a limited theatrical release in the United States in 2003 and eventually went on to gross $77.7 million worldwide.[6]

The film was produced at the height of a specific manifestation of multiculturalism in Britain. Variously used to describe a sociological process, a policy, a set of ideologies or the demographic composition of a specific community, 'multiculturalism' is a highly contested concept. In Britain, the intellectual notion of multiculturalism was strongly influenced by the work of Stuart Hall, who used the term 'adjectively' to 'describe the very different societies in which people of different ethnic, cultural, racial, and religious backgrounds live together . . . and are not formally segregated into distinct separate segments'.[7] As Hall explains, multicultural societies are not contemporary phenomena, but their presence and visibility increased after the Second World War.[8] In the British context, immigration policies implemented after the Second World War resulted in an influx of immigration from nation states within the Commonwealth.[9] Initially, the government's attitude towards immigration and increased multiculturalism foregrounded assimilation – meaning that minoritarian cultures should assume the habits, values, beliefs and practices of the majority. In the 1960s and 1970s, however, there was a shift towards an emphasis on integration, which emphasized cultural diversity and the coexistence of cultures alongside one another.[10] Despite shifts in political leadership in the 1980s and 1990s, integration remained a central tenet of British multiculturalism in the latter half of the twentieth century. In the early 2000s, however, attitudes towards British multiculturalism began to shift, and following a series of high-profile events – including 9/11 in the United States and a series of racially motivated riots in north England in 2002 – assimilation began to re-emerge as a prevailing attitude towards multiculturalism. The film was produced before this shift, and with its diverse case of characters and cross-cultural story, *Bend It Like Beckham* registered the ethos of British multiculturalism in the late 1990s that valued, and even celebrated, the peaceful coexistence of multiple cultures within the British nation state.

With its emphasis on women's sport and British South Asian characters, *Bend It Like Beckham* was a unique entry in the British cinema landscape in the early 2000s. But, its themes were not new to the film's director Gurinder Chadha. Chadha – who was born in Nairobi and moved to West London with her family when she was two years old – had long been exploring the lives of British South Asian communities, with a series of short documentaries for the British Film Institute in the 1980s and her first feature film, *Bhaji on the Beach* (1994), a comedy about an intergenerational group of mostly British South Asian women who go to the Blackpool Illuminations.[11] *Bhaji on the Beach* received widespread attention and was nominated for Best British Film of 1994 by the British Academy of Film and Television Arts. Across her early works, Chadha combined comedy and drama to explore issues relating to British South Asian experiences and particularly the lives of British South Asian women. *Bend It Like Beckham* picked up and expanded on these themes. It also bolstered Chadha's career, and following the film's international success, Chadha has co-written and directed several films that explored various facets of women's lives, British South Asian experience and intergenerational relationships in films like *Bride and Prejudice* (2004) and *It's a Wonderful Afterlife* (2010). By adapting the story for the musical format, *Bend It Like Beckham: The Musical* functions as a continuation of these themes and a re-imagining of through-lines from the original film.

The musical was workshopped in London in 2013 and 2014.[12] In the workshopping process, the team worked to translate the film's story arc for the stage. As Chadha explained during a panel in 2014, 'What we're doing all the time is distilling. Distilling away from the film but keeping the essence of the film.'[13] *Bend It Like Beckham: The Musical* premiered at the Phoenix Theatre in London's West End, with previews taking place in May 2015 and an official opening night on 24 June 2015. During the workshopping process, Chadha expressed a desire to retain the film's core themes. She explained: 'I'm a very populist filmmaker. I'm very much about the audience and taking the audience on a journey that is musically stimulating, creatively stimulating, and politically stimulating. But, at its core, [the film] is entertaining. And, that's really what *Bend It Like Beckham* was about. It was a hugely entertaining film about racism.'[14]

It's noteworthy that Chadha highlights racism as a central – if underlying – theme of the film, as the musical integrates the significance of racism in Jess's journey but places more significant emphasis on the themes of familial celebration and multicultural celebration. This marks one of a few minor distinctions between the film and musical. Indeed, while much of the story remained in the West End production, a few key changes were made. The musical keeps the original 2001 time setting but moves the location Hounslow – which is near Heathrow airport – to Southall, which is a district known for its significant British South Asian population. Second, the importance of the love triangle is diminished while the portrayal of Sikhism and the depictions of mother–daughter relationships are both enhanced. And, finally, the Bhamra home plays host to a wider variety of scenes, which places increased emphasis on domestic space and familial relations. The show received a Critics' Circle Theatre Award for Best Musical and ran for nine months, before closing in March of 2016. In December 2019, the musical had its North American premiere with a three-week run at the St. Lawrence Centre for the Arts' Bluma Appel Theatre in Toronto.[15]

In keeping several of the film's story elements, *Bend It Like Beckham: The Musical* extends and re-performs the movie's central themes and ideas, including friendship between young women, female empowerment in sport, cross- and multi-culturalism, intergenerational conflict and hybrid identities within the British South Asian community.[16] By virtue of the distinction between mediums, however, the musical offered a novel articulation of these ideas. Examining different types of knowledge transmission, Diana Taylor distinguishes between 'archival memory' which she suggests 'exists as documents, maps, literary texts, letters, archaeological remains, bones, videos, films, cds, all those items supposedly resistant to change', and what she calls the repertoire, which 'enacts embodied memory: performances, gestures, orality, movement, dance, singing – in short, all those acts usually thought of as ephemeral, nonreproducible knowledge'.[17] For Taylor, the repertoire is equally important to the archive because 'embodied and performed acts generated, record, and transmit knowledge'.[18] Even though the film is a recording – and, therefore, falls within the purview of the archive – the enactment of these skills by the filmic actors activated facets of the repertoire: in kicking a football Parminder Nagra, who portrayed Jess, performed a gesture from the repertoire of football. Significantly, however, Nagra – like the other film actors – did not perform this skill in front of audience members; her physical and vocal performance was framed and registered through recording technologies and later pieced together with editing technologies. As is consistent with the musical theatre form, performers' enactments were not framed by cameras, recorded or edited for audience members; rather, performers' entire bodies appeared 'live' in front of audience members. As an examination of enactments from the repertoires of football, bhangra dance and musical theatre demonstrate, this helped imbue the musical with nuanced performances of identity and multiculturalism.

Performing nation: Football, David Beckham and the British national body

From a dramaturgical perspective, *Bend It Like Beckham* shares important overlaps with another British musical *Billy Elliot: The Musical* (2005). In *Billy Elliot*, the main character is eleven-year-old Billy, who lives in a working-class town in England and discovers his love of ballet, but his father objects to Billy's dance ambitions because of gendered stereotypes about ballet. Both musicals are film to stage adaptations that depict a story involving British youth, both stories hinge on a young person's desire to participate in a specialized areas of practice (football for Jess, ballet for Billy) and, like *Bend It Like Beckham*, *Billy Elliot* utilizes a specialized area of practice to amplify themes relating to gender, intergenerational tension and nuance within British communities. The genealogies of football and ballet, however, inflect the musicals' distinctive emphases. Ballet developed in Italian and French courts in the fifteenth and sixteenth centuries.[19] It is strongly associated with nobility and 'high arts' such as opera and classical Western music. And, since the end of the nineteenth century, ballet has also been linked with Western conceptualizations of femininity. In *Billy Elliot*, the history of ballet – and its associations with aesthetics, nobility and femininity – is in sharp contrast to the masculine-oriented working-class British culture in Billy's small town. Association football, on the other hand, has strong roots in masculine, British culture, which offers an opportunity for *Bend It Like Beckham* to activate a multi-layered set of memories and knowledges through the performance of football skills.

The opening sequence – which features Jess daydreaming about playing for the English national team alongside her idol David Beckham – establishes the significance of football in Jess's life. Following this scene, football is incorporated into the musical at multiple levels. It is a key element of plotting, as Jess's desire to play football creates conflict in the Bhamra family and also facilitates the connections between Jess and Jules, Jess and Joe, and Jess and the Harriers. Themes relating to football feature in numbers including 'Glorious', 'Just a Game' and 'Result'. Jess, Jules and members of the Harriers' football team – often appearing on stage in football kit – enact football skills. Alongside themes and costumes, footwork drills and skills such as kicking or heading the ball are often integrated into choreography. The enactment of these skills on stage is significant because it means that sport is not only part of the discourse. Characters manifest their relationship with sport through performance, and in so doing, they actuate the histories and memories embedded in the repertoire of football. Critically, several facets of these memories are inflected by British history.

In the opening daydream sequence, Jess imagines herself playing alongside the English national team. In international sports, players can figuratively represent nation, but they also function as literal national representatives, who are selected to play on behalf of nation states. As the sequence reveals Jess's inner world, this suggests Jess's strong association with British national identity, where she desires to both literally and figuratively represent the English nation. The specific manifestation of Jess's desire is noteworthy, as it adds further layers to the invocation of British cultural memory through performance. Jess idolizes a male player (Beckham) and fantasizes about playing with the men's national team. It's possible to read this fantasy through the lens of gender as Ann Hall suggests, sport was traditionally considered a 'masculinizing project, a cultural practice in which boys learn[ed] to be men and male solidarity [was] forged', and while the landscape has shifted, the traditional association between sport and masculinity remained throughout the twentieth century.[20] Undoubtedly, the gendered dimension of sport is an important backdrop to the action, but it is not the main source of conflict. To this end, while both Mrs Bhamra and Jules's mother Paula disapprove of their daughters' participation in football, the story does not hinge on women's access to sport: the community has enough players to form the Harriers team, and while Mr Bhamra forbids Jess from playing football, this decision is fuelled by his fears of racism, not gender norms.[21] Jess's dream of playing alongside David Beckham, then, has less to do with a desire to be accepted as equal alongside men and more to do with being considered equal alongside white men.

During the early history of association football – when it was developing in English public schools – the rules of the game were not yet standardized, and there were different versions of the game, some of which allowed catching and use of the hands and the others of which did not.[22] Over time, games that permitted hand-use morphed into sports such as rugby and gridiron – also known as American – football while those that forbade hand-use became association football. This bifurcation shaped the distinct character of the different sports. Tackle-based ball sports such as gridiron football and rugby tend to emphasize principles such as roughness, physical durability and sacrifice of the individual body in service of the group, as these are necessary to excel in games.[23] Association football, on the other hand, tends to emphasize individual skill mastery, strategy and teamwork. And, the behavioural codes of association football, both historically and now, play much stronger emphasis on decorum than do the behavioural codes of other kinds of football.[24] As such, association football oriented towards an embodiment that emphasized decorum, strategy and virtuosic skill. This resonates with facets of David Beckham's style of play. During his career, Beckham's individual kicking skills and strategic play were highly regarded, and Beckham was, for twenty years, one of England's most revered professional players.[25] In idolizing Beckham, Jess envisions herself embodying a distinctly British style of football play.

The significance of this style of play is emphasized in the climactic sequence. Jess leaves Pinky's wedding to play in the Harriers' game, and during the game, Jess is fouled by the opposing team, giving her the opportunity to take a penalty kick. Though the entire action is not depicted on-stage (the moment combines live-action and projections), it is implied that the ball curls around the opponent, meaning that Jess successfully 'bent' the ball like her idol. In so doing, Jess actualizes sporting and cultural success by winning the game and enacting a virtuosic, and distinctly British, football embodiment. In the moments that follow, the effects of this successful performance crystallize, and Jess is celebrated by her teammates for her contribution to their collective success. Taken in isolation, this might suggest that the musical subsumes cultural difference through football. However, the musical's showcasing of additional areas of specialized practice, and especially bhangra dance, facilitates a more expansive performance of cultural identities.

Dance, bhangra and the performance of British South Asian culture

In the show's first major ensemble number, 'UB2', the audience is introduced to the Southall neighbourhood as well as to the main cast of characters. Unlike the opening sequence, which focuses on Jess's relationship to football, 'UB2' employs dance and music to develop character and embody different facets of British culture. In addition to introducing the main cast of characters, the number introduces the Southall neighbourhood, a district that is colloquially known as 'Little India'. At the beginning of the number, the ensemble is organized into four lines of dancers. Signalled through costuming – such as women in saris and Sikh men wearing pagris – British South Asian middle-aged and older adults dance stage right. Stage left, younger characters with various cultural identities wear T-shirts, jackets and hooded sweatshirts. In the first line of the second verse, the characters stage right sing,

'And it's a little bit of Punjab/Hey!'[26] Their counterparts on stage left immediately reply, 'A little bit UK/Braa!'[27] The call-and-response-style lyrics repeat: from stage right, 'A little splash of saffron'; from stage left, 'on a backdrop of grey'.[28] Alongside the lyrics and blocking, dance is used to differentiate between the two groups. The British South Asian characters on stage right enact dance moves that combine musical theatre and bhangra, while the characters on the right perform a mix of musical theatre and hip-hop inspired moves. This is indicative of the show's broader use of dance, which invokes the cultural histories of dance – and particularly bhangra dance – to contrast the sporting enactments, deepen British South Asian characterization and perform cultural and cross-cultural identities.

Bhangra dance is a type of Indian folk dance that originated in the Sialkot region of Punjab.[29] An up-tempo style of dance that involves kicks and leaps frequently alongside upward arm motions, it was originally associated with the season of harvesting and was performed by Punjabi farmers. The formalization of bhangra presentation took place in the context of post-independence in India, when cultural forms such as dance were used to bolster notions of regional and national identity. It was this form of bhangra that influenced the development of the form in Britain, when British South Asian youth began performing and experimenting with bhangra in the 1960s and 1970s. Influenced by African Caribbean music and culture, bhangra began to incorporate styles from a range of cultural traditions, and the style that is known as 'British Bhangra' started to emerge in the 1970s and 1980s. In the 1980s and 1990s, British Bhangra incorporated sounds from a range of musical styles and cultural traditions including popular Western music, reggae, grime and soul. This mixing of sounds and dance has continued into the present, and contemporary British Bhangra styles often combine elements of hip-hop dance alongside more conventional bhangra movement patterns.

The mixing of sounds was particularly important to Chadha in the workshopping process. As she explained at the 2014 panel, 'What we're at great pains to do is something that is uniquely British and that is that combination of the two [British, British South Asian].'[30] This combination is demonstrated in the music and accompanying choreography that infuses bhangra music and movements into conventional British musical theatre song and dance numbers to expand characterization. Predominantly enacted by British South Asian characters, bhangra-inspired movements help demarcate the British South Asian community within the musical. In wedding-related numbers, movements associated with traditional bhangra such as the miming of sword-based movements, the imagined playing of the *sapps* (a percussion instrument) and gestures that mimic farming activities are performed predominantly by male characters, while female characters enact movements from traditional women's dances such as the Giddha.[31] Meanwhile, the younger generation of British South Asian characters – Pinky and her friends, in particular – enact movements that combine traditional bhangra arm movements with hip-hop-influenced lower-body movements. Such gestures enliven Punjab and British South Asian cultural memories and histories embedded in the repertoire of bhangra dance, contributing to the embodiment of these cultures on stage.

Significantly, as with football, the activation of the repertoire spurred by bhangra dance movements offers a multifaceted embodiment of British South Asian culture. As noted earlier, the history of bhangra dance involves styles that reflect 'traditional' and 'modern' styles, wherein the first refers to movement patterns that extend directly from the form's early history in Punjab and the second denotes types of dances that integrate influences from multiple cultures. These two styles of bhangra are inflected by tension between generations. As Jerri Daboo explains, 'This "modern" Bhangra created conflict with some members of the elder generation who felt that it was "polluting" the "traditional" and "authentic" sound of Bhangra, and that this was a reflection of the younger generation losing touch with their culture and being contaminated by immoral influences of the West.'[32] This tension is staged in the musical's choreography. Throughout, the older British South Asian women tend to perform movements associated with traditional women's bhangra, whereas the younger generations tend to enact gestures that are more strongly influenced by hip-hop. These enactments are frequently supported by scoring and orchestration. Describing Pinky's engagement number, 'Look at Us Now / Golden Moment / Get Me', orchestrator Kuljit Bhamra explains:

> The idea was to pit the elders dancing to traditional Bhangra against the youngsters dancing to a hip hop bhangra, a sort of face-off. Howard [Goodall] constructed the piece based on a traditional Punjabi *toombi* riff that he played on electronic instruments. [. . .] The sections with the younger generation had hip hop beats added, and the cousins chanted 'Go Pinky! Go Pinky!' during her dance bit.[33]

While the number might have been conceptualized as 'a sort of face-off', there are no winners or losers. Rather, the scene performs nuance within the British South Asian community, demonstrating how characters are at once connected through their shared knowledge of the repertoire of bhangra and separated from each other by their performance of moves from different branches of the form. In conversation with the performance of football, this might suggest that specialized areas of practice are predominantly used to signal difference within the musical. The repertoire of musical theatre, however, offers an opportunity to forge connections across communities.

Singing your feelings: Embodying intergenerational conflict

Unlike bhangra or football – which emerge from the story – the specialized practice of singing derives from the use of the integrated musical form. In musicals that use integration, numbers usually contribute to story, expand on character or advance the plot. The film used soundtrack music – as well as dance sequences – to display facets of Jess's inner world, but characters did not repeatedly express their feelings through song or dance. In the musical, singing recalls the history of musical theatre and deepens connections across communities, particularly through the characterization of the mother–daughter relationships.

In the film Mrs Bhamra and Paula Paxton receive narrow characterizations, and their respective disapprovals are frequently used for comic effect. Mrs Bhamra is a stereotypical British South Asian mother who criticizes her daughter and constantly invokes Punjab values and culture while Paula Paxton serves one of the film's running jokes, when she (incorrectly) suspects that Jess and Jules are in a lesbian relationship. In the musical, the comic function of the mothers is decreased while the significance of intergenerational tension is amplified. At the beginning of the musical, both Jess and Mrs Bhamra's and Jules and Paula's relationship is strained, as neither mother understands her daughter's passion for football. The parallel mother–daughter conflicts are brought into conversation with one another in the Act One number 'Tough Love'. Featuring all four characters, the pairings sing their frustrations with one another in alternating verses. Then, in the final verse, the four women sing together:

> Too bad, tough love
> Since we're all stuck with love
> With love
> Love[34]

The number forges a matrix of relations between characters: Jess and Jules; Jess and Mrs Bhamra; Jules and Paula; Paula and Mrs Bhamra. These connections are bittersweet in relation to the lyrics, which emphasize the mutually experienced disconnect between mothers and daughters. At the same time, the harmony in the final verse activates a connection between the two families: despite their distinct situations and their seemingly separate cultural backgrounds, both mother–daughter pairs are facing similar challenges.

The embodiment of intergenerational conflict is nuanced, and expanded, by Paula and Mrs Bhamra's solo numbers. Both characters are part of the long line of fully developed, and sometimes complicated, mothers in English-language professional musical theatre such as Mama Rose from *Gypsy* and Fantine from *Les Misérables* (1985). As with these characters, Paula and Mrs Bhamra espouse their anxieties through song. In the second act number, 'There She Goes', Paula is afforded the opportunity to express her perspective. Following a four-bar piano solo, Paula sings her first line, 'There she goes/there she goes'.[35] Aligned with the conventions of Broadway musical theatre, the performer – and by extension Paula – uses her lower vocal register to continue: '/Full of fear, full of rage/Far from here, from the cage of my heart . . .' As the number goes on, a violin joins the piano, and Paula expounds: 'And there's nothing, no nothing/we mothers can possibly say/All our weeping and wailing won't ever dissuade/them from sailing away'.[36] Paula's fear of losing connection with Jules is paralleled in the Bhamra family. In dialogue, Mrs Bhamra consistently chides Jess for lack of engagement with traditional Punjab cultural practices such as cooking. While Mrs Bhamra's nagging is sometimes played for comic effect, her motivations are revealed in her second act solo number 'Heer'. Before Pinky's wedding, Mrs Bhamra hopes to pass down cultural and familial tradition, telling Jess that she must 'learn these old songs like I did from my mother'.[37] A few lines of dialogue later, she begins to sing in Punjabi. As the number progresses, lines sung in English by British South Asian elders espouse a range of motivations for immigrating to Britain. As they sing about their children's lives – which include the integration of traditional Punjab values with financial success – they proclaim, 'This is what our dreaming was for'.[38] Like Paula, the musical number offers insight into Mrs Bhamra's perspective and her constant nagging of Jess: Jess's life path is connected to her own dreams and her perception of her own successes as a mother.

Mrs Bhamra and Paula's solo numbers not only deepen characterization but also subtly re-orient a common musical theatre trope. In musicals such as *Oklahoma!* (1943) and *Guys and Dolls* (1950), it is often the case that romantic story arcs – wherein a man and a woman begin as distinct, usually opposing, individuals but overcome their differences through romantic love – represent the forging of broader communal bonds. As Stacy Wolf explains, the heterosexual union between two characters often 'signifies and more importantly, performs the unification of the entire community'.[39] *Bend It Like Beckham* does include a heterosexual romance between Jess and Joe, but their storyline is tertiary to other conflicts and receives limited focus in musical numbers. This effectively dampens the harmonizing potential of their union. Instead, the trope of community unification through romantic love is reoriented towards familial bonds. As noted earlier, 'Tough Love' explicitly establishes the parallel relationships between the mother–daughter pairings, and in act two, 'There She Goes' and 'Heer' furthers these connections by highlighting the mothers' shared desire to make sense of their children's lives. Moreover, the two songs draw a thread between the emotional experiences of parents across cultures. In 'There She Goes', Paula laments that there's 'nothing we mothers can possibly say'[40] to discourage children from leaving home; meanwhile, the elders in 'Heer' explain their desire to be recognized by their children: 'We hoped/We coped/We kept our nerve/Now don't you think/That We deserve/To take a bow?'[41] These emotional expressions concretize and deepen a thread of connection between the two families – and by extension the different communities – wherein parents struggle to reconcile intergenerational difference. As an analysis of the final numbers reveals, the theme of familial love is significant, in part, because it contributes to the musical's harmonious conclusion.

Conclusion

Describing the effect of the repertoire for performance, Diana Taylor argues that 'performance makes visible (for an instant, live, now) that which is always already there: the ghosts, the tropes, the scenarios that structure our individual and collective life'.[42] Throughout *Bend It Like Beckham: The Musical*, the enactment of specialized areas of practice deepens facets of characterization and invokes the memories and knowledges – the 'ghosts' as Taylor might put it – embedded in the repertoires of football, bhangra dance and musical theatre. In the climactic number, 'The Wedding & Football Final: Sadaa Charhi Kalaa', these repertories converge, realizing the musical's multicultural ideal. Dramaturgically, the number weaves together Pinky's wedding celebrations with the Harriers' final match. The opening captures the celebratory character of the wedding, beginning with up-tempo dhol drum rhythms. Attendees of Pinky's wedding – including the Bhamra family – sing the first verses in Punjabi. In the chorus, they repeat 'Sadaa Chardhi Kalaa' – a reference to the Sikh concept of Chardi Kala, meaning to have an optimistic and joyful mindset. Midway through the chorus, they perform the same notes and rhythm but switch to English, singing, 'Stand up, stand up and live. Stand up, Stand up, and sing!'[43] This shift signals the number's broader integration of cultural traditions. After the chorus, Tony convinces Jess to leave the wedding celebrations so that Jess can play in the second half of the Harriers' game. Noticing his daughter's downturned mood, Mr Bhamra gives his support, saying: 'This is the only way I know to see you smiling . . . at your sister's wedding. Then, go now! But, when you come back, I want to see you happy on the video.' Thematically, Mr Bhamra's permission demonstrates an expanded intergenerational and familial relation where Jess can at once fulfil her familial obligations and pursue her own dreams. This expansion is performed through music and choreography. Reprising musical motifs from previous numbers including 'UB2', 'Result!' and 'Glorious' alongside the multilingual 'Sadaa Chardhi Kalaa' refrain, the choreography and blocking draw together movement patterns from both bhangra (enacted by the wedding guests) and football (performed by the Harriers).

As the football action unfolds, Jess is fouled and receives a penalty shot. Before the shot, there is a frozen moment, where Jess prepares. Mrs Bhamra steps forward and instructs,

'Remember who you are.' This recalls her line from the opening sequence, wherein she urged her daughter to remember her British South Asian identity. By this moment, Jess has already fulfilled her responsibilities to her British South Asian heritage by attending Pinky's wedding, and it is time to shift her attention. She takes a breath and kicks the ball, performing her footballer-self by scoring the winning goal. Stage right, guests perform bhangra dance and rejoice at Pinky's wedding. Stage left, Jess and the Harriers celebrate their win. In the number's final moments, Jess and Pinky are lifted onto the shoulders of ensemble members in parallel motions. This celebrates Jess's sporting accomplishment and marks her successful negotiation between family and football. The moment also subtly extends its reorientation towards the cohesive power of family by positioning the sisters at the centre of the celebration. In combination with Mr Bhamra's intergenerational encouragement, the number performs an expanded notion of familial and community achievement, where both Pinky and Jess's choices are commended and where different live-paths, passions and views can be valued alongside one another.

The family achievement is supported by the number's overall festivity, which hinges on harmonious enactments by distinct cultural groups. In the final moment, the distinction between integration and assimilation is embodied. Music, again, provides the connective thread, and in the number's final two minutes, musical influences and ensemble voices harmonize. The wedding guests and footballers remain separate, but the blocking and choreography presents them as two parts of an on-stage community. Bhangra and football are performed side by side, and in the instant that Jess and Pinky are lifted into the air, the coexistence of cultures is championed. This final moment strongly resonates with late-twentieth-century multicultural ideals, wherein differences within and across British identities were praised. In isolation, then, the articulation of multiculturalism that 'Sadaa Chardi Kalaa' performs could be interpreted as a triumphant moment, both onstage and in the context of professional British musical theatre more broadly. Within the musical's production context, however, the musical's multicultural ideal is haunted by the shifting political landscape in Britain in the twenty-first century.

Since the turn of the twenty-first century, government policies and majoritarian discourse have unsettled twentieth-century notions of British multiculturalism. In the 2010s, a series of political events – including 2013 anti-immigration campaigns, the 2015 general election and the 2016 Brexit vote – were inflected by an apparent resistance to twentieth-century notions of multiculturalism. In the 2020s, it might be argued that 'British multiculturalism' at once describes a demographic situation – people from multiple cultures, races, ethnicities and religious backgrounds coexist within the British nation state – and a contested idea about how coexistence does, or should, function. In adapting the film for the stage, the creators chose to keep the film's turn-of-the-twenty-first-century setting. In a conversation with *Times Out London* in 2015, Andrzej Lukowski notes the significance of this shift in a conversation with Chadha, commenting that if '"Bend It Like Beckham" is a social document it's surely one of a happier Britain that embraced multiculturalism and believed it might win a football tournament?'[44] To this, Chadha replied: 'Absolutely. It's set in 2001 and we made the film pre-9/11, when Beckham was still at Man U. There's not very many times where we Londoners set out to celebrate the fact we're culturally diverse, and there are plenty of times that that is knocked.'[45]

The exchange gestures to increasing societal division and suggests how this shifting political landscape created a potential gap between the musical's multicultural ideal and its production context. As Jerri Daboo suggests, 'Though the musical was produced in London's West End in 2015 . . . there is a sense of an idealised conviviality of multiculturalism that is perhaps at odds with the current state of the nation.'[46] The performance of multiculturalism in *Bend It Like Beckham* invokes ideals associated with the musical's 2001 setting and simultaneously registers the realities of its production context. Importantly, the full scope of the musical's meanings is not yet fully realized. In 2019, the show received its first international production in Toronto, Canada, a city that is also known for its multicultural impulses. In coming decades, it is possible that further international productions could contribute to the musical's performance history and impact. So, while the musical does reflect an early 2000s articulation of multiculturalism in Britain, the meanings of this articulation are likely to become more layered with time. As one of the only professional British musicals to feature British South Asian culture as well as the depiction of multiple cultures on stage, these meanings will further the musical's already significant position within the British musical theatre landscape.

Notes

1. Descriptions of the show are based on my consultation of a range of sources, including the official cast album, promotional images and videos, unofficial recordings, and descriptions by Jerri Daboo in *Staging British South Asian Culture: Bollywood and Bhangra in British Theatre* (London: Routledge, 2018).
2. Benditlive, 'Glorious (Opening)- Bend It Like Beckham- Natalie Dew', *YouTube*, 20 February 2016, https://www.youtube.com/watch?v=b0nm5tQPCbY.
3. Benditlive, 'Glorious (Opening)- Bend It Like Beckham- Natalie Dew'.
4. Diana Taylor, *The Archive and the Repertoire: Performing Cultural Memory in the Americas*. (Durham: Duke University Press, 2003), 84.
5. 'Bend It Like Beckham - Rotten Tomatoes', *Rotten Tomatoes*, accessed 15 April 2022, https://www.rottentomatoes.com/m/bend_it_like_beckham; Tejinder Jouhal, 'BFI Screenonline: Bend It Like Beckham (2002)', accessed 15 April 2022, http://www.screenonline.org.uk/film/id/475636/index.html.
6. Jouhal, 'BFI: Screenonline'.
7. Stuart Hall, 'The Multicultural Question', *The Political Economy Research Centre Annual Lecture*, Firth Hall, Sheffield, England, 4 May 2000, https://red.pucp.edu.pe/wp-content/uploads/biblioteca/Stuart_Hall_The_multicultural_question.pdf.
8. Hall, 'The Multicultural Question'.
9. Richard T. Ashcroft and Mark Bevir, 'British Multiculturalism after Empire: Immigration, Nationality and Citizenship', in *Multiculturalism in the British Commonwealth Since 1945: Comparative Perspectives on Theory and Practice*, ed. Richard T. Ashcroft and Mark Bevir (Berkeley: University of California Press, 2019), 24.
10. For more on this topic, see: Ashcroft and Bevir, 'British Multiculturalism after Empire', 25–45.
11. 'BFI Screenonline: Chadha, Gurinder (1960-) Biography', *BFI Screenonline*, accessed 15 April 2022, http://www.screenonline.org.uk/people/id/502103/.
12. Sonia Friedman, 'Bend It Like Beckham Edges Closer to West End?', *WestEndTheatre*, 7 May 2014, https://www.westendtheatre.com/26782/news/stage-spy/bend-it-like-beckham-edges-closer-to-west-end/.

13. Gurinder Chadha, MTN & MMD Joint Musical Theatre Conference, Almeida Theatre, London, 21 March 2014.
14. Gurinder Chadha, MTN & MMD Joint Musical Theatre Conference, Almeida Theatre, London, 21 March 2014.
15. '"Bend It Like Beckham" Musical to Make North American Debut in Toronto', *CTV News*, accessed 15 April 2022.
16. For analysis of these topics in Chadha's films see: Guido Rings, 'Questions of Identity: Cultural Encounters in Gurinder Chadha's Bend It Like Beckham', *Journal of Popular Film and Television* 39, no. 3 (2011): 114–23; Linda McClain, 'Bend It Like Beckham and Real Women Have Curves: Constructing Identity in Multicultural Coming-Of-Age Stories', *Depaul Law Review* 54, no. 3 (2014): 701–54; Mary Ann Chacko, 'Bend It Like Beckham: Dribbling the Self through a Cross-Cultural Space', *Multicultural Perspectives* 12, no. 2 (2010): 81–6.
17. Taylor, *The Archive and the Repertoire,* 20.
18. Taylor, *The Archive and the Repertoire,* 20.
19. For more on the history of ballet, see: Marion Kant, ed., *The Cambridge Companion to Ballet* (Cambridge: Cambridge University Press, 2011).
20. Ann Hall, *The Girl and the Game: A History of Women's Sport in Canada*, 2nd edn (Toronto: University of Toronto Press, 2016), 1.
21. In both the film and the musical, Mr Bhamra experiences racial discrimination in England during his experiences with cricket.
22. Graham Curry and Eric Dunning, 'The Folk Antecedents of Modern Football', *Association Football: A Study in Figurational Sociology*, 2015, doi:10.4324/9781315738369.
23. Curry and Dunning, 'The Folk Antecedents of Modern Football'.
24. For more on decorum and behavioural codes in association football, see: Fédération Internationale de Football Association 'FIFA Disciplinary Code', Zurich, Switzerland, 2023. https://digitalhub.fifa.com/m/59dca8ae619101cf/original/FIFA-Disciplinary-Code-2023.pdf.
25. Sam Tighe, 'David Beckham: Tactical Evolution of Man Utd, Real Madrid and L.A. Galaxy Star', *Bleacher Report*, accessed 15 April 2022. https://bleacherreport.com/articles/1424372-david-beckham-tactical-evolution-of-man-utd-real-madrid-and-la-galaxy-star.
26. Howard Goodall and Charles Hart, *Bend It Like Beckham: The Musical Original Cast Album*, recording date unknown (Sony Music Canada, 2015).
27. Goodall and Hart, *Bend It Like Beckham.*
28. Goodall and Hart, *Bend It Like Beckham.*
29. The description of the history of bhangra dance draws from a range of sources: Ananya Jahanara Kabir, 'Salsa/bhangra: Transnational Rhythm Cultures in Comparative Perspective', *Music and Arts in Action* 3, no. 3 (2011): 40–55; Dabo, *Staging British South Asian Culture*; G. Schreffler, 'Situating Bhangra Dance: A Critical Introduction', *South Asian History and Culture* 4, no. 3 (2020): 384–412; Sangita Gopal and Sujata Moorti, *Global Bollywood: Travels of Hindi Song and Dance* (Minneapolis: University of Minnesota Press, 2008).
30. Gurinder Chadha, MTN & MMD Joint Musical Theatre Conference, Almeida Theatre, London, 21 March 2014.
31. In addition to the combination of sources used to describe action sequences, observations about bhangra dance moves draw from Jerri Daboo's experience and subsequent analysis of the show in Daboo, *Staging British South Asian Culture.*
32. Daboo, *Staging British South Asian Culture.*

33. Gurinder Chadha qtd. in Daboo's *Staging British South Asian Culture:*.
34. Goodall and Hart, *Bend It Like Beckham*.
35. Goodall and Hart, *Bend It Like Beckham*.
36. Goodall and Hart, *Bend It Like Beckham*.
37. Goodall and Hart, *Bend It Like Beckham*.
38. Goodall and Hart, *Bend It Like Beckham*.
39. Stacy Wolf, *Changed for Good: A Feminist History of the Broadway Musical* (New York: Oxford University Press, 2011), 2.
40. Goodall and Hart, *Bend It Like Beckham*.
41. Goodall and Hart, *Bend It Like Beckham*.
42. Taylor, *The Archive and the Repertoire,* 143.
43. Goodall and Hart, *Bend It Like Beckham*.
44. Andrzej Lukowski, 'Gurinder Chadha on "Bend It Like Beckham" the Musical, Cultural Diversity and a Spare Golden Horse', *TimeOut London*, 21 June 2015, https://www.timeout.com/london/theatre/gurinder-chadha-on-bend-it-like-beckham-the-musical-cultural-diversity-and-a-spare-golden-horse.
45. Gurinder Chadha qutd in Lukowski, 'Gurinder Chadha on "Bend It Like Beckham" the Musical, Cultural Diversity and a Spare Golden Horse'.
46. Daboo, *Staging British South Asian Culture,* 163.

References

'Active Lives October 2018: Tables 4–7 Twice in the Last 28 Days' (2019), *Sport England*, May, https://www.sportengland.org/know-your-audience/data/active-lives/active-lives-data-tables.

'Active Lives April 2020: Spectating' (2020), *Sport England*, April, https://www.sportengland.org/know-your-audience/data/active-lives/active-lives-data-tables.

Ashcroft, Richard T. and Mark Bevir (2018), 'Multiculturalism in Contemporary Britain: Policy, Law and Theory', *Critical Review of International Social and Political Philosophy*, 21 (4): https://doi.org/10.1080/13698230.2017.1398443.

Ashcroft, Richard T. and Mark Bevir. (2019), 'British Multiculturalism after Empire: Immigration, Nationality and Citizenship', in Richard T. Ashcroft and Mark Bevir (eds), *Multiculturalism in the British Commonwealth Since 1945: Comparative Perspectives on Theory and Practice*, 25–45. Berkeley: University of California Press.

'BFI Screenonline: Chadha, Gurinder (1960–) Biography', *BFI Screenonline*, http://www.screenonline.org.uk/people/id/502103/ (accessed 15 April 2022).

'"Bend It Like Beckham" Musical to Make North American Debut in Toronto', *CTV News*, 7 May 2019, https://www.ctvnews.ca/entertainment/bend-it-like-beckham-musical-to-make-north-american-debut-in-toronto-1.4412205?cache=svysufqcvzxhsyhq%3FclipId%3D1921747 (accessed 15 April 2022).

'Bend It Like Beckham - Rotten Tomatoes', *Rotten Tomatoes*, https://www.rottentomatoes.com/m/bend_it_like_beckham (accessed 15 April 2022).

Benditlive (2016), 'Glorious (Opening)- Bend It Like Beckham- Natalie Dew', *YouTube*, 20 February, https://www.youtube.com/watch?v=b0nm5tQPCbY.

Chacko, Mary Ann (2010), 'Bend It Like Beckham: Dribbling the Self Through a Cross-Cultural Space', *Multicultural Perspectives*, 12 (2): 81–6.

Christensen, Paul (2012), *Sport and Democracy in the Ancient and Modern Worlds*. Cambridge: Cambridge University Press.

Curry, Graham and Eric Dunning (2015), 'The Folk Antecedents of Modern Football', *Association Football: A Study in Figurational Sociology*, doi:10.4324/9781315738369.

Daboo, Jerri (2018), *Staging British South Asian Culture: Bollywood and Bhangra in British Theatre*. London: Routledge, 2018.

'David Beckham', *ESPN UK*, http://www.espn.co.uk/football/sport/player/72740.html (accessed 15 April 2022).

Fédération Internationale de Football Association (2023), 'FIFA Disciplinary Code', Zurich, Switzerland.

Friedman, Sonia (2014), 'Bend It Like Beckham Edges Closer to West End?', *WestEndTheatre*, 7 May, https://www.westendtheatre.com/26782/news/stage-spy/bend-it-like-beckham-edges-closer-to-west-end/.

Gruneau, Richard S. (1983), *Class, Sports, and Social Development*. Champaign, IL: University of Massachusetts Press.

Goodall, Howard and Charles Hart (2015), *Bend It Like Beckham: The Musical Original Cast Album*, recording date unknown. Sony Music Canada.

Gopal, Sangita and Sujata Moorti (2008), *Global Bollywood: Travels of Hindi Song and Dance*. Minneapolis: University of Minnesota Press.

Gordon, Robert, Olaf Jubin and Millie Taylor (2016), *British Musical Theatre Since 1950*. London: Bloomsbury Methuen Drama, an Imprint of Bloomsbury Publishing Plc.

Hall, M. Ann (2016), *The Girl and the Game: A History of Women's Sport in Canada*, 2nd edn. Toronto: University of Toronto Press, 1.

Hall, Stuart (2000), 'The Multicultural Question', *The Political Economy Research Centre Annual Lecture*, Firth Hall, Sheffield, England, 4 May, https://red.pucp.edu.pe/wp-content/uploads/biblioteca/Stuart_Hall_The_multicultural_question.pdf.

Harvey, Adrian (2013), 'The Emergence of Football in Nineteenth-Century England: The Historiographic Debate', *The International Journal of the History of Sport*, 30 (18): 2154–63. https://doi.org/10.1080/09523367.2013.839551.

Horne, John, Alan Tomlinson and Garry Whannel (1999), *Understanding Sport: An Introduction to the Sociological and Cultural Analysis of Sport*. London: Routledge.

Jouhal, Tejinder, 'BFI Screenonline: Bend It Like Beckham (2002)', http://www.screenonline.org.uk/film/id/475636/index.html (accessed 15 April 2022).

Kabir, Ananya Jahanara (2011), 'Salsa/bhangra: Transnational Rhythm Cultures in Comparative Perspective', *Music and Arts in Action*, 3 (3): 40–55.

Kant, Marion, eds (2011), *The Cambridge Companion to Ballet*. Cambridge: Cambridge University Press.

Kerrigan, Colm (2005), *Teachers and Football: Schoolboy Association Football in England, 1885–1915* (version 1st edn), 1st edn. Woburn Education Series. London: RoutledgeFalmer.

Lukowski, Andrzej (2015), 'Gurinder Chadha on "Bend It Like Beckham" the Musical, Cultural Diversity and a Spare Golden Horse', *TimeOut London*, 21 June, https://www.timeout.com/london/theatre/gurinder-chadha-on-bend-it-like-beckham-the-musical-cultural-diversity-and-a-spare-golden-horse.

Major, John (1995), *Department of National Heritage. Sport: Raising the Game*. Great Britain: Her Majesty's Stationery Office, 2

'Manchester United | English Football Club | Britannica' (2023), https://www.britannica.com/biography/David-Beckham (accessed 15 April 2022).

McClain, Linda (2014), 'Bend It Like Beckham and Real Women Have Curves: Constructing Identity in Multicultural Coming-Of-Age Stories', *Depaul Law Review*, 54 (3): 701.

O'Hanlon, Dom (2016), 'Bend It Like Beckham the Musical Announces Full Cast', *London Theatre*, 8 June, https://www.londontheatre.co.uk/theatre-news/news/bend-it-like-beckham-the-musical-announces-full-cast.

Rings, Guido (2011), 'Questions of Identity: Cultural Encounters in Gurinder Chadha's Bend It Like Beckham', *Journal of Popular Film and Television*, 39 (3): 114–23.

Schreffler, G. (2013), 'Situating Bhangra Dance: A Critical Introduction', *South Asian History and Culture*, 4 (3): 384–412. doi:10.1080/19472498.2013.808514.

Taylor, Diana (2003), *The Archive and the Repertoire: Performing Cultural Memory in the Americas*. Durham: Duke University Press, 20.

Tighe, Sam (2012), 'David Beckham: Tactical Evolution of Man Utd, Real Madrid and L.A. Galaxy Star', *Bleacher Report*, 27 November, https://bleacherreport.com/articles/1424372-david-beckham-tactical-evolution-of-man-utd-real-madrid-and-la-galaxy-star (accessed 15 April 2022).

Wigglesworth, Neil (2007), *The Story of Sport in England*. Student Sport Studies. London: Routledge.

Wolf, Stacy Ellen (2011), *Changed for Good: A Feminist History of the Broadway Musical*. New York: Oxford University Press, 2.

Preeya Kalidas interview

Performer *Bend It Like Beckham*

What is your favourite British musical?

If I can only choose one – which is hard – I'd say *Miss Saigon*. When I was seven years old my mum taped *The Heat Is On: The Making of Miss Saigon* documentary and it was after seeing that that I fell in love with musicals.

What's your favourite British musical theatre song?

So many to choose from! But 'Tell Me It's Not True' from *Blood Brothers*. I can't listen to it without getting teary.

What training did you do for your career?

I went to Sylvia Young Theatre School from the age of ten to sixteen, mainly thanks to my local council where I grew up, as the termly fee was difficult for my parents to afford. Fortunately the school had an agency that kept me on as a client and I would be sent to auditions. So, a lot of my training I ended up learning on the job.

Do you consider *Bend It Like Beckham* to be a key British musical?

It was absolutely a key musical and one that I believe should have had a longer run for so many reasons. It was and still is a hugely successful hit around the world and connected with so many people. Today, the story is just as important and relevant as it was then, representing a young woman with dreams and aspirations layered with cultural expectations.

The world in which it's set, amalgamated with rich and relatable characters, made for a fantastic show. Musically, the audience experienced a hybrid of musical theatre/Classical Indian and Punjabi Music, the perfect combination to represent the melting pot in which we live. These are musical styles you don't often get to hear on a mainstream stage.

Please could you describe your contribution to *Bend It Like Beckham*?

The show was in development for five years with various workshops over this period. I was involved from the very first workshop to the last. I helped to re-create the role of Pinky (Jess's wedding-obsessed sister) for the stage. Pinky was a wonderful character, who really came to life in the show, particularly with the opportunity to add singing and dance numbers which Pinky (and I) absolutely relished!

You appeared in both the original *Bend It Like Beckham* movie, and the stage adaptation (albeit in different roles) – can you tell us a little about that experience?

It was early in my career that I worked on the film. It was a great experience working with director Gurinder Chadha (also director for the musical) whom I stayed in touch with and invited to come and see me, a few years later, as the narrator in *Joseph and the Amazing Technicolour Dreamcoat* at The Adelphi. It was in my dressing room that she mentioned they were in development creating the musical version of *Bend It Like Beckham*. You cannot compare stage and screen but the experience of being part of both only made it that extra bit more magical for me. During filming for *Bend It Like Beckham* was also when I found out I would be playing my first leading role in the workshop for a new musical, produced by Andrew Lloyd Webber, AR Rahman's *Bombay Dreams*. I was given the fantastic opportunity to play the leading lady in the original West End production and this is where I learnt a lot about developing a character for the stage, which helped when I joined the *Bend It Like Beckham* musical.

How would you describe the rehearsal/production process for this show?

It was exciting but also nerve-wracking! This was a brand new musical, which had more pressure added because it was adapted from a hit film and not all films translate onto the stage. But having been part of the workshops, and working with the incredible team, I had no doubt that this would work on stage.

How do you feel about *Bend It Like Beckham* now?

I have such fond memories of that show and I loved playing Pinky eight shows a week. I still have people mention how much they loved it even though it's been nearly seven years since it was on, which to me is a clear indication that it should be revived!

How did the experience of working on *Bend It Like Beckham* shape your future work, if at all?

Thanks to playing Pinky, I was nominated for a prestigious Olivier Award. I'm not someone who works just for accolades but this felt more special due to the fact that the character represented a community that is rarely seen in musical theatre. I think it's important for young aspiring talent to be able to see themselves represented on a mainstream stage.

Are you still working in musical theatre?

Is that a real question? Of course! As a performer I am grateful to have had the opportunities to work on stage and screen to represent different worlds and characters. Musicals are another way of expressing yourself in stories that you care about. I have also been writing a musical[1] to represent and create more opportunities for South Asian women.

Where do you see the British musical in 5/10 years?

I can't predict that, but I hope that British musicals continue to reflect the society in which we live, and new writing and original narratives are given more platforms.

What changes do you think need to happen to ensure musical theatre in the UK flourishes?

Investment in new writing talent and representation across the board in every department.

What advice would you give aspiring writers?

Don't think about what an audience would want to hear, write from a place of passion for the story YOU want to tell.

Note

1. *Out The Box*, with music and lyrics by Kalidas and Craig Shenton, and a book by Kalidas and Arun Blair-Mangat, was presented at the Turbine Theatre, London, as part of MT Fest 2023.

5 *Flowers for Mrs Harris*

Covid-19, women's work and the musical's 'some kind of bliss'

SARAH K. WHITFIELD

Remembering lockdown in a living room, the West Midlands, UK April 2020

On 23 March 2020, British prime minister Boris Johnson announced the first lockdown in the UK, responding to the rising rates of the new Covid-19 virus. Looking back on this period, it is hard to remember back to those first months of lockdown with any clarity. I do remember the complicated and exhausting feeling of relief at being safe while being exhausted from attempts to simultaneously home-school two children and work a full-time job.

Somehow in the middle of that frightening period, I remember watching an on-demand digital stream of a musical, *Flowers for Mrs Harris*, slightly more clearly than you might expect – like I am remembering a little light in the dark. The musical, adapted from Paul Galileo's 1964 novel *Mrs 'Arris Goes to Paris* by composer and lyricist Richard Taylor and librettist Rachel Wagstaff, was shared as an on-demand stream during this early period of lockdown by Chichester Festival Theatre (CFT). And even though thinking back is hard (did we really queue for hours for the supermarket? did I really think I could teach times tables?), I seem to remember precise details of my encounter with the show, I think because putting on *Flowers for Mrs Harris* was like unwrapping a special present, all for myself.

Despite being a musical theatre lecturer, as a parent of young children I had not seen many musicals or live theatre in the intervening years since my daughters' births. So counter-intuitively, during spring and summer 2020, I ended up watching more theatre from my living room than I had for years. This was not because I did not want to go to the theatre, and I had always intended to see *Mrs Harris*, having heard snippets about the show in both of its incarnations, its original Sheffield 2016 production, and later 2018 revival at Chichester Festival Theatre (CFT). Reality meant that I never quite made it. Watching the show from my sofa was an opportunity that did not come with hefty childcare costs attached or accessibility to navigate as a disabled theatregoer. So again, in one of the hardest moments that I have experienced as a Mum, *Flowers for Mrs Harris* met me where I was. I precisely recall the moment when Ada Harris (played by Clare Burt) finds the Dior dress for the first time, and when she gets to watch the dress parade of extraordinary Dior-inspired frocks. I know that I cried when I watched the magical arrival of the many flowers in the emotionally expansive finale, in the moment that Ada realizes she is not alone. It is one of the clearest moments of theatrical joy that I can ever recall, since it offered me what Ada herself calls 'some kind of bliss.'[1]

Reconfiguring the theatrical encounter in a time of Covid-19

At the beginning of lockdown in the UK, theatres quickly moved to offer comfort to a frightened population who were stuck at home for the foreseeable future by releasing pre-existing recordings of material from their back catalogues. From April to July 2020, the National Theatre launched weekly Thursday night streams from their existing NT Live back catalogue. When the CFT began their streaming program in April 2020 with *Mrs Harris*, Daniel Evans, as both the musical's director and the theatre's artistic director, explained that while the recording had only ever been intended to be 'no more than an archive recording, [. . .] we felt that the themes of kindness and compassion might bring a bit of joy to people's lives during these very difficult conditions'.[2] Many other theatres began streaming work from their own catalogues. This provision was keenly taken up: the NT broadcasts were seen by an astonishing global audience of fifteen million people.[3] One report, commissioned by Arts Council England on arts participation during lockdowns, found that home-based arts and cultural activities like theatre streams meant that between March and May 2020 'around 1 in 5 people [reported] increasing their arts activity engagement'.[4] The counter-intuitive potential that accessing theatre at home offers is an important theme of this chapter.

Several musical theatre organizations also streamed pre-recorded productions, as a gesture of solidarity, kindness and comfort, and eventually of fundraising for unemployed practitioners and theatres facing a total lack of income. Andrew Lloyd Webber's 'The Show Must Go On' began streaming musicals from the Really Useful Group's catalogue (RUG) each Friday evening from April 2020, shows which included *Jesus Christ Superstar* and *Joseph and the Amazing Technicolor Dreamcoat*. Shows were then made freely available on YouTube for forty-eight hours afterwards. RUG's viewers were invited to donate to charities supporting unemployed theatre workers such as the Actors' Benevolent Fund, Broadway Cares and Acting for Others. In the UK, the four national Arts Councils launched emergency funding schemes to rescue arts professionals whose entire income had paused, and who fell outside of the Government furlough scheme for salaried workers because of their complex work histories. Similar schemes were offered for theatre institutions who were facing perilous financial situations. Despite these efforts to support institutions and divert funding, the impact of Covid was devastating on individuals and arts institutions. In February 2022, *The Stage* reported that 'England's largest subsidised venues lost more than £116 million in revenue during the first year of the Covid-19 pandemic [and] Chichester Festival Theatre's income plummeted from £15.8 million to £5.6 million, a decrease of 64%'.[5]

The isolated encounter of watching theatre during the first Covid lockdown is a particular scenario that no theatre or individual could have possibly predicted. Critically exploring the stream of *Flowers for Mrs Harris*, as I intend to do here, requires a serious care and ethical engagement. During the first Covid lockdown, any theatre performance in an auditorium was illegal because of public health restrictions on public gatherings indoors or outdoors. Schools, offices, entertainment spaces and places of worship were shut down, as well as playgrounds and seating areas in parks, some park benches were 'taped up to prevent sitting'.[6] In the UK, people were only allowed out of their homes for a limited list of reasons which included exercise for one hour once a day, or to obtain food or other vital supplies, or if they were key workers instrumental to the safety and well-being of the country. Domestic spaces became homes *and* classrooms, home offices, and make do children's activity centres. This had drastic implications for houses with multigenerational occupants, those facing overcrowding or a lack of garden/outdoor space. Being able to watch a theatre screening at all reveals layers of privilege at work: safety, leisure time, manageable caring roles, financial stability and access to high-speed internet and devices, and, quite probably, access to multiple rooms and viewing spaces within the home.

The unspoken crucial luxury to watching digital theatre during Covid-19 lockdowns is the implied health and well-being to be able to do so during the pandemic. In the UK, to date, over 206,000 people have died with Covid-19 listed on their death certificate. The pandemic had disastrous and disproportionate consequences for millions of women in Britain through financial, personal and health consequences. Women were in 'the majority of employees in industries with some of the highest Covid-19 job losses', which led to more women than men being furloughed.[7] Kate Power notes: 'unpaid childcare provision [fell] more heavily on women, which has constrained their ability to work.'[8] Women experienced higher levels of domestic abuse and violence, to such an extent that it was described as the 'epidemic beneath a pandemic'.[9] These problems were exacerbated for Women of Colour.[10] In the UK, Black and South Asian women's experiences and health outcomes were far worse than white women. Public Health England confirmed in August 2020 that 'risk of dying was higher for those in Black, Asian and Minority Ethnic (BAME) groups than in White ethnic groups'.[11] This disparity was also felt in increased job losses, financial insecurity and care responsibilities, and with resulting impacts on child poverty.[12]

This chapter then is part of the growing field of scholarship responding to Covid's initial and continuing impact on the live entertainment industry and theatre production.[13] These approaches draw on existing digital theatre studies which has tended to focus on the digital streaming of live theatre productions, as well as the theatre industry's negotiation of immersive technology and social media. In musical theatre studies, digital theatre scholarship has considered the production and reception process of musical theatre in a 'digital age',[14] considering how production processes have shifted to utilize fan and digital spaces and even staged digital spaces (*Dear Evan Hansen*).[15] Approaches have considered individuals like Lin-Manuel Miranda's utilization of digital opportunities to market and build fanbases around their shows.[16] In addition, digital access is particularly important for new British musical theatre, which may be less likely to receive a full cast album or maintain an online presence after an original production. The preservation of new musicals like Gus Gowland's *Pieces of String* (Mercury Theatre, Colchester, 2018) and Ian Watson and Craig Adams' *Lift* (Soho Theatre, 2013) through the Digital Theatre Plus resource allows vital access to this repertoire for audiences and for teaching. Understanding digitally mediated encounters with performances, and with musicals, continues to be a growing area of scholarship for musical theatre studies.

Digital theatre studies has sought to analyse and quantify how audiences encounter live performance outside of traditional theatrical spaces, and to address questions of what liveness might mean in such scenarios. One particular concern has been live performance which is taking place on some kind of stage that is being concurrently transmitted through another means of production (i.e. a cinema or digital stream) to a *different* place of reception. The elusive ephemeral quality of live theatre is a seductive quality that has shaped digitized encounters and caused extensive academic discourse. As a result, the NT Live simulcast broadcasts to cinemas have received extensive scholarly attention. Clare Read's work on live streams of theatre notes the preserved sense of 'liveness despite the inevitable distance between the performers and the digital audiences'.[17]

To watch a live cinema stream of a theatre production suggests two sites of audience: the main in-theatre one (who experience a co-spatial event), and the secondary in-cinema one who cannot immediately impact the performers but are co-temporal (they are experiencing the event at the same time as it is taking place). As Read suggests, the desire for 'liveness' is a guiding one. NT Live streams start at the same time in the cinema and at the theatre, as if to reassure the cinema audience, we are all *together* in being the audience for *this* performance. The importance of the unique event and its 'you-had-to-be-there' quality is potentially eroded by cinemas re-screening NT Live 'live broadcasts' that extend the audience while maintaining the structural apparatus of liveness (an interval, shots of the audience, etc.). Academics have explored the ways in which cinema streams might build new audiences or divert local audiences away from regional theatres. Meuser and Vlachos note that there needs to be some caution as there is as yet little evidence for live audience building or detracting within the UK.[18]

To return to the March 2020 context, theatre screenings occurred in a radically re-conceptualized performance space during which co-temporality and co-presence with theatre performers were impossible. Arianna Maiorani argues that the pandemic instigated a new phase in live streaming – what she calls 'live at home'.[19] Although Maiorani's work is specifically focused on ballet livestreams, her work is particularly useful in considering how the CFT on-demand recording of *Flowers for Mrs Harris* could be seen to reconfigure the performance space:

> With streamed ballet, the space of this interaction is embedded in the home space and experienced as 'live' as it has acquired spatio-temporal coordinates, not through the physical sharing of the theatre environment.[20]

When everything is out-of-time, and shared theatre place is not an option, *Flowers for Mrs Harris* finds new 'spatio-temporal coordinates' by allowing a different kind of sharing.

Telling women's stories and feminist possibility

In this particular moment, *Flowers for Mrs Harris* staged women's experience, friendship and labour in my living room, in a way no one involved with the production could ever have foreseen. Though domestic musical theatre in April 2020 might be a singular kind of theatrical encounter, there is much that can be untangled from *Flowers for Mrs Harris'* unusual feminist potential. *Mrs Harris* is an unusual musical: not only does it start and end in the eponymous Mrs Harris's own living space (well in this case, her kitchen), but it also allows a woman to be at the centre of a musical without focusing on her romantic pursuits. Mrs Harris, played on each outing by the incomparable Burt, is a fifty-three-year-old working-class woman. This is not an identity usually placed at centre of a musical. One critic noted her own surprise that '[Mrs Harris] is a downtrodden London charlady, yet she is *not* the sidekick or the comic turn, but the heroine'.[21] Wagstaff notes, 'there's something inherently exciting about writing a musical for and about women in their fifties, territory not frequently explored in musicals.'[22]

Flowers for Mrs Harris opens into grey world of post-war 1950s London, with rationing still going and smog filling the air. London after the Second World War was a city in mourning: while 384,000 British troops died during the war, a further 70,000 British civilians were killed largely through sustained aerial bombing, almost half of these deaths being Londoners. The musical's opening song, 'All I Ever Needed', presents us with Mr and Mrs Harris celebrating their wedding anniversary in their small Battersea kitchen in 5, Willis Gardens. Ada tells us how happy she is with her life and its 'penny blooms' (i.e. cheap flowers). The song acts as oppositional to the expected 'I want' song that usually provides our early introduction to a main protagonist. Mrs Harris does not want to fulfil anything, and seems content with what is clearly her fairly meagre lot in life. However, when Ada's friend appears we learn that Mr Harris has died during the war and that the ghostly figure of the previous song has been helping Ada in her grief. Ada's friend Mrs (Violet) Butterworth has also experienced terrible loss, and her husband too has died (it is later revealed at Passchendale). Violet, note the flower, offers Ada true friendship; she is a central support to Ada and is another important working-class figure in the story. Ada and Violet are both cleaners, and when Ada helps her friend by taking on one of her clients for a day, the wealthy Lady Dant (Joanna Riding); everything is set up for the musical's real conflict to emerge.

When Mrs Harris cleans Lady Dant's glamorous house she sees the aristocrat's dressing room, with a Christian Dior dress. In both the published script and director Daniel Evans's careful staging, we do not see the dress, only Ada as she sees the thing and her life is irrevocably changed. The sequence allows Ada to be the focus of the realization that 'There Is More to Life'. This is not a revelation about Ada wanting *expensive* dresses but, rather, wanting *beautiful* things (undeniably, this beautiful thing is not exactly cheap). Ada decides she must have such beauty close to her. The brusque Lady Dant quickly reveals (perhaps to the benefit of anyone in the audience who might be unaware of the wealth differential between London charladies and Dior dress owners) 'the little price tag ensures the dress remains exclusive.'[23] This is echoed by Violet, who later reminds her friend, 'those dresses aren't for the likes of us.'[24] In fact, Violet finds the idea that Ada might own a dress not only preposterous but even worse, something of a betrayal of their friendship (she is in the end won over by the sincerity of Ada's desire). The rest of Act One shows us the terrible lengths Mrs Harris has to go to in order to scrape together the means for an unlikely flight to Paris, finally selling her late husband's watch. She continues to transform the lives of those she is working for by encouraging them to follow their passions or supporting their dreams.

In Act Two, Mrs Harris continues to face obstacles to acquire her dream. Denied entry because she looks like a cleaner (and proudly acknowledges that she is one), Ada finds her way into a private dress showing because the Marquis de Chassagne (played by Mark Meadows) is impressed by her persistence and insists she is allowed to join him. Many of the small cast are in doubled roles to create the busy world of the Dior house, with its seamstresses and dressmakers. In the 'Dress Showing', the full beauty of the dresses is unleashed for the first time. Dramaturgically the magical sequence sits where the dream ballet sequence would traditionally have done; it is underscored with an economy that allows a space to simultaneously be transported by the music, the vision of the gorgeous costumes (designs inspired by Dior's New Look collections by Lez Brotherstone with associate costume designer and costume supervisor Irene Bohan). Harp arpeggios are gently echoed by brass and wind sections (Taylor also orchestrated the score), as the Marquis and Ada's counterpoint responses become entwined in flights of imaginative responses that 'life won't get better than this'. The libretto is woven in, as Madame Colbert tells us about the dresses we are seeing, and the whole effect is nothing short of magic. As Ada instructs herself to 'take all of this in, squeeze every moment of everything', it seems an invitation to the audience too: 'For these few precious hours | I might wallow in some kind of bliss.'[25]

Though Act Two of the musical clearly features Paris and Paris fashion, it is essential to note that the musical does not do any Cinderella style transformation with Mrs Harris wearing the nice dress and having all her problems solved. Instead, when her dress is ready, and Mme Colbert asks if she would like to try it on, Ada says she would 'rather just take it home'.[26] Instead, just as she did in London, Ada transforms the lives of those around her in Paris. Faced with the obstacle of customs, with no money to pay for customs duty, she simply tells the truth that she has a Dior dress in her suitcase. The customs officer finds the idea hilarious and sends her straight through. At the very last moment she faces yet another implausible obstacle, which edges dangerously close to irritating the audience out of their suspension of disbelief: Ada lends her brand new dress to Pamela (one of her beleaguered clients) before she has even taken the dress home, and due to Pamela's carelessness, the dress gets ruined. Somehow, the twist remains *just* the right side of melodramatic, mainly because it serves the function of making sure we know that the dress was never the centre of the story.

Once again distraught by the loss of the object she has fought so hard for, letters and bouquets of flowers start to pour into 5 Willis Gardens from her new friends. All of her kindnesses are returned to her in the song 'Flowers (Something for You)', the drab kitchen is transformed and the stage is filled with flowers. Lady Daunt gives her a Dior handbag, her friends at Dior invite her back and her next trip to Paris is hastily arranged from the happy couple she has encouraged who are now planning their wedding. Ada gets Albert's watch back, having had to sell it in Act One. Transformed, Ada accepts his death and the new direction of her life as full of meaning. In the show's glorious finale, 'The Garden of Eden', the orchestra underpins her acceptance of all that she has achieved, and her acknowledgement that she has been lonely and now she will not be any more, she bids her husband's ghost goodbye.

Though *Mrs Harris* resists it, transformation sequences are a long established part of theatre and more specifically musicals. Musicals have often used transformations to show character fulfilment, progression or development, and the *Cinderella*-style transformation sequence has been a crucial part of many Broadway musicals about women. Maya Cantu has explored these types of stories at length, in what she calls 'Cinderella fashion musicals',[27] noting the need for two key principles, haute-couture fashion and haute-couture fashion that comes *from Paris*. Cantu explains that these musicals often feature working-class women and shifted their protagonist from fairy tale to a working-class 'shop girl', where 'clothing [. . .] functions as a means of her transformation and ascent'.[28] She argues that such stories might disrupt women's expected place in social class structures through such transformations: noting that in her case studies working-class women 'are all represented as spirited, assertive and resourceful characters, with sharply articulated goals and ambitions'.[29] In many respects Mrs Harris fulfils this characterization, but with the profound exception that she never wears the dress. To be clear, I am not arguing this could not have been a feminist musical if Ada wore the dress, but noting that *Flowers for Mrs Harris* is up to something different.

Director Daniel Evans positions *Flowers for Mrs Harris* clearly in regard to the presumption of fashion based transformations: 'The mistake that people might make is that it's all about a woman wanting a dress – but it's not about the dress at all [. . .] It's about what it awakens in her and how she finds the courage to act on that change in herself.'[30] Wagstaff and Taylor, in their introduction to the musical, emphasize this: 'This was never a story about [a] woman wanting a dress. It is about a lonely, widowed cleaning lady, needing something or someone of her own. [. . .] This show is a celebration of an ordinary woman, who has no idea how extraordinary she really is, in her courage and her unfailing care for others.'[31] Actor Joanna Riding, who plays both Lady Daunt and Madame Colbert, echoes these themes: '[Ada's] journey has never been about the dress. It is about doing something to fill the black hole that was the loneliness in her life.'[32] The musical shows Ada building a rich and complex community that provides her with a support network and care that is led by women.

Careful encounters with the musical: Conclusions

Flowers for Mrs Harris is a musical which both stages Mrs Harris's care for others, and in its domestic encounter provides it – as a gift for its audience. Yet the musical had another kind of encounter which again challenged the use of theatrical space during lockdown, the recording of a cast album on 29 July 2020, on the main stage of the CFT. Edward Seckerson's review of the recording notes its unique status: 'This wonderful souvenir of the Chichester production, recorded during lockdown (and all that that imparts), rejoices in all the benefits of a true ensemble company wherein the band, as in each and every instrumentalist, are as much characters in the drama as those on stage.'[33]

Three months after the on-demand stream of the musical, theatrical performances with audiences remained illegal, because of the risk of mass infection at a time when the vaccine was in its earliest stages. The recording was made possible by a legacy from the composer, Richard Taylor's mum, who had died in autumn 2019. Taylor explained, 'I don't come from a musical family at all, my Mum actively disliked music most of the time. She came to see things I wrote, didn't usually like them and would tell me, but she came to see Mrs Harris and she loved it.'[34] He used the money from her estate to make the recording – the recording provided very necessary work to musicians facing an unprecedented collapse in their working lives. In order to reduce the risk of transmission, the main stage of CFT was used to do the recording rather than a recording studio, with the orchestra as spread out as widely as possible.

An accompanying YouTube video was made to preserve the cast recording, watching it is profoundly moving. We see Laura Llewellyn Jones, a French horn player, rehearsing with her children in the garden on a trampoline: 'From the moment I got the email [. . .] I've got something to prepare for.'[35] Women musicians talk about the risks to mental health of musicians, to the financial devastation Covid has wrought to the arts, changes which have placed them on

Universal Credit or turning to new businesses. Nicki Davenport, double bass player, talks about her own history with the musical, noting it was her first job as a new parent and by the time of the recording her four-year-old son was able to sing 'little bits of *Flowers for Mrs Harris* round the kitchen'. Taylor's remarks capture the joyful nature of the recording: 'All these people are getting a lot of joy out of being here, and doing what they do after being caged up for so long.'[36]

Looking back on these reconfigured theatrical encounters in Covid-19, and the particular kinds of care that those around *Flowers for Mrs Harris* extended to its audiences and its company suggests particular possibilities for British musical theatre. It offers an invitation to tell women's stories and different women's stories and to showcase friendship and joy. It also extends the possibility to offer new kinds of encounters for theatre that might continue to meet audiences where they actually are, as Maria Chatzichristodoulou et al caution:

> While we are all eager to be back in real space with our colleagues, audiences and communities, the sudden gaps between us that technologies bridged, quite profoundly, through performance during the pandemic must give us pause – for breath.[37]

Some theatres such as the Young Vic have instigated ongoing schemes to enable audiences to watch from home, something particularly important for groups including immunosuppressed disabled people who are still facing exclusion from venues. In October 2021 however, *The Guardian* reported research that found that 50 per cent of UK theatres that had streamed during Covid had reverted to in-person theatre only. Disabled director and theatre maker Jamie Hale shared his concern that this reversion means 'it will become less possible for people living in rural areas, people with caring and parenting responsibilities, not just disabled people like me, to access the theatre we want to'.[38] As for me in my living room, I don't get to see very much theatre anymore, though I certainly will not forget the gift of *Mrs Harris*. British musical theatre could learn a lot from the possibility that the musical *Mrs Harris* offered to reach audiences wherever they may be.

Notes

1. Rachel Wagstaff, *Flowers for Mrs Harris*, Acting edn (London: Samuel French, 2022), 89.
2. Giverny Masso, 'Coronavirus: Chichester Festival Theatre to Make Shows Available Online for Free', *The Stage*, 6 April 2020, https://www.thestage.co.uk/news/production-news/coronavirus-chichester-festival-theatre-to-make-shows-available-online-for-free.
3. British High Commission Nicosia, 'How the National Theatre Tackled the COVID-19 Challenge', GOV.UK, 8 March 2021, https://www.gov.uk/government/news/how-the-national-theatre-tackled-the-covid-19-challenge.
4. Alexandra Bradbury, Katey Warran, Kei Wan Mak and Daisy Fancourt, *The Role of the Arts during the COVID-19 Pandemic* (London: University College London and Arts Council, 1 August 2021), 3.
5. Georgia Snow, '"Dreadful Storm" – Covid's Assault on Theatre Finances Revealed', *The Stage*, 16 February 2020, https://www.thestage.co.uk/news/dreadful-storm--covids-assault-on-theatre-finances-revealed.
6. (Some schools were open to the children of key workers). Heritage Fund, 'Parks in a Pandemic: What Have We Learned?', from 'Parks for People: Why Should We Invest in Parks?',

18 January 2021, https://www.heritagefund.org.uk/about/insight/evaluation/parks-people-why-should-we-invest-parks.

7. Women's Budget Group, 'Women and Employment during Covid-19', Spring Budget 2021: Pre Budget Briefing, Spring 2021, UK: Women's Budget Group, https://wbg.org.uk/wp-content/uploads/2021/03/Women-and-employment-during-Covid-19-1.pdf.
8. Kate Power, 'The COVID-19 Pandemic Has Increased the Care Burden of Women and Families', *Sustainability: Science, Practice and Policy* 16, no. 1 (2020). doi:10.1080/15487733.2020.1776561.
9. June Kelly, 'Coronavirus: Domestic Abuse an "Epidemic beneath a Pandemic"', *BBC News*, 23 March 2021, sec. UK, https://www.bbc.com/news/uk-56491643.
10. See L. Kelly, 'Direct and Indirect Impacts of the COVID-19 Pandemic on Women and Girls', *K4D Helpdesk Report*, Institute of Development Studies, 2021, doi:10.19088; Nicola Newson, 'Covid-19: Empowering Women in the Recovery from the Impact of the Pandemic', House of Lords Library (blog), 8 March 2021, https://lordslibrary.parliament.uk/covid-19-empowering-women-in-the-recovery-from-the-impact-of-the-pandemic/; Office for National Statistics, 'Coronavirus (COVID-19) and the Different Effects on Men and Women in the UK, March 2020 to February 2021 - Office for National Statistics', UK: Office for National Statistics, 10 March 2021, https://www.ons.gov.uk/peoplepopulationandcommunity/healthandsocialcare/conditionsanddiseases/articles/coronaviruscovid19andthedifferenteffectsonmenandwomenintheukmarch2020tofebruary2021/2021-03-10. [NB. The majority of Government and institutional reports around Covid-19 only refer to two genders, and do not specifically track the experience of genderfluid/queer people.]
11. Public Health England, 'Disparities in the Risk and Outcomes of COVID-19', Public Health England, August 2020, https://assets.publishing.service.gov.uk/government/uploads/system/uploads/attachment_data/file/908434/Disparities_in_the_risk_and_outcomes_of_COVID_August_2020_update.pdf.
12. Women's Budget Group, 'New Data Reveals "Crisis of Support" for BAME Women', *Women's Budget Group* (blog), 8 June 2020, https://wbg.org.uk/media/new-data-reveals-crisis-of-support-for-bame-women/.
13. For example: Barry Houlihan and Catherine Morris, 'Introduction–Performing in Digital in the COVID-19 Era', *Research in Drama Education: The Journal of Applied Theatre and Performance* 27, no. 2 (2022): 157–67 and Nkululeko Sibanda and Cletus Moyo, 'Theatricality in the Midst of a Pandemic: An Assessment of Artistic Responses to COVID-19 Pandemic in Zimbabwe', *Journal of African Media Studies* 14, no. 2 (2022): 295–308.
14. Jessica Hillman-McCord, ed., *IBroadway: Musical Theatre in the Digital Age* (London: Palgrave Macmillan, 2017).
15. Clare Chandler and Simeon Scheuber-Rush, '"Does Anybody Have A Map?": The Impact of "Virtual Broadway" on Musical Theatre Composition', *The Journal of Popular Culture* 54, no. 2 (2021): 276–300.
16. Jessica Hillman-McCord, 'Lin-Manuel Miranda: Digital age diva', *Studies in Musical Theatre* 12, no. 1 (2018): 109–22.
17. Claire Read, '"Live, or Almost Live . . .": The Politics of Performance and Documentation', *International Journal of Performance Arts and Digital Media* 10, no. 1 (2014): 67–76. doi:10.1080/14794713.2014.912502.

18. Daniela Mueser and Peter Vlachos, 'Almost Like Being There? A Conceptualisation of Live-Streaming Theatre,' *International Journal of Event and Festival Management* 9, no. 2: 183–203 (2018). doi:10.1108/IJEFM-05-2018-0030.
19. Arianna Maiorani, 'Selling the Past and the Present Alike: Streaming Ballet for Live Audiences During Lockdown', *Journal of International Culture & Arts* 1, no. 4 (2020), https://hdl.handle.net/2134/17048609.
20. Maiorani, 'Selling the Past and the Present Alike', 7.
21. [Emphasis added]. Sarah Crompton, 'Why Are There No Middle-Aged Women in Musicals?', *The Independent*, London: Independent Digital News & Media, 13 June 2022.
22. 'Creating Mrs Harris, an Interview with Richard Taylor and Rachel Wagstaff', Digital program for *Flowers for Mrs Harris*, 2018, https://www.cft.org.uk/archive/flowers-for-mrs-harris-2018.
23. Wagstaff, *Flowers for Mrs Harris*, 24.
24. Wagstaff, *Flowers for Mrs Harris*, 26.
25. Wagstaff, *Flowers for Mrs Harris*, 89.
26. Wagstaff, *Flowers for Mrs Harris*, 123.
27. Maya Cantu, 'Clothes Make an Awful Difference in a Girl': *Mlle. Modiste*, *Irene* and *Funny Face* as Cinderella Fashion Musicals', *Studies in Musical Theatre* 9, no. 1 (2015): 13–30.
28. Cantu, 'Clothes Make', 14.
29. Cantu, 'Clothes Make', 28.
30. Dominic Cavendish, '"Not Everyone in Sussex is Retired Or Rich": Having Turned Sheffield into a Theatrical Hit-Factory, Artistic Director Daniel Evans is Heading South. Dominic Cavendish Met Him', *Daily Telegraph*, 16 May 2016, 26.
31. Rachel Wagstaff and Richard Taylor, 'Authors' Notes', in *Flowers for Mrs Harris*, Acting edn (London: Samuel French, 2022), viii.
32. 'Chichester: Joanna Riding and the Art of Discovering What Really Matters', *The West Sussex Gazette*, 25 September 2018, ProQuest.
33. Edward Seckerson, 'TAYLOR Flowers for Mrs Harris', *Gramophone*, accessed 15 November 2022, https://www.gramophone.co.uk/reviews/review?slug=taylor-flowers-for-mrs-harris.
34. Chichester Festival Theatre, 'Flowers For Mrs Harris | Cast Album Recording', YouTube, 2020, https://www.youtube.com/watch?v=b3H7FAKy72k.
35. Chichester Festival Theatre, 'Flowers For Mrs Harris | Cast Album Recording'.
36. Chichester Festival Theatre, 'Flowers For Mrs Harris | Cast Album Recording'.
37. Maria Chatzichristodoulou, Kevin Brown, Nick Hunt, Peter Kuling and Toni Sant, 'Covid-19: Theatre Goes Digital – Provocations', *International Journal of Performance Arts and Digital Media* 18, no. 1 (2 January 2022): 1–6, 5. doi:10.1080/14794713.2022.2040095.
38. Harriet Sherwood, '50% of UK Theatres Streaming Shows Online during Covid Revert to In-Person Only', *The Guardian*, 10 October 2021, sec. Stage, https://www.theguardian.com/stage/2021/oct/10/50-of-uk-theatres-streaming-shows-online-during-covid-revert-to-in-person-only.

Works Cited

Bradbury, Alexandra, Katey Warran, Kei Wan Mak and Daisy Fancourt (2021), *The Role of the Arts during the COVID-19 Pandemic*. London: University College London and Arts Council, 1 August.

British High Commission Nicosia (2021), 'How the National Theatre Tackled the COVID-19 Challenge', *GOV.UK*, 8 March.

Cantu, Maya (2015), '"Clothes Make an Awful Difference in a Girl": *Mlle. Modiste, Irene* and *Funny Face* as Cinderella Fashion Musicals', *Studies in Musical Theatre*, 9 (1): 13–30.

Cavendish, Dominic (2016), '"Not Everyone in Sussex is Retired or Rich": Having Turned Sheffield into a Theatrical Hit-Factory, Artistic Director Daniel Evans is Heading South. Dominic Cavendish Met Him', *Daily Telegraph*, 16 May.

Chandler, Clare and Simeon Scheuber-Rush (2021), '"Does Anybody Have A Map?": The Impact of "Virtual Broadway" on Musical Theatre Composition', *The Journal of Popular Culture*, 54 (2): 276–300.

Chatzichristodoulou, Maria, Kevin Brown, Nick Hunt, Peter Kuling and Toni Sant (2022), 'Covid-19: Theatre Goes Digital – Provocations', *International Journal of Performance Arts and Digital Media*, 18 (1): 1–6, 5. doi:10.1080/14794713.2022.2040095.

Chichester Festival Theatre (2020), 'Flowers for Mrs Harris | Cast Album Recording', *YouTube*, https://www.youtube.com/watch?v=b3H7FAKy72k.

'Creating Mrs Harris, an Interview with Richard Taylor and Rachel Wagstaff' (2018), Digital program for *Flowers for Mrs Harris*, Issu.com/chichesterfestivaltheatre/docs/cft18_flowerformrsharris_programme.

Crompton, Sarah (2022), 'Why Are There No Middle-Aged Women in Musicals?' *The Independent*, London: Independent Digital News & Media, 13 June.

Heritage Fund (2021), 'Parks in a Pandemic: What Have We Learned?', from 'Parks for People: Why Should We Invest in Parks?', 18 January.

Hillman-McCord, Jessica, ed. (2017), *Broadway: Musical Theatre in the Digital Age*. London: Palgrave Macmillan.

Hillman-McCord, Jessica (2018), 'Lin-Manuel Miranda: Digital Age Diva', *Studies in Musical Theatre*, 12 (1): 109–22.

Houlihan, Barry and Catherine Morris (2022), 'Introduction–performing in Digital in the COVID-19 Era', *Research in Drama Education: The Journal of Applied Theatre and Performance*, 27 (2): 157–67.

Kelly, June (2021), 'Coronavirus: Domestic Abuse an "Epidemic Beneath a Pandemic"', *BBC News*, 23 March.

Kelly, Luke (2021), 'Direct and Indirect Impacts of the COVID-19 Pandemic on Women and GIRLS', K4D Helpdesk Report, *Institute of Development Studies*, doi:10.19088.

Maiorani, Arianna (2020), 'Selling the Past and the Present Alike: Streaming Ballet for Live Audiences During Lockdown', *Journal of International Culture & Arts*, 1 (4): 1–9.

Masso, Giverny (2020), 'Coronavirus: Chichester Festival Theatre to Make Shows Available Online for Free', *The Stage*, 6 April.

Mueser, Daniela and Peter Vlachos (2018), 'Almost Like Being there? A Conceptualisation of Live-Streaming Theatre', *International Journal of Event and Festival Management*, 9 (2): 183–203. doi:10.1108/IJEFM-05-2018-0030.

Newson, Nicola (2021), 'Covid-19: Empowering Women in the Recovery from the Impact of the Pandemic', *House of Lords Library* (blog), 8 March.

The Newsroom (2018), 'Chichester: Joanna Riding and the Art of Discovering what Really Matters', *The West Sussex Gazette*, 25 September.

Office for National Statistics (2021), *Coronavirus (COVID-19) and the Different Effects on Men and Women in the UK, March 2020 to February 2021 - Office for National Statistics*. UK: Office for National Statistics, 10 March.

Power, Kate (2020), 'The COVID-19 Pandemic Has Increased the Care Burden of Women and Families', *Sustainability: Science, Practice and Policy*, 16 (1). doi:10.1080/15487733.2020.1776561.

Public Health England (2020), 'Disparities in the Risk and Outcomes of COVID-19', *Public Health England*, August.

Read, Claire (2014), '"Live, or Almost Live . . .": The Politics of Performance and Documentation', *International Journal of Performance Arts and Digital Media*, 10 (1): 67–76. doi:10.1080/14794713.2014.912502.

Seckerson, Edward, 'Taylor: Flowers for Mrs Harris', *Gramophone* (accessed 15 November 2022).

Sherwood, Harriet (2021), '50% of UK Theatres Streaming Shows Online during Covid Revert to In-Person Only', *The Guardian*, 10 October.

Sibanda, Nkululeko and Cletus Moyo (2022), 'Theatricality in the Midst of a Pandemic: An Assessment of Artistic Responses to COVID-19 Pandemic in Zimbabwe', *Journal of African Media Studies*, 14 (2): 295–308.

Snow, Georgia (2020), '"Dreadful Storm" – Covid's Assault on Theatre Finances Revealed', *The Stage*, 16 February.

Wagstaff, Rachel (2022), *Flowers for Mrs Harris*, Acting edn. London: Samuel French.

Wagstaff, Rachel and Richard Taylor (2022), 'Authors' Notes', in *Flowers for Mrs Harris*, Acting edn. London: Samuel French.

Women's Budget Group (2020), 'New Data Reveals "Crisis of Support" for BAME Women', *Women's Budget Group* (blog), 8 June.

Women's Budget Group (2021), *'Women and Employment during Covid-19'*, Spring Budget 2021: Pre Budget Briefing, Spring. UK: Women's Budget Group.

Rachel Wagstaff and Richard Taylor interview

Writer and Composer *Flowers for Mrs Harris*

What is your favourite British musical?

Richard I don't really have one but I'm gonna say *Blood Brothers* only because I love that it's so comfortable in his own skin.

Rachel There are so many I love. Perhaps *Matilda?*

What's your favourite British musical theatre song?

Richard I have struggled with this. But I'm going to choose 'Let's Have Lunch' from *Sunset Boulevard*. I'm pretty so-so about the rest of the show but I admire that song a lot. The rhythms of it. And I think it's a brilliant interwoven character piece, very seductive. It's probably everybody else's least favourite bit of *Sunset Boulevard*, which also probably is why I like it!

Rachel How can you choose?! Can I go for three?

Richard You can't have three!

Rachel Oh, go on! 'When I Grow Up' from *Matilda,* 'Call Me Rusty' from *Starlight Express* and 'Electricity' from *Billy Elliot*.

What training have you done for your careers?

Rachel I always wanted to write but didn't realize that it was possible to get a job as a writer. I directed a few plays at university and learned a great deal from that. I had always loved musicals but it was only when I directed a musical at university, I thought 'this is it!' This is what I want to do. But I had no idea how to get a job doing it. I had a place to do a PhD in literature at Cambridge and I had a place to study Text and Performance as an MA at RADA and King's College London. My friends thought I was crazy when I decided to do the London one but I had a really exciting year. Then, for my dissertation, my tutor, Lloyd Trott, encouraged me to write my first play. This was put on at the Edinburgh Festival, an agent picked it up and it went from there. I wrote plays, entered competitions, joined the young writing programmes at The Royal Court and the Soho Theatre and began, very slowly, while also having other jobs, to earn a living writing.

Richard I auditioned at the Royal Northern College of Music as a pianist and also for the composition course. When I was offered either I chose composition, having always written music since I can remember. I was there for five years, studying pure composition, mostly concert music. At the time it was very blinkered and focused only on the cutting edge contemporary scene. No acknowledgement of cross art-forms, or encouragement to investigate other areas. Even so, nearly all the pieces I wrote there had some sort of theatricality, or external stimulus. I couldn't write music just for music's sake. I needed that added thing. A story, actors, visuals.

As soon as I left college I started working for theatre companies, writing music for plays mostly. I worked with some wonderful directors and fantastic actors, and that's where I learned, and continue to learn, everything about theatre really, and how music can drive and underpin a narrative. When I'm writing a musical theatre score I tend to have the same mindset as if I'm underscoring a play, namely, keeping the music rather low-key. I often avoid the big splashy 'look at me' moments that most musicals are built on. I prefer to let the story and characters take centre stage, and let the music work more intravenously, under the radar, so the audience aren't so conscious of when someone is singing or not. Then when the music rises up and does take the spotlight it's all the more powerful for it. That's certainly how *Flowers for Mrs Harris* works anyway, taking its cue from the humble central character. It's not in her nature to stand up and sing a 'big number'.

Mrs Harris has been one of the most well received British musicals in recent years. Do you, or did you at the time, see this as a key British musical?

Richard It's certainly not for us to say if it's a key musical. It's a key British musical in my house! We wrote the piece we wanted to write and tried to find a truthful way of doing it, and a way that worked for us. But we weren't conscious of purposely trying to be different for the sake or making a big statement. I think that would be a disastrous mindset while writing. It is a piece that is very dear and important to us, though, I know that.

Rachel Agreed! It's incredibly important to us, but I can't speak for everyone else. I carry the music with me the whole time. It was, still is, such an important part of my life – I had two babies during the making of it. I wrote Act One pre-babies, Act Two post-babies. I remember bringing one baby to the first set of rehearsals . . . It was difficult, getting up to London, commuting during rush hour with a pram, so by the time I got to the rehearsal room, I was exhausted! But I couldn't bear to leave him behind, as he was only a few months old . . . The first production was in Sheffield so I went up with two young children and spent the time running between the flat in which we'd been put up, and the theatre. It was pretty intense. I remember getting on the train from Sheffield station on the way back, wrestling with the double buggy, thinking 'oh my goodness, was that really worth it?!' And then Vicky Graham, the producer who had brought us the book in the first place, came racing down the train, with a big smile on her face. She wanted to tell me that we'd 'just got five stars in *The Guardian*!' Perhaps more importantly, audiences seemed to respond to it really well . . . but it can be very difficult to predict what work will live on, and what work, for whatever reason, doesn't.

How would you describe your writing process for *Flowers for Mrs Harris*?

Rachel Collaborative. We both talked with Vicky Graham, the producer who initially commissioned it, about the story, why we loved it, what it was, why it needed to be a musical. Then Richard and I spent hours and hours talking on the telephone, or in person when we could, about the show. We both instinctively felt it wasn't a show that demanded a big chorus of twenty-five cleaning ladies. It was about one woman and her dream of having something beautiful, having something to come home to. So, we would discuss and plan, then I would go away and write a scene, or a few scenes, putting in bold whatever I thought could or should be musicalized, and send to Richard. Richard would then work away on the song moment, or interweaving singing or lyrics with the scene, and send back to me. Then I would rework, send back and so on.

Richard The aim became when you hear the piece you shouldn't really know where Rachel starts and where I start and stop. It should feel like it's been written by one pair of hands. And I think if there's a small triumph in it, I think it's that we managed to do what we did on our first piece together, actually.

Rachel We were lucky in that we were given quite a few workshops in which we could test out sections of the show, as we were writing it. We were also very lucky that Daniel Evans joined us as director for several of these workshops, and both productions. We had utterly brilliant dramaturgical input from him. At every stage, we kept interrogating the best way of telling the story, which is always the problem with any adaptation. It's not what's the story. It's which elements can we keep in and how do we make this work best on stage? With Daniel at the helm, we created something we found magical.

How do you feel about the show now? Obviously, you've said there's a great love for it.

Richard Personally I like to write pieces that are in some way attempting to explore The Meaning of Life. That dive into the human condition and ask big questions. *Mrs Harris* absolutely does that. It's about why we're alive and what matters. And I think you go to the theatre to be moved and to hopefully come out of that shared experience thinking about your own existence and where you fit into things and perhaps a little bit changed, if not a little wiser. I feel very privileged to have been given the opportunity to tell her story and get under her skin. It means such a lot to me that so many people were deeply affected by it.

Rachel Yes, I love the story so much but particularly, I love the main character, Mrs Harris, and how her tireless kindness and generosity touches the lives of everyone around her. I love the music. And I loved both productions. It will always live with me, whether it happens again or not.

Has the experience of *Flowers for Mrs Harris* shaped other work that you've done?

Richard We performed one of the songs from the show at an award ceremony. Afterwards people were very complimentary about it and asked why on earth we'd cut the song from the show. And this was by people who had seen the show! We'd actually done no such thing, it had always been there, but because it was *so* integrated, *so* under-the-radar, it just kind-of came out and didn't make a splash of itself and then went back into the score. So that was very telling, and has certainly shaped my practice since. I can sometimes try so hard to keep my head down and not allow the music to be gratuitously *placed* that actually it doesn't make an impact when it should. It's pretty obvious really, but you live and learn. Always.

Rachel I've mostly learnt about the joy of rewriting. I have a producer friend who always reminds me that a musical isn't written, it's rewritten. When you're young and naive, you think you can just dash out a work of genius! But now I think that for anything to be truly good, you have to work and rework. It also really helps if you work with a brilliant creative team who constantly push it, and *you*, to be better, right up until closing night! And, even now, there are a couple of things I want to change – sorry Richard! – for another life because it's only really when you see it or feel your show in an auditorium with people listening, that you think, 'oh, actually we could do with taking out that little bit', or 'that bit needs to be fuller'. So it's taught me to keep challenging myself, constantly, and never to be satisfied.

What advice would you give to aspiring writers and composers?

Richard I would say write in your voice, find what your voice is, and don't try to copy what anybody else's voice is, because what works for them won't necessarily work for you, and you could end up merely a pale imitation. Musical theatre scores have in some ways never been more varied, whatever music you write, there is room for you. If anything, the *Hamilton*s and *SIX*s give hope to writers that are ploughing their own path. I mean, they both seem such unlikely prospects for success, on paper. But they create their own worlds and do so uncompromisingly. That's fantastic.

Rachel Never set out to be successful. Set out to write something that is utterly truthful to what you believe in. Otherwise, as Richard says, you're imitating, you're *trying* to be something rather than being it.

6 'You're him and he is you'

Identification with the disabled 'freak' in *The Grinning Man* (2016)

ELLEN ARMSTRONG

'You're him and he is you.'[1] So sing those who gaze upon the Grinning Man, and so too echo fans of the show. However, the Grinning Man is a fictional disabled freak show performer from a bygone age, and you are a contemporary theatregoer being entertained by the theatricalization of his plight.

Adapted from Victor Hugo's novel *The Man Who Laughs* (1869), *The Grinning Man* (2016) is a macabre fairy tale that is at times dark and gothic, and at others, laughably absurd. Through intricate layers of metatheatre and puppetry it tells the story of Grinpayne, a disfigured freak show performer tormented by the secret horrors of his past and desperate to uncover his true identity. Travelling with his blind adopted sister, Dea; a fatherly puppeteer, Ursus; and a wolf named Mojo, the freak show arrives at the capital where Grinpayne's startling visage captivates the attention of the city. From here, Grinpayne is quickly swept into the dark and twisted world of the aristocracy where his tortured past is finally revealed.

With a book by Carl Grose, music by Tim Phillips and Marc Teitler and lyrics by Carl Grose, Tom Morris, Tim Phillips and Marc Teitler, *The Grinning Man* premiered at the Bristol Old Vic in 2016, before being revived for a West End run at the Trafalgar Studios in 2017.[2] From its initial run, the show quickly developed a small, almost cult-like following of fans (known as Grinners or Grinlettes) who felt a strong affinity for the outcast characters. Two such fans were invited to join the cast and crew in a discussion panel filmed for release with the recorded show. During this panel, fan Lizzie Cavanagh articulated that the Grinners affinity for the show comes from being able to connect to the characters as being different, outsiders and freaks, despite not sharing any particular details with them.[3] This feeling of relating to, or identifying with, the characters was reinforced by several Grinners who kindly shared their experiences with me over social media.

This chapter uses theories from literary studies to explore how *The Grinning Man* nurtured strong audience identification with the titular character despite the unique and macabre narrative of the show. It investigates how the narrative and metatheatrical techniques deployed throughout *The Grinning Man* pertain to these literary theories and further facilitated identification. Finally, as a disabled academic myself, I question the political implications of such identification by situating *The Grinning Man* within the context of both disability and the historic freak show. Here, in line with Adams[4] and Church,[5] this chapter uncovers how identification with the protagonist may be nurtured as a problematic form of subcultural capital by way of identification with the Other.

Identification: Abstraction and projection

Mar and Oatley state that 'the abstraction performed by fictional stories demands that readers and others project themselves into the represented events'.[6] These abstractions therefore create spaces between representation and reality in which multiple readings and identifications can occur depending upon the unique experience that each audience member brings. *The Grinning Man* fashions these spaces between representation and reality in a number of ways, including through a displaced narrative, puppetry and layers of plays-within-plays.

The show opens in front of a closed theatre cloth where court jester Barkilphedro directly addresses the audience and welcomes them to 'a time in history that never was'.[7] From the outset, this establishes the show as a construction removed from reality. The audience are not permitted to fully enter this construction but are instead encouraged to engage more actively (or cognitively) with the text due to the direct address, and visibility of the cloth, emphasizing the distance between the audience and soon-to-unfold drama. This effect is amplified through Barkilphedro describing the setting as a 'world wildly different and yet weirdly similar to your own'.[8] This warns us not to expect reality; however, it also encourages us to draw parallels between our own lives and the story about to unfold. It can therefore be read as encouraging projection into the space being created by abstraction.

This setting is a type of narrative displacement common to both literature and theatre. From Shakespearian drama (*The Tempest*, 1611), to opera (*Pelléas and Mélisande*, 1902), fictional and folkloric settings have been used as a way of exploring social and political themes while maintaining a distance from reality (often to avoid censorship). Sternfeld describes how in *The Phantom of the Opera* (1986) historical distance functions to 'cushion' the audience from the discomfort of its inevitably tragic ending.[9] In *The Grinning Man* it may be seen as a way for the audience to engage with themes of marginalization or trauma without the discomfort of engaging directly with disfigurement or with their own particular marginalization. However, *The Grinning Man* is specifically described as a fairy tale.[10] In this genre, distant coordinates can 'place the story not in time or place of external reality, but in a state of mind'.[11] This is a state in which 'internal processes are externalized and become comprehensible as represented by the figures of the story and its events'.[12] The setting of *The Grinning Man* could therefore act as a tool with which to work through one's own experiences. This could explain why one fan praised the show for its 'healing narrative' and claimed it to be 'a balm for the wounded souls in the audience'.[13] *The Grinning Man*'s ambiguous title and the protagonist's name – which reads as a character portrait: *grin-pain* – also support this. Here, according to Bettelheim, generic titles and descriptive names 'demonstrate that the fairy-tale is about everyman' and is a way of 'facilitating projections and identifications'.[14] Thus, the abstractions performed by this far-off setting and everyman-narrative allow for audience introspection and provide a canvas onto which they may project their own identities and inner conflicts.

Our introduction to the world of *The Grinning Man* is also a form of metatheatre, a term which describes the use of theatrical devices – such as direct address and the play-within-the-play – that draw attention to the artifice of the production. Here Roberts states that 'the limits of representation' – abstractions, or the gap between representation and reality – can be exposed through *representing* representation.[15] This is epitomized by the play-within-the-play which features throughout *The Grinning Man* both as a framed and an inset play. The first is evident during the opening scene – discussed earlier – which continues with Barkilphedro introducing the aristocracy through a tableau in which they pose behind large ornate picture frames. This physically separates the metatheatrical framing device of Barkilphedro from the literally framed, framed play. This draws attention to the construction of the production and emphasizes the distance between reality and representation. The first of the inset plays is introduced when we later see the travelling show perform within the world of the play. This layers the metatheatrical content, presenting the inset play (the travelling show) within the framed play (the world of the aristocracy), which itself is within a framing device (Barkilphedro's narration). When we are introduced to Grinpayne it is within this inset play, thus, placing him at the furthest point from the audience. He is an actor playing a character, playing a character and as such he exposes the gap between representation and reality.

As with the aristocracy before him, Grinpayne is first presented in tableau, though here he resembles a puppet, rotating slowly, his upper body shaking subtly as though he is suspended on string or in a music box. We then see his silhouette behind a screen as he conducts a shadow puppet exposition of his story. These two-dimensional presentations expose the limits of representation and do not encourage the audience to read him as a three-dimensional character. Instead, they perform an abstraction through which he is primed to become a symbol or metaphor. This position is maintained when we see Grinpayne within the world of the framed play, as the ongoing use of metatheatrical devices continue to distance the audience from Grinpayne. For example, Grinpayne's disfigurement is presented through the use of a non-realistic mask, the wolf Mojo is represented by a puppet and characters such as Barkilphedro and Osric repeatedly break the fourth wall.

Grinpayne's potential as a metaphor functions in the same way as the displaced narrative. Discussing plays-within-plays, Kayner suggests that 'to "distance the evidence" about the extra-performative referent to the never-never land of myth, legend or autonomous stage metaphor [results in] stimulating the spectator's suggestive interpretive intervention'.[16] In other words, the spectator plays a more active role in completing the narrative when that narrative is distanced from their own reality. They fill in any narrative gaps using their own imagination. Therefore, the distance created between representation and reality in this two-dimensional introduction to Grinpayne – sustained by reminding us of his artifice through metatheatrical techniques – can be seen as encouraging the audience to make their own interpretation of the character. Further, Mar and Oatley suggest that 'a fictional text may prompt more constructive imaginative processes, which then create an experience that has some of the attributes of actuality'.[17] An interpretation of Grinpayne may therefore come from how the spectator uses their own specific lived experience to fill the gap between representation and reality and thus co-create meaning with the text. Consequently, this metatheatrical distancing works in the same way as abstraction in fiction; it requires the audience to project themselves into the space, filling any representational deficiency with their own experiences in order to complete and make sense of the text. Further, since these experiences will be specific to the particular audience member, they have the ability to nurture deeper and highly personal connections to the characters. The audience can therefore identify with Grinpayne, forming a deep connection with him despite his unique narrative, because they are mapping their *own* experiences onto him through a constructive imaginative process.

The potential for projection continues during the inset play (the travelling show performance) when we are introduced to Grinpayne and Dea as young children. These younger versions are represented by life-sized humanoid puppets, inspired by Japanese Bunraku puppetry, which are each animated by visible puppeteers who include the actors playing their adult counterpart. Caldwell and Olié – co-designers and directors of puppetry in *The Grinning Man* – propose that this puppetry 'invites the audience to take part in the story being told' and that the audience 'are, in a sense, co-creators who invest in the life of the thing that they are watching'.[18] This may be possible due to the puppet's humanoid form and visible manipulation on stage exposing an abstraction which encourages further constructive imaginative processes (allowing for the co-creation of the text), and creates a space into which projection can occur resulting in audience identification with and investment in the characters.

Grinpayne and Dea's puppets are also specifically representative of children, an image which in Jungian analysis is a symbolic form 'detached from ideas of living, breathing children'.[19] Child Grinpayne is therefore doubly removed from reality: through both the metatheatricality of puppetry and the archetype of the child, with this combination creating space for projection. This is in addition to child Grinpayne also being removed from reality through belonging to the inset play (though this world later spills out into the framed play). The child is also often representative of 'the inner child', a role which returns us to the use of stories as a safe space into which one can project and work through internal processes. Here, child Grinpayne can embody the spectator's inner child, allowing the audience to engage with trauma from a safe(r) distance. Further, Hancock identifies that 'the socially and culturally defined category of "childhood" is the broadest category of "other" which is known to adult world'[20] and therefore it can be suggested that the puppet child reinforces an otherness which – as will be discussed – is prescribed by Grinpayne's disfigurement. Consequently, the audience member may be encouraged to map their inner narrative of marginalization onto Grinpayne's own, forming a deeply personal shared identity of Other that is strengthened through projection rather than any specific shared experience.

These examples demonstrate how deeply personal identifications with Grinpayne can be nurtured through the abstractions performed by various narrative and metatheatrical devices creating an ambiguous or liminal space into which the audience can project their own identity or political cause. However, as we will see, this becomes problematic when we recognize that at the heart of *The Grinning Man* is a disability narrative; a protected characteristic, the abstraction of which comes with political and real-world implications.

Disability

Disability is classified under the UK's Equality Act 2010 as a physical or mental impairment that 'has a substantial and long-term adverse effect on P's [a person's] ability to carry out normal day-to-day activities'.[21] In the UK, disability is predominantly understood through the social model, whereby 'disability is presented as a social and political problem that turns an impairment into an oppression either by erecting barriers or by refusing to create barrier-free environments'.[22] This means that it is not physical or mental difference that defines disability, but the social response to impairment and the barriers that prevent a person from equitable engagement in society. A commonly cited example is a wheelchair user being disabled by the lack of ramps or elevators into and in a building. Through both the Equality Act and the social model of disability, a severe disfigurement such as Grinpayne's can be recognized as a disability.

Disabilities including disfigurement have long played a narrative role on our musical stages. From signifiers of social and racial inequality (*Porgy and Bess*, 1935) and physical manifestations of depravity (*The Phantom of the Opera*) to reinforcing non-disabled values (*Light in the Piazza*, 2005) disability has been used as a narrative shorthand to embody otherwise invisible characteristics and ideologies. Examining several musicals, Knapp documents disability figuring 'as an instance of stigmatized difference, [and] as the basis for overcoming or transcending difficulties',[23] highlighting its use as both metaphor and plot device. Both of these can also be found in *The Grinning Man*, where Grinpayne's disfigurement serves as a visible reminder of his outsider status, as a metaphor for generalized othering (onto which the audience can project) and as a narrative shorthand (prompting the responses of those around him and driving him to seek revenge on those that disfigured him). His disability is used to justify his obsession and anger. Mitchell and Snyder describe this use of disability as a 'narrative prosthesis', claiming that 'disability has been used throughout history as a crutch upon which literary narratives lean for their representational power, disruptive potentiality, and analytical insight'.[24] This may be because, as Garland Thomson states, 'corporeal departures from dominant expectations never go uninterpreted'.[25] The desire to read disability as a signifier is then further perpetuated in the theatre where 'audiences are trained by convention to read disability as a metaphor, or meaning-maker'.[26] Consequently, disability is relentlessly analysed for significance.

A prevalent form of narrative prosthesis found in musical theatre is the use of disability to mark the corporeal Other. This may be understood though Michell and Snyder's claim that 'one might think of disability as the master trope of human disqualification';[27] the disabled character is therefore primed to be read as the antithesis of the onstage community. Grinpayne thus signifies as Other, a position supported by our previous reading of the child puppet. With a focus on *The Phantom of the Opera,* Sternfeld explores the dramaturgical function of the Other in relation to disability, defining the role as 'an outsider who must eventually be welcomed into the community or be banned from it'.[28] She explains how given the Phantom's inability to assimilate into society, his symbolic death becomes inevitable.[29] This is a common musical theatre narrative in which disability frequently figures. For example, Grizabella in *Cats* (1981) – disabled though ageing – cannot assimilate and so is removed to the Heaviside layer. Elphaba in *Wicked* (2003) – whose green skin may equally be read through racial theory – is doubly removed through her staged (faked) death and then her voluntary retreat from Oz. On the other hand, some characters do assimilate into society; for example, both Colin in *The Secret Garden* (1991) and the titular character in *Tommy* (1993) achieve assimilation through a miraculous cure which removes their status as Other. Each of these resolutions is rooted in ableism, with death or cure being the only options. *The Grinning Man* complies providing a metaphorical death, as the show ends with Grinpayne and Dea leaving to find a new life. Their removal from the community is then further emphasized by their physical removal from stage as they leave the proscenium arch and make their way through the audience. Consequently, while their ending may seem optimistic, they are denied the opportunity to simply exist as they are.

However, othering is not the only problematic use of narrative prosthesis. Mitchell and Snyder also argue that it obscures the complex real-life experience of those with disabilities.[30] Thus, while disability may be hyper-visible through a narrative, it may also be conspicuously absent in any way that is authentic or meaningful in relation to disabled people[31] or disability politics. Fox touches upon this phenomenon in her analysis of disability within *Light in the Piazza* when she identifies that the show works 'with disability metaphor and ways of representing the disabled that are less about realism and more about projecting social anxiety about gender onto the disabled body'.[32] Likewise, the abstraction that allows the audience to project themselves onto Grinpayne also erases the lived experience of disability in favour of its use as metaphorical device. Without this lived experience, these devices perpetuate the same damaging misconceptions and tropes of disability which negatively impact upon how society interacts with disability on a daily basis. For example, Dea is given a compensatory strength for her blindness; she is able to physically feel emotions in the air. Though fantastical, this plays into and encourages expectations that a disabled person must have exceptional skill in order for them to be of value in society.

We are, however, beginning to see changes in the theatre industry where there has been building momentum towards cultivating equality, diversity and inclusion beyond a narrative use of protected characteristics. Primarily, this involves disabled people having the power to represent themselves and can be summarized by the slogan: 'nothing about us without us'. This drive for change is coming from multiple levels, for example #WeShallNotBeRemoved is a political movement in the UK that was founded in response to the COVID-19 pandemic. It recognizes that disabled artists have been disproportionately affected by the pandemic and campaigns for better support to facilitate them in the industry. In the North of England, the Disabled Artists Networking Community is a group that establishes dialogue between disabled practitioners and the decision-makers and gatekeepers in the industry. They promote the talent of D/deaf and disabled creatives and provide educational opportunities for those working in the field. Meanwhile, the Arts Council of England provides regular reports on diversity employment in National Portfolio Organisations in order to encourage wider participation. In terms of visibility on stage in musical theatre, disability-led companies have produced musicals featuring disabled artists (Graeae's *Reasons to be Cheerful*, 2010 and Ramps on the Moon's *Tommy*, 2017) and disabled performers such as Beth Hinton-Lever (*Hadestown*, 2018) and Amy Trigg (*Mamma Mia: Here We Go Again*, 2018) have garnered commercial success. Most notably, in America, Ali Stoker (*Oklahoma!*, 2019) brought attention to disabled artists when she became the first wheelchair user to be nominated for and win a Tony Award in 2019.

Despite progress being made, narratives of disability are still predominantly examples of narrative prosthesis, and disabled actors still struggle to find training and casting opportunities. This is particularly evident in musicals, which Knapp argues are 'fundamentally exclusionary to the disabled', and 'celebrate, through performance, physical abilities'.[33] Yates expands on this concept, suggesting that the multiple skills of the triple threat performer may actually be read as a form of hypercapacity,[34] thus implying that musical theatre venerates not only the nondisabled but also the hyper-capable body. This becomes particularly evident when non-disabled actors are cast in disabled roles. Often referred to as 'cripping up' or 'disability drag', Yates defines this practice as 'disability simulation'[35] and with the example of *Side Show* (1997, 2014) demonstrates how this 'relies on the exceptional able-bodiedness of the actors'.[36] He follows this to say that 'this copy [the simulation] is predicated on imprecise assumption or second-hand information about what a disabled body is, does or can be'.[37] Consequently, not only does disability simulation venerate the hypercapable non-disabled body, but it actually erases disability, once again producing an abstraction which removes it from any real-life experience.

The disability presented in *The Grinning Man* may be read as a disability simulation which strips disfigurement of its real-life context and reinforces it as a marker of generalized otherness. While the political identity of the actors is unknown and cannot be assumed, their bodies on stage visibly present as non-disabled, and even as hypercapable through their command of puppetry, their vocal dexterity and the meticulous body control displayed during the stylized movement of the in-play performances. This is subtly evident during Grinpayne's first scene where he rotates his body at an almost imperceptible slowness while maintaining balance and pose. The disability presented to the audience is a fabrication, with the use of actual prosthetics supporting the narrative prosthetic. Here, Grinpayne's disfigurement is physically fabricated through the use of a disfigured mask, and Dea is marked as blind through the use of white contact lenses. This visible construction of disability highlights the simulation performed by the actors, which thus resists a reading of authenticity and instead encourages the disabilities to be read as narrative device. The effects of this simulation then combine with the use of the puppets which can be read as literally objectifying the character, and thus dehumanizing Grinpayne. This dehumanization allows disability again to be read as a metaphor while simultaneously creating a space for projection that does not directly engage with the disabled identity (Figure 3).

Figure 3 *The Grinning Man*, 2017 revival cast. Credit: Helen Maybanks.

The freak show

The Grinning Man not only portrays disability, however, but specifically references the 'freak show',[38] a practice that has both featured in and inspired a number of musicals, most notably *Barnum* (1980), *Side Show* (1997) and *The Greatest Showman* (2017). The term 'freak show' refers to a historic practice, summarized by Bogdan as 'the formally organized exhibition of people with alleged and real physical, mental, or behavioural anomalies for amusement and profit'.[39] Bogdan also stresses, however, that '"freak" is a way of thinking, of presenting, a set of practices, an institution – not a characteristic of an individual'.[40] This set of practices provide a useful tool with which to explore Grinpayne's performance, as this contextualization sheds light not only on how specific techniques were used and received historically but also how they may be read today.

Despite freak not being 'a characteristic of an individual',[41] a reading of Grinpayne as freak is also useful beyond the confines of his freak show presentation. This is in part because as the narrative progresses, the lines between framing device, framed play and inset play begin to blur, collapsing the boundaries between representations, reality and fiction. For example, the puppet children who were established as belonging to the world of the inset play later appear within the framed play through the memories of Barkilphedro.

A giant puppet head, introduced during the freak show, also appears later in the framed play. Meanwhile, Barkilphedro flits between framing device and framed play, eventually interacting with the puppets from the inset play, and as the show ends, Grinpayne and Dea transcend all three layers and physically enter the world of the auditorium. Blurring these boundaries erases any neat lines drawn between the freak show and the containing narrative and as such Grinpayne may be read as freak throughout. Additionally, while the characters in the show encounter Grinpayne in both his freak show presentation and as himself offstage, for the theatre audience every presentation of Grinpayne is a performance removed from the individual, and so any of these presentations may be read as freak.

Moreover, as with the freak show performance, the entire production is a highly stylized presentation which actively encourages the audience to stare at the Other. Grinpayne's disfigurement is physically fabricated through a ghastly oversized lower face mask which for majority of the show remains hidden beneath a blood-stained bandage. Being denied the opportunity to observe his disfigurement, there is a growing anticipation of the reveal until the audience are finally given the horrific grin they have been waiting for; the mask is unveiled, quickly accompanied by a giant, distorted and bloody puppet head that floats above the stage in a horrific theatricalization of his disfigurement. This anticipation and reveal has parallels with *The Phantom of the Opera* – which Sternfeld refers to as a modern-day freak show – where 'the audience is there to see the intriguing, grotesque, frightening Phantom, just as spectators went to see side shows and other novelty displays or performances in many different times and cultures'.[42] In this way, it is possible, and useful, to read *The Grinning Man* as a freak show in its own right.

While the exhibition of people with anomalous bodies can be found throughout history, what we retrospectively refer to as the freak show was a specific, highly stylized and deeply popular form of entertainment. At the beginning of the nineteenth century people with disabilities were regularly displayed by parents, priests and philosophers in the back rooms of pubs and taverns in what Bogdan describes as a 'sleazy operation on the fringe of Victorian America'.[43] During the nineteenth century, advances in science pathologized the disabled figure, transforming the discourse from disability under godly jurisdiction towards Mendelian and Darwinian phenomena. This captured Victorian imagination, and under the guise of 'education' the dime museum was born, moving human oddities from backroom exhibitions to professional establishments. This iteration of the freak show then experienced a fifty-year golden age, during which the dime museum was received as a somewhat respectable establishment that traded in on the popular-science of the day and offered to quench a growing thirst for knowledge. The key figure of this period was P. T. Barnum who owned the American Museum from 1841 and provided the inspiration for the musicals *Barnum* and *The Greatest Showman*.

Chemers describes the golden age of the freak show as 'one marked by sensational presentation, extreme professionalism, and high controversy'.[44] Traditionally, there were two methods of presentation: the aggrandized and the exotic. The aggrandized 'emphasized how, with the exception of the particular physical, mental, or behavioural condition, the freak was an upstanding, high-status person with talents of a conventional and socially prestigious nature'.[45] For example, little person Charles Stratton was presented as General Tom Thumb, with this military position aggrandizing his presentation. Stratton was fictionalized in both *Barnum* and *The Greatest Showman* retaining this aggrandized presentation. His character in *The Greatest Showman* was then joined by fictional bearded woman Lettie Lutz, whose exaggerated femininity through costuming, hair, make-up and impressive vocal talents are juxtaposed against her facial hair, again aggrandizing her presentation. Lutz demonstrates how the aggrandized method is perhaps well suited for musical theatre representation, where the physical and vocal demands placed upon the artist can emphasize the exceptional talent of hypercapable actors juxtaposed against their disability simulations. As previously discussed, however, this accentuates the talent of the actor rather than revealing any truth about disability. Further it perpetuates the idea that the disabled figure is only valued when they have a compensatory strength.

The exotic method, on the other hand, constructed an exaggerated *difference* between the freak and the audience, presenting the person 'so as to appeal to people's interest in the culturally strange, the primitive, the bestial, the exotic'.[46] This method of presentation is perhaps the most ethically troubling as it strips the humanity from the subject. Examples of this method include the presentation of people of colour and people with microcephaly as Darwin's 'missing link': that is the hypothetical evolutionary step between our anthropoid ancestors and modern humans. This placed the person as less-than-human. Further, these were often enslaved people and disabled people that did not have the capacity to consent. Grinpayne's presentation may be read through this exotic method, with his mask and giant puppet head inflating his disfigurement into a macabre and brazen display of exaggerated otherness that identifies him as monstrous or inhumane. This view is also encouraged through characters who are horrified by his image and by the creator's description of him as 'a beautiful monster'.[47] However, Conroy claims that 'to associate disability with the monstrous, the evil or the unusually saintly is to prevent others from responding straightforwardly to the individual'.[48] This presentation therefore dehumanizes Grinpayne and encourages the audience to view his characteristics as a metaphor.

The exaggeration of the mask and giant head also work metatheatrically, where a play 'may present actions that are alien, stylized or absurd to distance audience from the theatrical illusion on the stage'.[49] Consequently, the audience are not simply reminded of the difference between them and the character but are distanced from the theatrical illusion itself, thereby alerting them to the relationship between performance and reality with the space between these two elements encouraging the constructive imaginative process. This may further be aided through reading the giant head as 'grotesque'. Discussing Bakhtin's seminal work on the subject, Chemers articulates that 'the grotesque body seems to transcend its own individuality, accessing, in its swellings and protuberances, parts of other bodies, unpredictably morphing into new identities and new shapes'.[50] This liminality, the ability of the grotesque to morph, allows the disabled body to act as a fruitful canvas onto which one can project their own experiences. It is at once undefinable and unlimited and therefore is a place in which multiple identities may converge, while simultaneously obscuring the lived experience of that body.

However, this description is how he presents theatrically to the modern-day audience. The characters within the framed play are receiving a different show, presumably witnessing his true disfigurement accompanied by the narrative of his life. This calls into question why – other than as spectacle – Grinpayne's disfigurement is so brazenly theatricalized for the modern audience while this level of exaggeration is absent from the plot. Chemers notes that the freak show is marked by a 'knee-jerk moralizing' in contemporary society.[51] It may be that the excessivity of the disfigured mask and puppet head serves to distance Grinpayne from any authentic disability, thereby making the freak show more palatable for the modern audience. In this way, the extravagant construction of disability allows the audience to not only accept but also enjoy the eccentric reception that Grinpayne's receives on stage, while also being assuaged of any guilt caused by their complicity in the freak show. It therefore trades in freak show iconography, without engaging with the politics involved in the practice.

The presentation received by the characters within the framed play does not fit neatly into either the aggrandized or the exotic methods of presentation, but rather aligns more closely with pre-golden age exhibition. Similarly, the modesty and isolation of Grinpayne's travelling show also situate it as pre-Golden Age. This timeline is then narratively reinforced when Grinpayne is refused admission onto a boat at the beginning of the show; its crewmen believing that Grinpayne's disfigurement is ungodly and that he will cause the boat to sink. This aligns with religious views of disability that were prominent before the development of science brought disabled performers into the dime museum. This pre-golden age setting differentiates *The Grinning Man* from the majority of musicals that reference the freak show, and which – like *The Greatest Showman* – trade on a sense of community and acceptance. Even *Side Show*, which is set post golden age, features an ensemble of freak show performers and carries themes of interpersonal (as well as literal) connection. In contrast, despite featuring romantic partnerships, *The Grinning Man* is more heavily focused on themes of personal identification and Grinpayne, though travelling with Dea and Ursus, is isolated from any golden age community. His otherness is not just marginalization from the dominant society, but from others like him, particularly when he shuns the affection of Dea. References to the 'freak' therefore serve to heighten Grinpayne's marginalization, whereas the term in relation to *The Greatest Showman* allows for empowerment through transgression and belonging.

This marginalization may function to provoke empathy from the audience, which returns us to audience identification. Mar and Oatley suggest that empathy, when towards fictional characters, manifests as *identification*.[52] Through empathy, Grinpayne therefore becomes primed as a site of identification; however, this is specifically encouraged in relation to the context of freakery. This is seen after the curtain call when the company unites to sing the line 'the age of the freak is at hand'. The united breaking of the fourth wall beckons the audience to join them, and having been removed from any true engagement with disability and the freak show, the audience are now free to identify with the freaks through mapping any personal experience of marginalization onto Grinpayne as Other. One audience member identified this as a prominent moment for her, claiming that

> So many of us feel we are freaks in one way or another . . . an outsider . . . whether it be not looking 'perfect' or having a disability or being the geek with non-geeks, or a theatre kid in a world of athletes. To have a show that underscores it's our time as well . . . that the underdog has their time to shine . . . it's a wonderfully uplifting message to anyone facing those types of challenges.[53]

Another wrote, 'I was welcomed to Trafalgar Fair as a fellow freak and I was thrilled to be part of it.'[54] These are sentiments shared by actress Gloria Onitiri, who played Josiana in the Bristol production. In a post-show panel she claimed that 'there's something about the freak that's in me that was enabled to come out, because of the story and because of how we put it together'.[55] While these messages portray an empowering and wholesome experience, they may read as an appropriation of freak terminology which negates the disability central to the production.

This is because contemporary understanding of freakery is largely shaped through the counterculture movement of the 1960s where the term 'freak' was re-appropriated by a youth culture that used it to describe their own rebellion against, and alienation from mainstream society. Rachel Adams identifies its use as an 'affirmative self-identification' that was endorsed by the likes of Jimi Hendrix and Frank Zappa who brandished 'freak flags' and used phraseology such as 'freak out'.[56] Consequently, the freak became a locus onto which a disenfranchized audience could project their own feelings of otherness while acquiring subcultural capital. In contemporary musical theatre this can be seen in 'Freak Flag' in *Shrek* (2008) where the term is appropriated by the fairy-tale characters oppressed by Lord Farquaad. Because of this history, Grinpayne's assertion, 'I am the freak show' may be read as encouraging a contemporary audience who feel ostracized from the mainstream to project their feelings of otherness onto Grinpayne's own freakery. This is problematic, however, as this projection onto Grinpayne takes place through an ironic distance, where Church argues that 'they can effectively distance themselves, as privileged (nondisabled) possessors of the ableist gaze, from the freakish objects of that gaze – even if they still identify on some level with the freak's marginalization'.[57] This detachment allows the counterculture to use the anomalous body as a symbol of its own marginalization but, as Church suggests, 'without critically engaging the politics of disability representation'.[58]

Conclusion

Disability in *The Grinning Man* is both hyper-visible, yet conspicuously absent; it is a crucial narrative prosthesis around which the show revolves, yet stripped of authenticity it becomes a site of potential identification for any marginalized individual. Parallels with the freak show demonstrate how Grinpayne's presentation encourage him to be read as Other, while the contemporary contextualization of the freak show demonstrates how identification with the Other may be used to gain subcultural capital without having to engage with the politics of disability. This identification is further supported by the use of metatheatrical techniques that expose the gap between representation and reality. This gap then encourages the audience to project their own identities into the narrative and co-create meaning with the text. Consequently, the identification felt with Grinpayne is strengthened through recognizing the parts of us that we have projected onto him through aligning our perceived otherness with his and claiming his marginalization as our own. If the audience member is disabled or has significant experience of disability, it is possible that their sense of otherness and marginalization align to some extent with Grinpayne's. However, it is likely that the majority of the audience will not identify as disabled – in 2019–20 one in five people in the UK reported having a disability[59] – and for those non-disabled spectators, *The Grinning Man* encourages identification with the Other while escaping any engagement with disability.

The Grinning Man may therefore have missed an opportunity. Arts Council England state that 'the arts can both stimulate and respond to change, but only if they better represent the contemporary world'.[60] Musicals therefore have the opportunity – and responsibility – to enact real social change. For example, 'by bringing disability on to the stage, it becomes more visible, more knowable, and thus gives the audience a chance to integrate the reality so they can see beyond their prejudices.'[61] We must therefore ask ourselves what are the stories that are being told, and who is telling them. As Fox states, 'we need to remain connected to a more nuanced understanding' of disability.[62] This means that instead of relying on the 'representational power' of disability, and perpetuating ideals about musical theatre bodies that continue to exclude disabled people, we have a responsibility to facilitate disabled creatives and performers and create disability narratives that reflect and include the community. By coming from a place of authenticity, the subsequent abstractions will not fully obscure the genuine representation that could take place and the positive shifts that they could encourage in our society. By coming from lived experience, identification with disabled characters may dismantle prejudice while championing the disabled community.

Notes

1. Carl Grose, Tim Phillips, Marc Teitler and Tom Morris, *The Grinning Man* (United Kingdom: Concord Theatricals, 2021), 33.
2. At the time of writing, a digital recording of the Bristol production has twice been available for streaming through the Covid-19 pandemic. It is this recorded production, with additional material from the published libretto that serves as the main reference for this chapter.
3. In Bristol Old Vic, 'The Grinning Man | Post Show Q&A | Bristol Old Vic at Home' [video], (streamed live 26 June 2020), accessed 21 August 2021, https://www.youtube.com/watch?v=5-bubbzbtAs.
4. Rachel Adams, *Sideshow U.S.A: Freaks and the American Cultural Imagination* (Chicagoand London: University of Chicago Press, 2001).
5. David Church, 'Freakery, Cult Films and the Problem of Ambivalence', *Journal of Film and Video* 63, no. 1 (2011): 3–17.

6. Raymond A. Mar and Keith Oatley, 'The Function of Fiction Is the Abstraction and Simulation of Social Experience', *Perspectives on Psychological Science* 3, no. 3 (2008): 173–92: 173.
7. Grose et al., *The Grinning Man*, 1.
8. Grose et al., *The Grinning Man*, 1.
9. Jessica Sternfeld, '"Pitiful Creature of Darkness": The Subhuman and the Superhuman in The Phantom of the Opera', in *The Oxford Handbook of Music and Disability Studies*, ed. B. Howe, S. Jensen-Moulton, N. W. Lerner and J. N. Straus (Oxford; New York: Oxford University Press, 2016), 795–813 (796).
10. Grose et al., *The Grinning Man*, Notes on production.
11. Bruno Bettelheim, *The Uses of Enchantment: The Meaning and Importance of Fairy Tales* (London: Penguin Books, 1978), 62.
12. Bettelheim, *The Uses of Enchantment*, 25.
13. In correspondence with the author.
14. Bettelheim, *The Uses of Enchantment*, 40.
15. David Roberts, 'The Play within the Play and the Closure of Representation', in *The Play within the Play: The Performance of Meta-Theatre and Self-Reflection*, ed. G. Fischer and B. Greiner (Amsterdam: Rodopi, 2007), 37–46 (37).
16. Gad Kayner, 'Play within the Fictitious Play in Israeli Stage-Drama', in *The Play within the Play: The Performance of Meta-Theatre and Self-Reflection*, ed. G. Fischer and B. Greiner (Amsterdam: Rodopi, 2007), 67–188 (167).
17. Mar and Oatley, 'The Function of Fiction Is the Abstraction and Simulation of Social Experience', 173–92 (180).
18. In The Space, '*The Grinning Man:* Puppetry' (n.d.), accessed 31 Dec. 2022, https://artsandculture.google.com/story/the-grinning-man-puppetry-the-space/KgVh4A0jolsOJw?hl=en-GB.
19. Susan Hancock, *The Child That Haunts Us: Symbols and Images in Fairytale and Miniature Literature* (New York: Routledge, 2016), 15.
20. Hancock, *The Child That Haunts Us*, 9.
21. 'Equality Act 2010, c.15', Legislation.gov.uk (2010), accessed 25 February 2022, https://www.legislation.gov.uk/ukpga/2010/15, Provision 6(1)b.
22. Lennard J. Davis, 'The End of Identity Politics: On Disability as an Unstable Category', in *The Disability Studies Reader*, ed. Lennard J. Davis, 4th edn (New York and London: Routledge, 2013), 263–77 (271).
23. Raymond Knapp, '"Waitin' for the Light to Shine": Musicals and Disability', in *The Oxford Handbook of Music and Disability Studies*, ed. B. Howe, S. Jensen-Moulton, N. W. Lerner and J. N. Straus (Oxford; New York: Oxford University Press, 2016), 814–35 (816).
24. David Mitchell and Sharon Snyder, *Narrative Prosthesis: Disability and the Dependencies of Discourse* (Michigan: The University of Michigan Press, 2000), 49.
25. Rosemarie Garland Thomson, *Extraordinary Bodies: Figuring Physical Disability in American Culture and Literature* (New York: Columbia University Press, 1997), 7.
26. Carrie Sandahl, 'Why Disability Identity Matters: From Dramaturgy to Casting in John Belluso's Pyretown', *Text and Performance Quarterly* 28, no. 1–2 (2008): 225–41 (236).
27. Mitchell and Snyder, *Narrative Prosthesis,* 3.
28. Sternfeld, '"Pitiful Creature of Darkness"', 795–813 (795).
29. Sternfeld, '"Pitiful Creature of Darkness"', 798.
30. Mitchell and Snyder, *Narrative Prosthesis,* 60.

31. In the UK, we predominantly use disability-first language, for example 'a disabled person', while in America it is more common to encounter person-first language, for example 'a person with a disability'. It is always recommended that when referring to any disabled person, you use the terminology that they personally prefer.
32. Ann Fox, 'Scene in a New Light: Monstrous Mothers, Disabled Daughters, and the Performance of Feminism and Disability in *The Light in the Piazza* (2005) and *Next to Normal* (2008)', in *The Oxford Handbook of Music and Disability Studies*, ed. B. Howe, S. Jensen-Moulton, N. W. Lerner and J. N. Straus (Oxford and New York: Oxford University Press, 2016), 775–94 (781).
33. Knapp, '"Waitin' for the Light to Shine"', 814–35 (815).
34. Samuel Yates, 'Spider-Man's Designer Genes: Hypercapacity and Transhumanism in a "DIY World"', in *The Matter of Disability: Materiality, Biopolitics, Crip Affect*, ed. David Mitchell, S. Antebi and Sharon Snyder (Ann Arbor: University of Michigan Press, 2019), 143–59.
35. Samuel Yates, 'Choreographing Conjoinment: Side Show's Fleshy Fixations and Disability Simulation', *Studies in Musical Theatre* 13, no. 1 (2019): 67–78.
36. Yates, 'Choreographing Conjoinment', 67.
37. Yates, 'Choreographing Conjoinment', 68.
38. While 'freak' is a controversial term within disability discourse, it is here used as a direct quote from *The Grinning Man* and in relation to the historical practice of the freak show. The freak show is a highly contested area that is fraught with debate over issues of agency and exploitation. It must be recognized that the freak show participated in the enslavement of people of colour and the presentation of people who may not have had the capacity to consent, for example, some people with microcephaly. However, while this is a critical part of the freak show's history and brings further debate to any use of the term 'freak,' these issues are beyond the remit of this chapter.
39. Robert Bogdan, *Freak Show: Presenting Human Oddities for Amusement and Profit* (Chicago: University of Chicago Press, 1990), 10.
40. Bogdan, *Freak Show*.
41. Bogdan, *Freak Show*.
42. Sternfeld, '"Pitiful Creature of Darkness"', 795–813 (802).
43. Bogdan, *Freak Show*, 32.
44. Michael M. Chemers, *Staging Stigma: A Critical Examination of the American Freak Show* (New York: Palgrave Macmillan, 2008), 67.
45. Bogdan, *Freak Show*, 108.
46. Bogdan, *Freak Show*, 105.
47. Grose et al., *The Grinning Man*, Notes on production.
48. Colette Conroy, 'Freaks and Not Freaks: Theatre and the Making of Crip Identity', *Lambda Nordica* 17, no. 1–2 (2012): 168–93 (174).
49. Liang Fei, 'Metadrama and Themes in Stoppard's *Rosencrantz and Guildenstern Are Dead*', *Canadian Social Science* 3, no. 3 (2007): 99–105: 100.
50. Michael M. Chemers, 'Le Freak, c'est Chic: The Twenty-First Century Freak Show as Theatre of Transgression', *Modern Drama* 46, no. 2 (2003): 285–304 (296).
51. Chemers, *Staging Stigma*, 139.
52. Mar and Oatley, 'The Function of Fiction Is the Abstraction and Simulation of Social Experience', 173–92 (181).

53. In correspondence with the author.
54. In correspondence with the author.
55. In Bristol Old Vic, 'The Grinning Man | Post Show Q&A | Bristol Old Vic at Home' [video].
56. Adams, *Sideshow U.S.A.*, 138.
57. Church, 'Freakery, Cult Films and the Problem of Ambivalence', 3–17 (13).
58. Church, 'Freakery, Cult Films and the Problem of Ambivalence', 12.
59. Department for Work and Pensions, 'National Statistics Family Resources Survey: Financial Year 2019 to 2020' (2021), accessed 21 August 2021, https://www.gov.uk/government/statistics/family-resources-survey-financial-year-2019-to-2020/family-resources-survey-financial-year-2019-to-2020#disability-1, Section 5.
60. Arts Council England, *Equality, Diversity and the Creative Case: A Data Report, 2017–2018* (2019), 2, accessed 10 December 2019, https://www.artscouncil.org.uk/sites/default/files/download-file/Diversity_report_1718.pdf.
61. Bonnie J. Eckard and Wendy Myers, 'Beyond Disability: A Dialogue with Members of the Improbably Theatre Company', *Research in Drama Education* 14, no. 1 (2009): 73.
62. 2016: 793.

Bibliography

Adams, Rachel (2001), *Sideshow U.S.A.: Freaks and the American Cultural Imagination*. Chicago and London: University of Chicago Press.

Arts Council England (2019), 'Equality, Diversity and the Creative Case: A Data Report, 2017–2018', https://www.artscouncil.org.uk/sites/default/files/download-file/Diversity_report_1718.pdf (accessed 10 December 2019).

Bettelheim, Bruno (1978), *The Uses of Enchantment: The Meaning and Importance of Fairy Tales*. London.

Bogdan, Robert (1990), *Freak Show: Presenting Human Oddities for Amusement and Profit*. Chicago.

Bristol Old Vic (2020), 'The Grinning Man | Post Show Q&A | Bristol Old Vic at Home' [video], (streamed live 26 June), https://www.youtube.com/watch?v=5-bubbzbtAs (accessed 21 August 2021).

Chemers, Michael, M. (2003), 'Le Freak, c'est Chic: The Twenty-First Century Freak Show as Theatre of Transgression', *Modern Drama*, 46 (2): 285–304.

Chemers, Michael, M. (2008), *Staging Stigma: A Critical Examination of the American Freak Show*. New York.

Church, David (2011), 'Freakery, Cult Films and the Problem of Ambivalence', *Journal of Film and Video*, 63 (1): 3–17.

Conroy, Colette (2012), 'Freaks and Not Freaks: Theatre and the Making of Crip Identity', *Lambda Nordica*, 17 (1–2): 168–93.

Davis, Lennard J. (2013), 'The End of Identity Politics: On Disability as an Unstable Category', in Lennard J. Davis (ed.), *The Disability Studies Reader*, 4th edn, 263–77. New York and London.

Department for Work and Pensions (2021), 'National Statistics Family Resources Survey: Financial Year 2019 to 2020', https://www.gov.uk/government/statistics/family-resources-survey-financial-year-2019-to-2020/family-resources-survey-financial-year-2019-to-2020#disability-1 (accessed 21 August 2021).

Eckard, Bonnie J. and Wendy Myers (2009), 'Beyond Disability: A Dialogue with Members of the Improbably Theatre Company', *Research in Drama Education*, 14 (1): 59–74.

'Equality Act 2010, c.15' (2010), *Legislation.gov.uk*, https://www.legislation.gov.uk/ukpga/2010/15 (accessed 25 February 2022).

Fei, Liang (2007), 'Metadrama and Themes in Stoppard's *Rosencrantz and Guildenstern Are Dead*', *Canadian Social Science*, 3 (3): 99–105.

Fox, Ann (2016), 'Scene in a New Light: Monstrous Mothers, Disabled Daughters, and the Performance of Feminism and Disability in *The Light in the Piazza* (2005) and *Next to Normal* (2008)', in B. Howe, S. Jensen-Moulton, N. W. Lerner and J. N. Straus (eds), *The Oxford Handbook of Music and Disability Studies*, 775–94. Oxford and New York.

Garland Thomson, Rosemarie (1997), *Extraordinary Bodies: Figuring Physical Disability in American Culture and Literature*. New York.

Grose, Carl, Tim Phillips, Marc Teitler and Tom Morris (2021), *The Grinning Man*. United Kingdom.

Hancock, Susan (2016), *The Child That Haunts Us: Symbols and Images in Fairytale and Miniature Literature*. New York.

Kayner, Gad (2007), 'Play Within the Fictitious Play in Israeli Stage-Drama', in G. Fischer and B. Greiner (eds), *The Play Within the Play: The Performance of Meta-Theatre and Self-Reflection*, 67–188. Amsterdam.

Knapp, Raymond (2016), '"Waitin' for the Light to Shine": Musicals and Disability', in B. Howe, S. Jensen-Moulton, N. W. Lerner and J. N. Straus (eds), *The Oxford Handbook of Music and Disability Studies*, 814–35. Oxford and New York.

Mar, Raymond A. and Keith Oatley (2008), 'The Function of Fiction Is the Abstraction and Simulation of Social Experience', *Perspectives on Psychological Science*, 3 (3): 173–92.

Mitchell, David and Sharon Snyder (2000), *Narrative Prosthesis: Disability and the Dependencies of Discourse*. Michigan.

Roberts, David (2007), 'The Play Within the Play and the Closure of Representation', in G. Fischer and B. Greiner (eds), *The Play Within the Play: The Performance of Meta-Theatre and Self-Reflection*, 37–46. Amsterdam.

Sandahl, Carrie (2008), 'Why Disability Identity Matters: From Dramaturgy to Casting in John Belluso's Pyretown', *Text and Performance Quarterly*, 28 (1–2): 225–41.

Sternfeld, Jessica (2016), '"Pitiful Creature of Darkness": The Subhuman and the Superhuman in The Phantom of the Opera', in B. Howe, S. Jensen-Moulton, N. W. Lerner and J. N. Straus (eds), *The Oxford Handbook of Music and Disability Studies*, 795–813. Oxford and New York.

Taylor, Millie and Dominic Symonds (2014), *Studying Musical Theatre: Theory and Practice*. London.

The Space (n.d.), *The Grinning Man: Puppetry*, https://artsandculture.google.com/story/the-grinning-man-puppetry-the-space/KgVh4A0jolsOJw?hl=en-GB (accessed 31 December 2022).

Yates, Samuel (2019), 'Choreographing Conjoinment: Side Show's Fleshy Fixations and Disability Simulation', *Studies in Musical Theatre*, 13 (1): 67–78.

Yates, Samuel (2019), 'Spider-Man's Designer Genes: Hypercapacity and Transhumanism in a "DIY World"', in David Mitchell, S. Antebi, and Sharon Snyder (eds), *The Matter of Disability: Materiality, Biopolitics, Crip Affect*, 143–59. Ann Arbor.

Toby Olié interview

Puppetry co-designer and co-director *The Grinning Man*

What is your favourite British musical?

I think for innovation, *London Road* at the National Theatre. To create a verbatim musical based on such sensitive subject matter was such an achievement. Plus the fact it came out of an experimental programme which partnered writers and composers is a testament to the subsidized sector and the risks it can and should take.

What's your favourite British musical theatre song?

'Naughty' from *Matilda*, it's such a good 'I want' song – but without the character actually knowing what she wants yet. She decides to fight back against her unjust circumstances, it encapsulates the whole show in a really brilliant way.

How did you train for this career?

I trained in puppetry at the Central School of Speech and Drama and was the only person on the course. This meant from day one I found myself working with students from lots of different creative disciplines in realizing projects and ideas, a fundamentally collaborative process that I still practice in my work today.

Finn (Caldwell, fellow co-founder of Gyre & Gimble) trained as an actor at Guildhall. He and I met while performing in the original cast of *War Horse,* and we realized that although we came from different disciplines, we were very much striving for the same attention to detail and nuanced levels of acting in puppetry.

We went on to create *The Elephantom* a show in The Shed – the National Theatre's 2013 temporary space – before founding Gyre & Gimble. And within a year of doing that director Tom Morris had got in touch with an invite to a reading of a new musical he was developing.

Do you see *The Grinning Man* as a key British musical?

It feels like the quirky underdog! The show started at the Bristol Old Vic in 2016 and over that relatively short initial run we saw more and more audience members coming in costumes or makeup inspired by the characters. It became evident that the piece resonated with people and its unique macabre style brought out their creative side.

So Tom and the producers immediately starting looking for a further life for the show, giving it another opportunity to build on this rapidly developing fan base. So we transferred to London's Trafalgar Studios in 2017 and it also streamed online in 2020's lockdowns. Each time it gathered more momentum and following, which was such a special thing to witness for such an off-piste musical where the hero and heroine aren't the usual kind of 'golden' boy or girl. It definitely struck a chord with people.

And how would you describe your contribution to the show?

There were several puppets in the show, the main three being younger versions of protagonists Grinpayne and Dea, and Mojo, their family's wolf guardian. The Grinpayne and Dea puppets feature in a flashback re-enactment of their past, which itself was seen as a puppet show told within the show. Whereas Mojo was a 'real' wolf within the present day world of the story, but he too appeared in the flashbacks – complicated right?!

So the more the script evolved, the more important, distinct, these different storytelling aspects felt. We settled on a carved aesthetic for the child puppets, with visible joints similar to traditional marionettes – not naturalistic, but at the same time their dextrous movements meant you still invested in them like they're a living character. Then with Mojo the wolf, he had an aspect of the children's carved, fluid shape about him for when he appeared in their flashbacks – but further dexterity in that his hind quarters were the legs of his second puppeteer. This made him an exciting hybrid of puppet and performer and gave him an additional dimension of reality and muscularity.

How did you contribute to the development of the show?

From our time in *War Horse* Finn and I were familiar with the speed at which Tom likes to work, and his improvisational approach. So initially it was about anticipating and responding to what was happening in the room. Usually by making simple prototype puppets out of everyday materials: scrunching children or rats out of paper and making a cardboard wolf to ensure Mojo felt like a character in the space at all times. Working alongside Tom, you begin to road-test ideas for staging or characters – and it's interesting to see what sticks when working at speed, what sorts of ideas allow the audience to invest their emotions. Working as both puppet director and puppet designer in the same instance you realize how intertwined the two roles are in creating characters that are both articulate and integrated.

How would you describe the rehearsal or the production process of the show?

Finn and I started work on the project during initial development workshops in summer 2015, a year and a half before we opened in Bristol. Those first workshops were centred around the script and songs, with the design members of the creative team listening and brewing up ideas in our sketchbooks. I remember Jon Bausor, who designed the show, showing a pencil sketch of a wide open mouth and saying 'That's our stage!', which felt extremely liberating and an immediate feel for the boldness of the alternate fairytale world. Further workshops focused more on staging and puppetry allowing the convention of the puppet show within the show to be fleshed out and consolidated.

With any new musical, you really have to be meticulous about where the focus of the narrative is and who the audience is rooting for – allowing the songs to be the backbone of the experience. However with *The Grinning Man* you have a world of quite fantastical, funny, often bizarre characters. So those development workshops and first weeks of the rehearsal process were vital in honing the focus of the story onto Grinpayne and his quest to find out where he came from. With the other fantastical characters feeding that rather than being an enjoyable distraction or interlude.

The big difference between the show's initial Bristol run and the London revival was the tightening up of the plot's twists and turns and consolidating who learnt what information and when. As we ran the risk of the pace dropping when the audience had seen characters learn information about Grinpayne before he did – only for them then to have to witness this played out again when he learns it. So a more 'whodunnit' mystery approach was created where pieces of the puzzle were drip fed via different characters throughout the show for Grinpayne to finally tie together for the audience in the finale.

As this narrative refining was happening, both Finn and I were making the puppets carry more emotional weight within the story: both affecting the story and being affected by it. This was particularly the case for Mojo, who could very easily have been a peripheral animal sidekick so finding ways to see his place within the family and the protection and care he provides made him an emotional crutch as well as fierce defender. I'm still really taken aback by the audience's reactions to Mojo, especially given that he wasn't a central, singing character. Their emotional investment and enthusiasm for him was apparent in their very vocal reactions – and one fan even got him tattooed on their leg!

How do you feel about the show now?

It was such a mad dash to the finish line both times we made the show. As not only was it a new musical with actor musicians, but also featured intricate visual and physical staging – so rehearsal time was always going to be tight. But in the end the hard work was worth it, and we were all so overwhelmed by the impact it had on audiences. I'll never forget the huge crowd gathered around the stage door on the final night as the cast left the theatre – and unbeknownst to them I was bundling past with bags full of puppets! It was a very collaborative process between cast and creative team, and also very discovery led throughout its development time right through to opening night of the revival. We became a strange breed of theatre-making archaeologists, chipping away to discover something and piecing something together, right till the very end. Something I'm sure gave the show its dynamic, heartfelt pulse.

How has the experience shaped your future work?

In a number of ways: the idea of a puppeteer's body being integrated into the puppet's form is something both Finn and I have enjoyed using since. A production of *Animal Farm* I created puppetry for used the technique for its entire cast of pigs, goats and dogs – and Finn put it to great use on the menacing Hyena in *Life of Pi*.

A lot of *The Grinning Man*'s design process encouraged me to not overthink, but to be bold and gestural. For example, both Grinpayne and Dea had carved spirals surrounding their eyes to add a mystic quality to the puppets, but I didn't want them to look like twins. In the end Grinpayne's spirals curled upwards to emphasize his mouth and jawline, whereas Dea's went downwards emphasizing her cranium and heightened cerebral senses. This was the first time I'd been so conceptual in a human puppet design, but with a subtle, subliminal emphasis on their character.

Are you still working in musical theatre?

In summer 2022 I created the puppetry for a new musical adaptation of *101 Dalmatians* at Regent's Park Open Air Theatre. It's such a famous title due to the many film adaptations, so going back to the original novel and combining elements of that with what's held in everyone's collective consciousness was an exciting springboard for a more modernized retelling. Developing a concept and staging language for the dogs and how the puppets would sing/speak was such an exciting challenge, one that eventually became extremely inter-woven into the production's DNA that I hope we get another chance to keep playing with it.

I'm also working on a musical adaptation of a Roald Dahl book – which hasn't been announced yet. But it promises to feature a very vibrant mix of musical styles that will appeal to audiences of all ages, and an extremely playful concept of how we see the performers bring the animal cast to life. I've started to explore the presence and function of the puppeteers a lot more in recent productions – of how the performers who have permission to be 'invisible' can be an access point for the audience into the narrative and its characters.

What advice would you give aspiring Puppet Designers and Puppet Directors?

Something that constantly excites me about puppetry is that there isn't a 'rulebook', it all comes down to your individual tastes and what the show requires. With every show you're defining your own set of rules and aesthetic while the production's concept evolves. So I think exploring ideas as early as possible even in rough, 3D form allows everyone in the process to engage and explore the form and its role within the storytelling.

7 'Something precious you don't simply give away'

Intersections of love and queer expression in *Everybody's Talking About Jamie*

HANNAH THURAISINGAM ROBBINS

Although musical theatre has been stereotypically associated with being a refuge for queer audiences and creatives, there are few examples of hit musicals that represent the 'everydayness' of queer life. Similarly, there are almost no roles for queers of colour that are not coded as the racial other within the works that do exist.[1] My chapter interrogates *Everybody's Talking About Jamie* as a stepping-stone musical that provides relatable queer representation for multiple communities of audiences and creatives. In addition to providing an unapologetically queer main character, *Everybody's Talking About Jamie* presents stigmatization of queerness as a moral failing. 'Debates' about the social and legal rights of trans, non-binary, and gender-divergent individuals, which are currently dominating British media, are not given power. Instead, allyship and self-belief are edified.

Everybody's Talking About Jamie was written for performance at the Crucible Theatre in Sheffield. *Jamie* was developed following the release of a BBC documentary *Jamie: Drag Queen at 16* (2011) about a real-life teenager Jamie Campbell, aspiring to be a drag artist while living in Durham, UK. Tom MacRae and Dan Gillespie Sells transposed this inspiration to Sheffield and created a new musical about a sixteen-year-old boy (Jamie New) who wants to be a drag star and to wear a dress to his school prom. The musical received very positive reviews during its short run in Sheffield in 2017 and *Jamie* was chosen for a West End transfer to the Apollo Theatre, Shaftesbury Avenue and national tour before being interrupted by the Covid-19 shutdown in March 2020. Having recently reopened, the West End production 'paused' in late September 2021, but the interrupted tour recommenced its journey around the UK and the film adaptation was released on Amazon Prime. The first international production of *Jamie* opened in Seoul in the middle of 2020 with few changes from the West End revisions (e.g. Jamie is seventeen rather than sixteen) and a Japanese production opened in August 2021. Members of different UK casts were brought together for the landmark American premiere, held in Los Angeles in 2022.

As a story based on 'real life', *Everybody's Talking About Jamie* offers a refreshing antidote to the historical suppression of queer stories on musical theatre stages.[2] Between Jamie, his supportive mother Margaret, their best friends Ray and Pritti, and Jamie's mentor, a former drag star called Hugo, we are provided with a snapshot of queer exploration and belonging, supported by invested friends and family. Through the music and direction of the stage musical, we glimpse details of nightclub culture that are regularly associated with queer youth as well as ballads and narrative songs about belonging and love. The nostalgic clubby feel, which hints at aspects of 1980s, 1990s and 2000s queer scenes, is echoed in the opening of the 2021 film adaptation, which incorporates a nightclub sequence in the opening number 'And You Don't Even Know It' and in footage of queer scenes in Camden and Soho (London) during the new song 'This Was Me'. The musical uses the songs to extend the fantasies of glamour and spectacle and to explore some of the harsher emotions experienced by Jamie and Margaret as they tussle about his newfound confidence, his absent father, and their relationship as he grows.

The joy of writing about *Everybody's Talking About Jamie* is that the musical offers so much. In his short overview of the show in Whitfield's *Reclaiming the Musical*, James Lovelock highlights how '*Jamie* offers a twist on the traditional coming-out story'.[3] He explains that this musical allows Jamie, already out and comfortable in his gayness, to explore his future as a drag performer. I would add that it also imagines a world where a questioning teenager can explore his gender identity and be happy, without finding definitive answers that transphobia, queerphobia and heteronormativity often require. I hope that future research will offer extensive coverage of the musical including areas such as the score, the representation of Sheffield, the centrality of working-class identities, the place of drag culture and the depiction of single parenthood. My chapter is invested in the possibilities that *Jamie* offers to queer spectators (and actors) of colour through the characterization of Jamie's best friend Pritti and his mum's best friend, Ray. Unlike casting in many contemporary musicals, Ray and Pritti are roles written for Asian women that do not exploit their race as part of the plot.[4] *Jamie* allows two actors of colour the chance to play fun, empowered characters with their own musical contributions to the score. They are also Jamie's emotional support network aside from his mother, Margaret. My chapter considers how Jamie's exploration of his gender and drag persona is bolstered by these two femmes. I reconcile the power of their agency and support of him with the limitations of the script and film adaptation.

Absent queerness

Before exploring my reflections on Pritti and Ray's contributions to the supportive environment framed in *Everybody's Talking About Jamie*, I want to clarify the context of analysing two hetero-, cis-passing characters in an essay about queer kinship. I define a community as two or more people in sympathy with one another, which can include large-group or collective sharing. For example, the title song 'Everybody's Talking About Jamie' shows Jamie's classmates gossiping together. They take on individual characters, breaking free from the homogenizing backing vocals and choreography they have provided to songs in Act One. In this spirit, I consider community as groups or relationships where there is interactive experience, intention in common, and/or a sense of belonging within the world of *Everybody's Talking About Jamie*.

I offer this clarity because the notion of 'queer community' has become both ubiquitous and meaningless. When queer histories were first being documented in American academic environments during the 1970s, the notion of a queer community – 'a social group with shared experiences and institutions' – was almost speculative.[5] Large communities of queer people existed before 1970 but they [we] were (and continue to be) unacknowledged and hidden in mainstream popular culture. I want to acknowledge that *Jamie* continues this trend. We do not see a substantial 'queer community' made real on stage or screen[6] during the performance or film. Instead, the musical is set in a domestic and school environment where Jamie is persistently seeking validation as someone 'different' from the others. Meanwhile, the images of love and protest in 'This Was Me' (only in the film version) do not translate into a community of friends or activists in the 'real time' plot. The absence of queer friendship feeds into an exceptional narrative of isolated queer individuals. The *Little Britain* sketch series about 'the only gay in the village' is a prominent example of this characterization in British television. By contrast, *Jamie* does not poke fun at the realities of being the only visible LGBTQIA+ individual in the school and home environments Jamie inhabits, but his star narrative is predicated on transcending difference as well as self-actualizing his drag and gender exploration.

The lack of queer allies in the core text of *Everybody's Talking About Jamie* is exacerbated by the fleetingness of the scenes in the drag club Legs Eleven. Contributions by the three drag queens Laika Virgin, Tray Sophisticay and Sandra Bollock are minimal. Although the Queens support Jamie's emotional and drag development, they do not provide sufficient space for a drag culture or relationships to be meaningfully formed. Superficially, the queens show that Jamie is allowed entry into a space where he is understood. However, Legs Eleven is presented as an adult environment where teenagers are guests and therefore the support Jamie receives is less nurturing and more practical than in other contexts of the musical. At Legs Eleven, Jamie is not special. He is there to perform like everyone else. Hugo's song 'Over the Top', which speaks over Jamie's anxieties about performing to his school bullies, is supported by the queens. They are part of Jamie's transformation, but they are not fully formed or present people in the musical. In the film adaptation, the banter between the queens before Jamie enters is extensively cut so that we get less sense of their ambiance as a group and as potential friends of Jamie. We see them support Hugo as Jamie transforms into his drag persona, Mimi Me, for the first time *and,* unlike the stage version, which drops the curtain for Act One at Mimi Me's reveal, the film shows Jamie's performance with Hugo and the queens rooting for him while his mum Margaret, Ray and Pritti cheer from the audience.

We might interpret these few minutes as an indication of the community that Jamie will enter *in the future*. For isolated queers, we might also find heart and hope from even the smallest indication of belonging. However, Jamie's aesthetic, music and aspirations outside of the club are never aligned with the drag representation we see from the older queens. He is frightened, inexperienced and afraid of the choices he is making. He is also ignorant of queer history. (This is implied in the stage musical and made evident in the film.) Hugo and the queens transport him through these emotions and absences, while Hugo takes on a surrogate father role, chasing thugs who attack Jamie when he runs away from home. Yet Hugo is not seen in community with the other people in Jamie's life until the finale. He is distanced and separate. Like all the adults, Hugo encourages Jamie's self-expression and his joyful imagining of a different self, but he also embodies a different generational angle on Jamie's hopes. For me, there is a conversation to be had about a coming-of-age story that does not provide or signpost Jamie with any peers of his own age. Given that this is a fictional imagining, we must acknowledge that the glimpses of queer fellowship are entirely removed from Jamie's immediate circle of friends and family even if he is surrounded by allies.

Love and acceptance: Pritti Pasha in *Everybody's Talking About Jamie*

On stage, Jamie's largest tangible community is the class he spends lots of time in and with. In the West End production, the cast of school children undertake most of the set movement so that they feel present throughout the musical regardless of the 'location' of the scene. Each of the teenagers has a different personality and context so their classroom is full of energy and different points of view. In 'And You Don't Even Know It', the song featured in the first scene of the musical, they act as Jamie's backing dancers during a careers lesson. While we get a sense of ensemble in 'And You Don't Even Know It', the number is an establishing song for Jamie and his dream of becoming a drag queen. In 'Everybody's Talking About Jamie', we hear about Jamie's performance but the students singing are themselves in the spotlight with their own singing and dance styles given short feature moments. Dan Sells cleverly captures the idea of students yelling across classrooms, of playground chatter, and the escalation of gossip as different characters report what they saw at Legs Eleven. When Jamie enters after the song, he anticipates his own reception by his classmates, showing a shared understanding of the dynamics of the group. We also learn that regardless of any playful viciousness that takes place in the classroom, most of the students are totally comfortable with Jamie being openly gay and with his exploration of gender. In the final scene, Pritti has the last word in the conflict to allow Jamie to attend a dress to prom, but Bex, Becca, Cy, Fatimah, Sayid, Mickey and Levi all argue for his inclusion before Pritti calls for a boycott of an event which is exclusive.

Jamie's relationship with Pritti is situated in the context of being schoolmates: they hang out between classes, do homework together and counsel each other in their bedrooms. The trends we see in Jamie's relationships at school hold up a mirror to the wider topics of the musical. In fact, *Everybody's Talking About Jamie* handles its insights into homophobia, racism, bullying and other forms of harm gently without dismissing their impact. Meanwhile, Jamie's best friend Pritti reveals the complexity of representation in musicals that were written (if not always interpreted) with foregrounded whiteness. On a surface level, Pritti is defined by the characteristics she is given in the musical's stage directions: a 'slightly chubby Muslim girl, wears a headscarf, super-smart but very shy'.[7] It would be easy to write an extensive section on the numerous allusions to Pritti's difference in her dialogue that are established through this description. For example, the script repeatedly foregrounds her non-white and non-Western backgrounds, her ambitions to be a doctor and her disinterest in 'girly' – implied to be immodest – things like prom and make-up. This characterization is distinct from roles like Jamie and Dean who are not given similar racial or cultural signposts in character descriptions or dialogue. Pritti also has undeniable proximity to the 'model minority' – a term used to distinguish between 'good' and 'bad' migrants (and their families), who are judged by their assimilative, financial and productive contributions to the society they are a part of. This is made most clear in the final scene of the musical when the other students react most strongly to hearing Pritti swear rather than to Jamie's defiance of Miss Hedge when he arrives at prom in a dress.

The framing of Pritti and Jamie's relationship shows the challenges and subversions of developing intersectional friendships without sharing the characteristics of the characters you are writing. In the construction of people of colour, and especially of Black and Brown women in stage musicals, we frequently see such relationships drawn through contrasts with 'neutral' (read: heterosexual, cisgender and white) and/or 'normative' personalities. This intersects with the representation of queer coded characters in musicals. For example, Albin's effusive persona is contrasted with Georges' less flamboyant, 'straight-passing' manner, which is set against the ultra-conservative heteronormativity of Anne's parents in *La Cage Aux Folles* (1983). There's also a component of this in the fraught scenes between Marvin and Whizzer in *Falsettos* (1992). To some extent, this compare-and-contrast lens is apparent in *Everybody's Talking About Jamie*. Pritti is bookish and academic. Jamie seems to struggle at school. Pritti is modest and shy. Jamie is bold and outgoing. Her counterpoint amplifies Jamie's queer expression and yet, there is awareness that their marginalizations are not the same.

In characterizing Pritti, *Everybody's Talking About Jamie* avoids the overweight virgin-nerd stereotype as well as the model minority trope. Pritti recognizes Jamie's career aspirations as equal to her own (doctor and drag queen respectively). Through Pritti and because of Pritti, Jamie is repeatedly emboldened. When Jamie shows Pritti his shoes, she doesn't initially get Jamie's wish 'to be a boy. Who sometimes wants to be a girl'.[8] But, she accepts his choice and situates them both as outsiders together. In the film adaptation, Pritti and Jamie then discuss people thinking that they are 'weird' in the cafeteria scene that prefaces 'Spotlight'. The screenplay adds a sarcastic line from Jamie that his 'being a drag queen in Sheffield' is not exactly like her being a Muslim girl with a Hindu first name. There is a tension in this addition because Jamie seems to minimize what Pritti is explaining about her difference. But this line also refuses to conflate Pritti's religious and racial experiences with Jamie's gender exploration. Then, when school bully Dean attempts to provoke Jamie and racially abuses Pritti, Jamie dresses him down, humiliating Dean in the process. Having watched Jamie's confidence and command of the situation, Pritti helps Jamie redirect his lack of self-belief by harnessing her own sense of confidence and belief in him. In 'Spotlight', the finale of the scene, she empowers him to be seen and enjoy it. Crucially, the opening lyrics of the refrain 'Out of the darkness / Into the spotlight' introduced by Pritti during this song become the basis of Jamie's most empowered anthem 'Out Of the Darkness (A Place Where We Belong)' at the end of the musical. Pritti gives words to Jamie's forward trajectory.

Importantly, we see Pritti accept and enjoy Jamie's self-expression. In the lead-up to the song 'Work of Art', she protects Jamie by claiming ownership of his bad make-up attempt. Although her lie is unsuccessful and Miss Hedge forces Jamie to attend class and face the students' ridicule, we see the reciprocity of their relationship in action. Pritti also carries the most understated song in *Jamie*. When Jamie is told by Miss Hedge that he will spoil prom for the others if he attends in a dress, he is able to be vulnerable with Pritti and give voice to the fears Miss Hedge activates. Pritti then turns this energy around and encourages Jamie to work on what he wants and who he knows himself to be.[9] The gentle ballad 'It Means Beautiful' disrupts Jamie's fear that he is ugly and unworthy of love without Mimi Me. In a soothing and still moment, Pritti showers Jamie with love by describing all the things he is to her, using the hook that Jamil (a version of Jamie) means beautiful in Arabic. In the West End staging, Pritti sings in a low-lit bedroom set with a planet lamp casting stars moving slowly across the set. Here, Pritti is given her own glitter ball. Her disco is not on a stage but in her imagination and in the love that she is able to offer Jamie.

Throughout *Jamie*, Pritti uses her own polycultural contexts to love and empower her friend but without ever losing her sense of self. Where critiques of the 'best friend' character look for blandness and a lack of richness, Pritti is well rounded. As highlighted above, she could be presented as the 'opposite' to Jamie but actually, their love and mutual respect is founded on the fact that they help each other and build each other's confidence rather than because they are both different. We see this when Pritti protests the decision to ban Jamie from entering the prom. Despite being shown as apart from her schoolmates, Pritti is able to persuade them to stand outside and stay with Jamie before leading the chant that ultimately changes Miss Hedge's mind. Pritti is not submissive or meek when she feels the need to make a stand but nothing, not her prom outfit, not her love of Jamie, not her personal ambition, is ever shown at odds with who she knows herself to be. Looking at the abundance of stereotyping that Muslim women face in British media, *Jamie* attempts to balance the real cultural dissonances that a young woman like Pritti might feel without defining her choices and loyalty by them. As wider research is conducted into the musical, we will need own voice, diasporic interpretations of both Ray and Pritti, which I (as a mixed-race, Black heritage person) cannot provide. Nonetheless, as a racialized 'other', I salute Pritti and Jamie's friendship. It may have been forged through their difference to others at school but the relationship we see is not defined by otherness. Instead, it is about laughter, acceptance and seeing each other for who we are.

Love and advocacy: Ray as a queer aunty

In contrast to his age-matched friendship with Pritti, Jamie has a raucous, but familial, connection to Ray, his mother's best friend. Ray is Jamie's unfiltered and fearless champion who is unapologetically invested in his happiness. She is fierce, loyal, loud and straight-talking. Throughout the musical, she shows Margaret and Jamie the love they both need without encroaching on their relationship. She helps throw Jamie's birthday party, buys him lipstick to continue his transformation after he has his birthday heels, and is willing to tell Miss Hedge exactly what she thinks of her while Margaret is caught up in worry. When Jamie appears in his badly tailored reworking of Mimi Me's red dress, Ray interrupts Margaret's fearful concerns about Jamie being 'too bold',[10] by leading the song 'Limited Edition Prom Night Special'. In this duet, Ray empowers Jamie by investing in his idea that his appearance at prom is a fabulous once-in-a-lifetime performance. 'Limited Edition' is an unruly song moment with a funky undertone that brings a contemporary disco feel. She and Jamie strut around the stage, belting in call and response, as Ray sings affirmations about Jamie's look and his future success at prom. In 'Limited Edition', Jamie is seen in dialogue with someone who understands and appreciates him as he is *in that moment*. It is the only example in the musical where Jamie participates in joy and excitement about his evolving confidence.

While spotlighting Jamie, 'Limited Edition', Ray's scolding of Miss Hedge, her ability to tell Jamie off in one breath and show him compassion in the next all hint at a rich understanding of her place in Jamie's community. From my own intersectional vantage point, she reminds me of various aunties in the Caribbean communities I grew up in. In fact, Ray embodies a South Asian tradition that has different but parallel roles: she is, ostensibly, Jamie's 'aunty'. In a TedTalk titled 'How to Be an Auntie', drag artist LaWhore Vagistan describes this role as: 'Women of our parents' age, they are not part of the nuclear family but they feel very present in the home. She belongs there even if she's not related, and she shows up even when she's not invited.'[11] It is unclear from the text if Ray was written in these terms, but the actresses that have embodied her have made this connection clear. Ray has meaningful communion with Margaret, Jamie (and Pritti) on their own terms. Her opinionated presence speaks to anyone she is around. She is able to mother and gossip, to defend and castigate, and to dance and cry unapologetically. There is also a hidden depth here as Vagistan (and others working in Critical Aunty Studies)[12] explain how the role 'aunty' exists beyond the heteronormative in Black and Brown LGBTQIA+ communities. In Vagistan's talk, she explains how drag queens and older LGBTQI+ individuals have found homefulness in their (related and constructed) family units through inhabiting the role of an aunty. Vagistan highlights the power of gossip and how this can protect queer individuals, signalling who to trust and why. She also highlights that aunties reclaim space and time using food and dance as part of their expression with the people they love. And we see Ray inhabit all these things.

I believe that Ray offers an exciting possibility to locate (and even extend) the queerness in *Everybody's Talking About Jamie*. By interpreting *and casting* Ray as genderqueer or trans femme, queer representation in *Jamie* would automatically extend beyond the cisgender whiteness that underpins the popularity of 'Instagram make-up gays' like the make-up artists Jeffree Star and James Charles. This parallel between *Jamie* and these individuals is important because the poster art for the musical and the final look he wears for 'Out of the Darkness' is closely reminiscent of these artists' make-ups where notions of femininity are connected to patriarchal models of womanhood (perfection, not ageing, supplication, etc.).[13] Because Jamie's relationship with Ray is neither parental nor linear, she is able to embody much of what Jamie aspires to be without compromising their mutual love and trust. She is not developing her identity. She is settled in herself. While giving him often needed confidence boosts, she also offers him a gateway into make-up and glamour as well as physical and personal confidence. As make-up, beauty, and posture (and corruptions of these things) are frequently used as manifestations of resistance for many queer individuals, Ray offers a counterpoint to Hugo who is written as a cis white man with a drag persona. Where Pritti reminds Jamie that there is power in his selfhood, Ray equips him and reminds him of the tools of selfhood that he already has.

In this chapter, I argue that *Everybody's Talking About Jamie* wants us to impose ourselves in its representation as the creators have worked very clearly to create *people you know* rather than people you relate to. It is (regrettably) possible to interpret Ray in the context of a heterosocial family environment where gender queerness and transness do not exist. However, an insistence on cisgender and heterosexual presence feels like an imposition that undermines the spirit of the musical. If we understand Ray in the role of Jamie's queer aunty, we locate a figure of joy and power who has the potential to develop his community in new productions of *Jamie*. Through Ray, we might receive a more powerful dialogue about drag culture and gender queerness that is never fully explored in the musical as it currently stands. Ray *understands and enjoys* Jamie's queerness in all its fullness. There is textual potential to have her performed in new ways which honour the music and embody the fluid and imprecise ideas of gender that *Jamie* explores.

Limited edition, missed potential

Given the varied possibilities of interpreting these characters, it feels especially bittersweet that Ray has a smaller presence in the music and drama of the 2021 film adaptation. 'Limited Edition' is cut entirely and her presence in conversations is muted. Instead, this version of *Jamie* provides us with a different queer context. It reimagines Hugo's drag lament 'The Ballad of Loco Chanelle', which fictionalizes his fall from stardom, as a poignant retrospective on British queer life in Hugo's youth. The new song 'This Was Me' (mentioned previously) shows a younger Hugo as Loco with his lover, surrounded by friends in gay nightclubs. As the lover becomes increasingly sick after contracting what we assume to be HIV, we see LGBTQIA+ protestors resisting the Conservative government and the introduction of Section 28 that prohibited the promotion of queerness in the UK, while also holding company with each other. Through this song, more of queer British history is made visible. Meanwhile, Hugo's tougher attitude to Jamie ('so get out there and fight')[14] is given more context. *Jamie* reminds us that lots of queer people do not know or have access to queer histories. 'This Was Me' opens Jamie's eyes to a bigger struggle that is not so evident in his isolated context.

Because the film moves Jamie's moment of musical acceptance away from Ray who is invested in his boldness from the perspective of a worldly adult, the film actually flattens the queer representation to one based in struggle and pain as well as dancing.

It is also important to acknowledge that many of the racial imaginings of *Everybody's Talking About Jamie* are shaped by narrow understandings of identity. I have highlighted the potential flatness of Pritti in the published script. However, the limitations are made most real in productions where Jamie is played by Black, mixed-heritage actors but Margaret is always portrayed as white. Therefore, it is Jamie's dad, a queerphobic deserter (and possible abuser), who embodies Blackness in his family unit. Ignoring the well-worn stereotype of absent Black fathers, the spectres of colonial racism lie in this implicit rejection of queer acceptance by Black people. Meanwhile, Blackness is seldom represented in any other principal role in *Everybody's Talking About Jamie* on stage in the UK and the film strips back the majority of representation in the named speaking cast. These challenges are compounded by the politics of Margaret's ambition to protect *and save* Jamie from his father. Similarly, we have not yet seen 'non-white' representation in the role of Hugo who, as Jamie's guide into the Sheffield drag scene, might show Black, Brown, Asian or multi-ethnic queerness as central to drag performance. Unfortunately, this role is not only owned by white men, but it is also widely played by white men known to be heterosexual. In contrast to the friendship matrix where someone 'different' is paired with someone 'normal', racial diversity is only embodied in this musical where it is written into the character, carried by Jamie who is repeatedly othered and feels outside of his environment, or by his father which is both a minor and unsympathetic part. While Jamie's cheerleaders are allowed to be Brown women, his heroes and mentors are otherwise ubiquitously white.

Perhaps this context sharpens the impact of Ray and Pritti's different loves for Jamie. His relationship with Pritti resists many stereotypes and lacklustre interpretations of cultural difference, even though she is sometimes described and labelled in unhelpful ways. The direction of the stage musical and film performances allow Pritti to take on something more than a background character. As I note earlier, Pritti also gives Jamie the music and vocabulary for his final song 'Out of the Darkness (A Place Where We Belong)' when he feels accepted by his school community, has been allowed to the prom by Miss Hedge, and Margaret, Ray and Hugo have gone about their own business. The party sequence at the end of the film adaptation transitions from the school prom to a street party reminiscent of the corporate scenes we see of UK Pride, which are also steeped in whiteness with Black and Brown actors as peripheral characters and extras. Yet, when Jamie says, 'Drag ... isn't just a TV show, it's a revolution' to Pritti earlier in the film, she tells him to join and he says he isn't brave enough. The visions of Hugo's lost love, the AIDS epidemic and the Section 28 protest in 'This Was Me' catalyse Jamie's intention to be himself but once again, it is Pritti who is unafraid of the confrontation it implies. She encourages Jamie to honour the acts of our queer elders. As the film cuts down Ray's interactions with Jamie and removes 'Limited Edition Prom Night Special', it is a relief that the seeds of empowered resistance are still embodied by a Brown femme.

Ray's character sits closely in the parallels between desi aunties and drag culture, which Kareem Khubchandan suggests can be 'mined for queer potentials: lewd jokes, transgressive femininity, self-exhibition, seduction, and innovative intertextualities'.[15] Ray is a model for Jamie's Mimi Me in her smarts, sexual confidence and fearlessness. Where Hugo and the drag queens perform 'Over the Top' as a combative march to compel Jamie onto stage, Ray is Jamie's hype person in 'Limited Edition'. She's not interested in how anyone else (including Margaret) feels and uses her confidence to buoy him up. She is crude and brash and loud. She knows all of his business. Fierce and intimidating in the self-confidence she exudes, Ray cuts against Pritti, who is also comfortable in her quieter selfhood, and Margaret, who is racked with insecurities. Where we locate queer, drag and trans potential in Ray, we are able to imagine an evolution of this musical where gender expression is not sensationalized but is intimately personal. It is exciting to think of the disruptive possibilities of future productions of *Jamie*, which reflect the queer love and expression of the text in the casting across all the principal roles.

A place where we belong

In *Everybody's Talking About Jamie*, we learn that ongoing community, love, and friendship activate new sites of joy even while the naysayers want that truth to disappear. We love Jamie and Jamie's people because they are the given richness that many secondary roles in musicals are refused. For Black and Brown audience members, we are also able to see ourselves in many contexts – as Ray, as Pritti and as children in his class and sometimes as Jamie too. There's more work to be done on the intersections of race and queerness, but as this chapter highlights, the queer potential in Ray is very exciting for future productions. Similarly, we may see amendments to international productions that route queer expression more firmly in 'non-white' communities. In the author's note that prefaces the published script, MacRae writes: 'every school kid has their own name, their own personality, their own story – and that should be reflected at every point in the production. [. . .] They each have their own full internal lives.'[16] This sentiment is crucial to the success of the show that is simultaneously about our star and about how a star is made and cherished. Hugo and the other drag queens are not window dressing. Rather, they hint at aspects of the drag scene that are left unexplored in this show while informing Jamie's possible future after the timespan of the musical. The addition of 'This Was Me' to the film provides Jamie a glimpse of the thriving queer scene that resisted bigoted government policies and navigated the AIDS epidemic in 1980s London. Jamie's ability to be himself is, then, situated alongside a history of disruptive but joyful queer expression.

In an essay about love and queer expression, it is vital to highlight that *Everybody's Talking About Jamie* is not a utopic musical. While it presents a positive and affirming picture of self-discovery and acceptance, it does not pretend that anything is simple. Instead, *Jamie* names lots of different challenges in the lived experience of its characters without providing a 'topic survey' of what is happening to its audience. For example, we gather (in the stage version) that Jamie's father has mistreated Margaret. This context helps explain Margaret's fears and the mythology of paternal acceptance that she builds for Jamie but we do not explore alcoholism or possible domestic violence in the dialogue of the show. We know everything and nothing about the parental relationship, but it is enough for us to intuit and empathize with the characters as they move through the story. One of the benefits of this approach is that MacRae and Sells allow the story to have different resonances with the varied lived experiences of those that see the musical or watch the film. For some, this will be a contentious choice that allows those who do not see the layers in the musical to take only superficial things from it. Yet, there's not much that's superficial about *Jamie*. We see a boy, who knows who he is, overcome bullying, parental neglect, low expectations and bigotry to find a form of self-expression as Mimi Me that empowers him and most of the people around him. No character that acts in good faith is left behind and there is restrained growth for some of the characters who have made Jamie's journey harder. In the relationship between Margaret and Ray, we are allowed glimpses of adult love as well as familial relationships and teenage 'besties'. In many ways, this musical allows all of its characters to maintain networks of love and disruption that ring true to life. So frequently, we hear 'this could never happen in real life' from musical theatre sceptics. Instead, *Everybody's Talking About Jamie* walks a line of performance and fantasy with relationship structures that resonate with people of many intersections. For queer spectators, we see the elders who affirm us, the allies that cheer us on, the people who love us **because of and not despite**, our peers who accept us even if they don't understand, and the bullies, critics, haters and harm get a say too.

As I wrote this chapter, I felt drawn to my previous research on queer fandom and *The Wizard of Oz*.[17] I craved the testimonials from other people about queer safety in musicals, about friends who are true to themselves without limiting you, and the possibility of creating homefulness for ourselves. *Everybody's Talking About Jamie* carries these narratives forward, standing on the shoulders of previous musicals including *La Cage Aux Folles*, *Hedwig and the Angry Inch*, *Kinky Boots* and (to some extent) *Fun Home*. It shows us real queer people thriving **because of and not despite** of the people around them and it allows Black and Brown people to exist in these spaces. I have endeavoured to highlight where the musical's representation is limited and to avoid arguing that this musical has all the answers because it doesn't, and it shouldn't. We only make those demands of work about marginalization for the non-marginalized who seek completeness. Instead, *Everybody's Talking About Jamie* allows us to see and hear some of the layers of community that exist in queer life, and, in chapters like this, conceptualize even greater richness. The musical allows queer joy to get the first and last word, and it is committed to representing people of many backgrounds in this context. I hope that anyone who sees this show is able to locate the power and joy in the camaraderie *Everybody's Talking About Jamie* cherishes. It reminds those of us seldom seen on stage that there really is a place where we belong.

Notes

1. Angel and Collins from *RENT* (1996) might be considered exceptions to this.
2. *A Strange Loop* (2019) provides a more recent example a commercially successful and critically acclaimed musical that foregrounds Black queerness. It will be exciting to see a body of literature emerge on this show.
3. James Lovelock, '"What About Love?" Claiming and Reclaiming LGBTQ+ Spaces', in *Reframing the Musical: Race, Culture, and Identity,* ed. Sarah Whitfield (London: Red Globe Press, 2019), 204.
4. I have deliberately used 'femmes' to include all actors who are willing to play a feminine role. That may include non-binary femmes and gender fluid actors who do not identify as 'female' or 'woman' but are comfortable interpreting a role situated with feminine characteristics. This chapter will explore the possibilities of representation in Ray's character, which might hopefully extend the queer tapestry of this musical soon.
5. John D'Emilio, *In a New Century: Essays on Queer History, Politics, and Community Life* (Wisconsin: University of Wisconsin Press, 2014), 123.
6. In all the performances of *Everybody's Talking About Jamie* that I have attended there has been a visible queer presence including people wearing slogan T-shirts and carrying various LGBTQIA+ liberation flags. This chapter is not a piece of audience research, but it is important to acknowledge that there certainly are mixed queer communities spectating the show.
7. Tom MacRae, Dan Sells and Jonathan Butterell, *Everybody's Talking About Jamie*, Acting edn (New York: Samuel French, 2017), 8.
8. MacRae et al., *Everybody's Talking About Jamie*, 30.
9. There is a double edge to her encouragement of Jamie in this scene because she empowers him to go and see his father who, unbeknownst to both of them, is embarrassed and ashamed of Jamie, whom he intends to disown. However, the impact of 'It Means Beautiful' is based on her love for her friend. It is not an action song like 'Over the Top' that is specifically calling Jamie to do something.
10. MacRae et al., *Everybody's Talking About Jamie*, 92.
11. LaWhore Vagistan, 'How to be an Auntie', *YouTube,* 13 May 2020, accessed 4 March 2022, https://www.youtube.com/watch?v=Z9IYJIC_VWY, 15-0:22.
12. You can find additional information on emergent research in this area from the 'Critical Aunty Studies' symposium website (https://www.criticalauntystudies.com/) curated by Kareem Khubchandan (LaWhore Vagistan), author of 'Aunty Fever: A Queer Impression', in *Queer Dance: Meanings and Makings* (Oxford University Press, 2017), who is currently working on a

special issue of *Text and Performance Quarterly* on 'unruly aunty figures that appear in sitcoms, memes, theatre, literature, drag, politics, and our everyday lives.'
13. Shirley Xue Chen and Akane Kanai, 'Authenticity, Uniqueness, and Talent: Gay Male Beauty Influencers in Post-Queer, Postfeminist, Instagram Beauty Culture', *European Journal of Cultural Studies* 25, no. 1 (2022): 98–9.
14. MacRae et al., *Everybody's Talking About Jamie*, 77.
15. Kareem Khubchandan, *Ishtyle: Accenting Gay Indian Nightlife* (Ann Arbor: University of Michigan Press, 2020) xiv.
16. Khubchandan, *Ishtyle*, 6.
17. Hannah Robbins, '"Friends of Dorothy": Queerness In and Beyond the MGM Film', in *Adapting The Wizard of Oz: Musical Versions from Baum to MGM and Beyond*, ed. Danielle Birkett and Dominic McHugh (New York: Oxford University Press, 2018), 143–60.

Bibliography

Chen, Shirley Xue and Akane Kanai (2022), 'Authenticity, Uniqueness, and Talent: Gay Male Beauty Influencers in Post-Queer, Postfeminist, Instagram Beauty Culture', *European Journal of Cultural Studies*, 25 (1): 97–116.

D'Emilio, John (2014), *In a New Century: Essays on Queer History, Politics, and Community Life*. Wisconsin: University of Wisconsin Press.

Khubchandan, Kareem (2020a), *Ishtyle: Accenting Gay Indian Nightlife*. Ann Arbor: University of Michigan Press.

Lovelock, James (2019), '"What About Love?" Claiming and Reclaiming LGBTQ+ Spaces', in Sarah Whitfield (ed.), *Reframing the Musical: Race, Culture, and Identity*, 187–209. London: Red Globe Press.

MacRae, Tom, Dan Sells and Jonathan Butterell (2017), *Everybody's Talking About Jamie*, Acting edn. New York: Samuel French.

Robbins, Hannah (2018), '"Friends of Dorothy": Queerness in and Beyond the MGM Film', in Danielle Birkett and Dominic McHugh (eds), *Adapting The Wizard of Oz: Musical Versions from Baum to MGM and Beyond*, 143–60. New York: Oxford University Press.

Vagistan, LaWhore (2020), 'How to Be an Auntie', *YouTube*, https://www.youtube.com/watch?v=Z9IYJIC_VWY (accessed 13 May 2020).

Rob Hastie interview

Artistic Director Sheffield Theatres *Everybody's Talking About Jamie*

What is your favourite British musical?

Jesus Christ Superstar, *Evita*

What's your favourite British musical theatre song?

At Chichester I was in a production of *Nicholas Nickleby*. It's not quite a musical, but there's original music in it. The second play ends with a beautiful setting of 'God Rest Ye, Merry Gentlemen' because it's all at Christmas and the first play ends with a rousing patriotic chorus. It's the most alive I've ever felt on stage, belting that out in a chorus with seven other people.

What training did you do for your career?

There isn't any kind of formal training for an artistic director. I studied English at university, and trained as an actor at RADA. I think my years as an actor trained me to be a director. Once I started directing my friend, Josie Rourke, took me under their wing and helped me figure out the bits of directing that were not visible to an actor. I didn't know all the stuff about how to work with a creative team, the design process, relationships with producers, with writers, with designers, what the casting process looks like. At that point, Josie was about to take over the Donmar Warehouse. I went to work as an associate director at the Donmar. That was my training to run a building, to run an organization artistically.

Do you consider *Everybody's Talking About Jamie* to be a key British musical?

It's been enormously key for Sheffield theatres. The Crucible has developed a reputation for musical theatre, that was strengthened by Daniel Evans, but he was building on a long tradition of musical theatre at the Crucible.[1] Recently we've picked up a bit more speed in generating new musicals. And in that sense, *Jamie* has been a really important show for us. It opened our eyes to the power of the locally generated story. It's absolutely about Sheffield in Tom's book, and Dan's music, particularly in Jonathan Butterell's perspective on it (because he's a Sheffield lad himself) it became a real expression of 'Sheffieldness'.

There are the classic examples of expressions of Sheffield in popular culture, like *The Full Monty*. These are often about underdogs who exist against a backdrop of industrial decline and social deprivation – it's a grim up north kind of thing. *Jamie* doesn't ignore that, it still feels like it's coming from a real place but I think it sort of neatly side steps that.

How would you describe your contribution to *Jamie*? And how did your role work within the context of it?

Jonathan Butterell had seen this documentary *Jamie Drag Queen at 16* and gone after rights to adapt it into a musical. By the time I arrived, there had already been workshops. Musicals are expensive to develop. They represent quite an investment of resources, and they're hard to get right. Daniel Evans was moving on from Sheffield and programmed, with real bravery as an artistic director, as much of the stuff that he had in commission as possible. Daniel put both of those shows fully into production. *Flowers for Mrs Harris* was the last thing he directed in Sheffield. And then he left a few months of programming for the next person to take on, and the last production was *Everybody's Talking About Jamie*.

A chunk of my job as artistic director is about deciding what it is that we'll do. But another really important chunk is about supporting the people who then come to do it, and shepherding that work through, or supporting it. Acting as a sounding board, as a kind of quality control, as an emergency phone-a-friend – all of those things that artistic directors do all the time in making the work the best it can be for an audience. Knowing that this programme was set, I had to get up to speed and invest in them as if I'd chosen them myself so that the artists and the directors were fully supported by the organization.

The first thing I did was to go around to Dan's studio and listen to him and Tom play through the musical. It was terrifying because I was thinking 'oh God, if I hate this, this is gonna be awful!' Halfway through the opening I started crying, partly because it's just such an enjoyable jubilant statement and it really hit me in the right place at that time. But also out of sheer relief. The confidence of this is so evident, the joy of it is so sure-footed. I could feel what the effect on an audience was going to be because it's such a brilliant opening. And thereafter I was fully on board.

How would you describe the rehearsal/production process?

By the time I attended the first readthrough quite a lot of the show was already in place. Most of the leads had played those roles already in workshops, particularly John and Josie. So the performances they gave at the first readthrough felt really developed. Budgeting a big show like that for a regional theatre, it was very, very tight. It had to take form really quickly.

Jonathan's leadership of the project was so personal and it really had come from him, he took that project through to fruition with what looks from the outside like confidence and ease – I'm sure it was terrifying at points. They rewrote a little in rehearsal, but not a lot. They had the confidence that they would get another go at it. The work had no future mapped out for it. It was entirely what it was for two and half weeks in Sheffield. And it would have ended there if it hadn't been good.

How do you feel about *Jamie* now?

It was the most enormous gift. It takes any artistic director time to find their feet. Those of us who started in the last five or six years were only just getting into our stride when Covid came along and tested us in ways that none of us had signed up for. To be able to set out with the headwind of something that popular and successful was an enormous gift and I'll always be really grateful to everyone in the organization who set that in motion. It also gave me the confidence to programme adventurously. The model for regional theatres that had persisted, certainly in Sheffield, was one that tended to be classic plays with the most famous person you could get into it. But what's been really thrilling about the last few years is that all of our biggest hits – *Everybody's Talking About Jamie*, *The Life of Pi*, *Standing at the Sky's Edge* – have been big, ensemble-led, new pieces of work that require an audience to take a kind of leap of faith when they buy their ticket. And they've been rewarded by being in at the start of something that has then gone on to much greater things. So I suppose the success of *Everybody's Talking About Jamie* both artistically and commercially gave me huge courage to back hunches and go for new work.

How did *Jamie* shape your future work?

I'd answer that in relation to *Standing at The Sky's Edge* which we're bringing back. It's a slightly different prospect in that it's working with an existing body of work. But the power of telling a local story and knowing that in the local you find the universal, that's something that *Standing at The Sky's Edge* and *Everybody's Talking About Jamie* really share. It couldn't be anywhere other than Sheffield but the characters in it are accessible wherever you're from. I think it's about trusting the principle that if you make work for the audience you have, other audiences will accumulate around it.

As an artistic director, that's the great privilege of working somewhere like Sheffield. You build up an audience's trust. The knowledge that people will come and see something because it's you rather than because of the title. Granted, that's easier when you are the only show in town, of course. But audiences in the north of England, we're not the only show in town. From York, you can head for an hour and half's drive in any number of directions and see great work. So it's not a monopoly. Therefore that relationship is really precious to us, that people trust us to give them a good night out. And that's going to get harder. We need to recognize there are hard times around the corner. Hard times are here, right? So, if we are asking audiences to part with their hard earned cash we need to make sure we're delivering that great night out.

What advice would you give aspiring writers/directors/artistic directors?

The reason you fell in love with theatre in the first place will feed you for decades, if you nurture it right. I chose *Jesus Christ Superstar* as my favourite musical because I had the cast album when I was ten. Don't underestimate those things. If you're very very lucky, you might get to work on some of your heroes; the fact that I got to do *Guys and Dolls*, that I'm getting to do *Miss Saigon*, that's really important to me. But you must never be defined or trapped by that because the ten year old is waiting to listen to the cast album of the thing you're doing now to inspire them. That gives us enormous responsibility because who are you wanting to inspire and enable and empower through the work that you make?

Note

1. *Chicago* had its European premiere at the Crucible, and *Five Guys Named Mo* had an early production there.

8 'One of a kind, no category'

Coding race, gender and excess in *SIX*

AVIVA NEFF, PHD

In August 2017, six actresses stormed the stage of a small theatre at Edinburgh Fringe to sing, dance and speak justice for the lives of Catherine of Aragon, Anne Boleyn, Jane Seymour, Anna of Cleves, Katherine Howard and Catherine Parr. These six women are better remembered by history as the ill-fated wives of Henry VIII. *SIX* (2017), written and composed by Toby Marlow and Lucy Moss, follows the six queens through a fantasy pop-rock concert in which they compete for the position of lead singer of a fictional band by regaling each other and the audience with stories from their failed marriages, each ex-wife eager to prove that she had the demonstrably worse experience with Henry VIII. Since its debut, *SIX* has been hailed as a '"must see" show of outstanding quality', with particular praise lauded on its smart lyricism and inclusive casting opportunities, propelling Marlow and Moss's femme-forward work onto stages throughout Europe, Australia and New Zealand, and North America.[1]

Despite the overwhelmingly positive press *SIX* has received, there is a dearth of conversation surrounding the impact of ahistorical casting, racial coding and typecasting within this piece. Contemporary predilections for colour blind – rather than colour conscious – casting and writing gives rise to patterns such as those visible in *SIX*, as demonstrated by the troubling fact that in the primary cast, only one woman of colour has taken the stage in the role of Jane Seymour, the righteous, beautiful and tragic queen.[2] This is further complicated by a pattern of casting almost exclusively Black actors in the aggressive and physically 'ugly' role of Anna of Cleves, who, historically, was rejected by Henry VIII due to her appearance. Like its contemporary *Hamilton* (2015), *SIX* relies on a progressive, racially liberal casting model which, through its inclusivity-minded script, seemingly balks at predominantly white, cis-gendered casting traditions, and welcomes Black, Brown, and queer actors onstage, embodying figures who, historically speaking, were white, likely heterosexual, and cis-gendered. Marlow and Moss may have successfully created a performance piece that unites many ideals of progressive politics, but does it create lasting, meaningful opportunities for non-normative actors?

In order to better contextualize the sociopolitical sphere in which *SIX* was created, this chapter includes an overview of relevant cultural events that shaped the late 2010s and contributed to the urgency of Marlow and Moss's work. *SIX* embodies much of what benefits *and* plagues millennial politics – democratized popular culture, body positivity, #MeToo, the

Black Lives Matter movement and historical revisionism have become de rigueur throughout the entertainment industry, but to what extent does this 'feminist Tudor musical' achieve the lofty goals of gender equity outlined within its nine songs?

'A story that you think you've heard before': The origins of SIX

The origin of this smash hit is oft framed as a story of seemingly accidental ingenuity, portraying Toby Marlow and Lucy Moss's rise from fringe theatre to London's West End as the ultimate show business fairy tale. According to media narratives, Marlow was in his final year at Cambridge in 2016 when he was commissioned by the University Arts Society to craft a new musical that would premiere the following year at the Edinburgh Fringe Festival, the largest theatre festival in the world.[3] Marlow recalls the early phases of development: 'I was trying to concentrate while [my instructor] was droning on about Wordsworth, imagining the songs, the costumes – I couldn't wait to get out of there and tell Lucy about it.'[4] Throughout interviews and articles that chronicle the genesis of SIX, there is an interesting presentation of SIX as a viral hit, suggesting that part of the musical's charm is in its rough and ready grassroots origins. A 2020 New York Times article, 'The Making of "Six": How Tudor Queens Turned into Pop Stars', breaks down Marlow and Moss's story into six seemingly replicable steps. From 'Step 1: Find a Friend' to 'Step 6: Go Big', Marlow and Moss's upbringing in arts-centric homes and subsequent attendance of Cambridge University is presented without commentary, obliquely suggesting that the pair were run-of-the-mill university students who stumbled upon a hit, rather than two highly trained, capable creatives attending a well-connected university: 'This is where the story gets a little woo-woo. Marlow had been reading Antonia Fraser's "The Wives of Henry VIII." When he tracked down Moss, it turned out she had just left Fraser's house – she was friendly with the author's grandson.'[5]

Audiences and critics at Edinburgh Fringe received SIX warmly, and while the show did not win any awards, as Vogue notes, fans sold out performances and queued for tickets to see six actresses illuminated by 'three lights' and sporting 'boohoo.com dresses' present a feminist re-presentation of the women known merely as the wives of one of England's bloodiest monarchs.[6]

Given the critical and financial success of SIX, it would seem as if Marlow and Moss's artistic instincts were keenly attuned to their cultural moment, as SIX was invited back to Edinburgh Fringe the following summer (2018), thanks to the support of several West End producers and a bit of business advice from a friend of Marlow's family, George Stiles of Stiles & Drewe.[7] According to a 2020 Vogue feature,

> However rough and ready the production appeared, people recognized its innate quality; producers began to circle. Marlow rang his family friend the composer George Stiles, who has known Marlow since he was a child, thanks to his friendship with his father, Andy. Stiles advised Marlow to sign nothing and then went to see the show. 'I immediately thought, this is just glorious,' Stiles says. 'There was an entirely young audience, but it didn't make me feel old.' Things then began to move fast, as Stiles assembled a producing team. The show was redesigned, reorchestrated, and recast. 'It went from being this low-budget whatever to this big, shiny, glitzy thing,' says Moss.[8]

While media narratives frame Lucy Moss and Toby Marlow's work as an overnight, viral sensation, it is crucial to foreground the writers' industry connections in order to understand the full dimensions of its popularity. This is not to detract from the quality of work presented by the company, but to question the so-called 'shiny, loud, subversive' musical supported by industry veterans and financed by one of the oldest universities in the English speaking world.[9]

The same year, *SIX* returned to Cambridge for a showing, but this time, thanks to George Stiles' advocacy, noted producer Kenny Wax was in the audience with his daughter.[10] Wax and Stiles quickly partnered with Wendy and Andy Barnes to produce *SIX*, resulting in a transfer to the Arts Theatre, thus marking Marlow and Moss's professional debut.[11] Sadly, as often happens when performances move into the professional realm, the original amateur cast was replaced by professional actors, a communication that Marlow and Moss claim to have handled 'poorly'.[12] *SIX* received a total of five Laurence Olivier Award nominations in 2019, including Best New Musical and Outstanding Achievement in Music, demonstrating its mass appeal to both audiences and critics.[13] In January 2019, *SIX* opened for a sixteen-week West End run, while the Chicago Shakespeare Theatre busily prepared to host the premier of *SIX* on North American shores.[14] Unfortunately, like thousands of companies across the globe, *SIX*'s performances were cut short by the emergence of the Covid-19 pandemic in the United States, the United Kingdom, and Australia and New Zealand.[15]

'Sorry, not sorry': *SIX* as a reflection of millennial politics

The cultural landscape in which *SIX* was conceived helped establish a strong foundation for a musical that captures the triumph and turmoil of the late 2010s – a decade that saw the end of Obama-era optimism in the United States and Britain's formal exit from the EU. *SIX* begins with 'Ex-Wives', an electro-pop opener which draws undeniable inspiration from *Chicago's* 'Cell Block Tango' (1975). Audiences of *SIX* are greeted by actors with dark skin, androgynous figures, natural hair and curvy waists, whose sexuality is displayed rather than hidden behind frumpy costumes. The six playfully dressed actors chant, 'Divorced. Beheaded. Died. Divorced. Beheaded. Survived', as lights gild their punked-out hair and studded corsets while they vie for the spot of frontwoman in a fictional rock band. Reminiscent of popular television shows such as *The X Factor* or *Making the Band*, *SIX* initially positions the women as competitors both in their vocal talent and in their intimate tragedy, pitting murder and maternal death against one another.

Each ex-wife introduces herself in turn, while in the midst of the song, a synth teases the melody of 'Greensleeves' and the actresses vow to 'do themselves justice'.[16] Marlow and Moss's chosen title, *SIX*, may suggest individualism, but their contemporary feminist reframing of the wives pushes the narrative towards unity, ultimately landing in a closing number which presents an historically revised conclusion for the six women. Herein lies the revisionist happily-ever-after; it is not their connection to Henry which grants common ground, but their voices in unison that heals their collective trauma. Lyrically, Marlow and Moss hinted at this conclusion in the opener 'Ex-Wives', which features the actors counting up from one to six, while 'Six', the finale, reverses their count from six to one – effectively marking the six queens as 'one of a kind'.[17] It is a stunning revelation, given the musical's debut amidst the popular height of the #MeToo movement in 2017, eleven years after the founder of #MeToo Tarana Burke, introduced the phrase and hashtag into the digital sphere.[18] The year 2017 saw mainstream celebrities such as Alyssa Milano co-opt the phrase and join the numerous accusations of sexual abuse against now-disgraced entertainment titan Harvey Weinstein, encouraging a shift in how survivors of abuse are treated both privately and by the media.[19] In many ways, *SIX* mirrors the tidal wave of support that was needed to expose abusers such as Weinstein and Broadway's Scott Rudin, for it was not the voice of one, but those of many in unison, that brought accountability to the entertainment industry. Although the majority of the women featured in *SIX* did not outlive their tyrannical husband, nor bring him to justice for murder, the musical rests a great deal of hope on Henry's final wife, Catherine Parr, who is repeatedly called 'the survivor'.

In 2020, in response to global devastation of the Covid-19 pandemic, Athena Collins, Danielle Steers, Maiya Quansah-Breed, Amelia Walker and Vidya Makan, who all played Catherine Parr in various stagings of *SIX*, virtually united to perform a cover of Destiny's Child's 'Survivor', which is audibly referenced by Marlow and Moss during Parr's solo in 'Ex-Wives'. While the actors may have recorded their '5 Parrt' cover as purely a pop-culture treat for fans, it is worth noting the connection between the significance of the word 'survivor' in a post-#MeToo entertainment industry and an historical woman who survived a violent, murderous husband.[20] Despite this serendipitous parallel, one of the striking commonalities about the collection of songstresses who have graced the stage as Catherine Parr is their stark physical difference in skin colour, hair texture and body shape. Marlow and Moss's 'survivor' is presented as an Everywoman, one who binds her fellow ex-wives and brings them to their penultimate realization: 'we don't need your love.'[21]

SIX cleverly toes the line between politics and mass media, staging the contemporary mainstream gender equity movement that scholars such as Dr Naila Keleta-Mae have deemed 'Beyoncé feminism'.[22] This popular, aesthetically driven brand of feminism espouses empowerment, intersectionality, sexual freedom and financial independence while (arguably willingly) ascribing to patriarchal tenants of society such as capitalism and the male gaze.[23] Keleta-Mae explains,

> At worst, Beyoncé's feminism is vacuous rhetoric wielded to monetize feminism and affix it to the Beyoncé brand. At best, her feminism is an extension of her astutely managed and highly successful career that was built, in part, by her ability to perch perfectly on the fence when it comes to her political views [. . .] a woman who rehearses and subverts capitalist patriarchy while she performs messages of female empowerment.[24]

In many ways, *SIX* engages with feminism-as-capital branding by boiling the Tudor-era topography of religion, nationality, and gender rights into anthemic messages that scratch our itch for historical revisionism-as-restorative justice. In a 2019 interview with the Sydney Opera House, Moss explained: 'So, while we did a little research, our main concern was making a statement about women's experiences in the present day, rather than delving too deeply into the dry facts and figures.'[25] It is not the responsibility of musical theatre to present a holistic and historically accurate representation of the past, nor can one performance end inequity in the arts, yet, *SIX* aspires to present the 'historemix', one that encourages audiences to dream of a shining throne room resplendent in the wonders of sex-positive queens who sing, dance and, most urgently, survive.

SIX emerged as a breakout hit among critical global social movements on gender and body equity, but it is perhaps most legibly affected by the Black Lives Matter movement, a digital and embodied resistance which was founded in the United States by Patrisse Cullors, Opal Tometi and Alicia Garza in 2013.[26] Created to protest the unlawful slaying of Black Americans, Black Lives Matter has grown to encompass advocacy for greater and better quality representation of Black life across entertainment media, including film, television and theatre.[27] Following the emergence of Black Lives Matter, social justice protests seized on the democratized opportunities offered by the digital sphere, using hashtags and memes to combat anti-Blackness in popular culture. In 2015, one year before Marlow was commissioned to create SIX, the Twitter movement #OscarsSoWhite was begun by April Reign, who noted that all twenty nominees for acting categories of the Oscars were white.[28] Encouraged by the wide response to calls for better representation in entertainment, studies, petitions and organizations were formed to track and analyse what diversity looked like in practice in US and UK theatre in the late 2010s. At a glance, SIX embodies much of what was campaigned for by organizers – prominent roles for actors of colour, imagining restorative justice for Black women and portrayals of Black speech and popular music as not only legitimate but also *crucial* to retellings of history.

Following the murder of George Floyd in 2020 and the fiery protests that swept the globe, the creative team behind SIX were eager to offer a message of solidarity, which was posted to their official Instagram:

> SIX is a show that has been seen to champion diversity and empower Black female-identifying voices, and we are so proud to have this position in the theatre community. We are also a show that is largely created and produced by white people – and like so many shows, SIX benefits from the talent and work of our Black cast members and colleagues everyday. It is therefore our duty to stand up for and support Black people always – and not just when it's trending – to be silent is to be complicit.[29]

Through this caption, the marketing team behind SIX acknowledge much of what troubles the dimensionality of 'representation' in Marlow and Moss's work – a predominantly white hierarchy that benefits from the work and creative talent of people of colour, especially Black women. Beneath its visible representation, SIX relies on the labour of women of colour to its core – as evidenced by the pop-diva 'queenspirations' Marlow and Moss rooted their work in.

'I ain't sayin' I'm a gold digger': Race-coding in SIX

According to Asian American Performers Action Coalition (AAPAC), a staggering 74 per cent of 2014–15 Broadway musical roles were awarded to white actors, despite nearly 80 per cent of those roles being eligible for 'non-traditional', sometimes conflated with 'colour-blind' casting.[30] Similarly, in 2016, the Andrew Lloyd Webber Foundation declared that UK theatre was experiencing a 'diversity crisis' and must make urgent change to save it from maintaining 'hideously white' casting and production practices.[31] Debuting two years after Lin-Manuel Miranda's *Hamilton*, SIX joined Miranda's work as a decidedly contemporary musical, not just for its style and content, but for its coronation as the latest mega-hit performance to demand that Broadway and the West End honour so-called 'colour blind casting'. In '"Bonding over Phobia": Restaging a Revolution at the Expense of Black Revolt', author Wind Dell Woods asks, 'When much of the discourse demonstrates an awareness of not only race, but the ways racially marked bodies shape the musical, what accounts for the persistent use of the phrase "colourblind casting?"'[32] Woods points to the erroneous assumption that ignoring the presence of race and raced individuals is a shortcut to eliminating racism. This practice has been called out by many as a harmful erasure of cultural heritage and representation, and a willing denial of the way race and ethnicity interact with metaphor, character and story in theatre. There are several schools of thought among artists, scholars and practitioners regarding the best way to ease the scarcity of roles for global majority actors, yet, the most popular approach, 'colour blind' casting, is fraught with cultural competency pitfalls. Reflecting on *Hamilton*'s similar revisionist casting, Woods writes, 'there must *also* be a deeper interrogation, not merely of what the play does *with* the past, but what it does *for* the present.'[33]

In 'From Color Blind to Color Conscious', author Robin Prichard defines 'colour blind' as 'a widely held belief that race is no longer a factor in a person's opportunities or well-being, nor in institutional policies and practices; it also encompasses the belief that ignoring race will lead to better outcomes than acknowledging it'.[34] Prichard's article, which addresses race in dance education, suggests that ignoring the presence of race in institutional and artistic settings creates problematic dynamics throughout the creative process, from development and casting to critique and performance reviews. Alternatively, Prichard offers 'colour consciousness' as a means to creating a more equitable artistic space: 'Color-consciousness acknowledges the different experiences of multiple ethnicities and races, including institutional discrimination and privilege.'[35]

However one chooses to engage with race during the creative process, it is vital to acknowledge that audiences will inscribe race and cultural markers onto a performance, often resulting in what is known as 'coding'. Within the sociopolitical sphere, race, gender, sexuality, ability and economic class are often culturally demarcated through 'coded' language, resulting in social issues becoming aligned with one or more minority groups rather than acknowledging the intersectionality of need and oppression. The National Education Association (US) defines 'coded language' as 'substituting terms describing racial identity with seemingly race-neutral terms that disguise explicit and/or implicit racial animus'.[36] Understood in the context of the performing arts and entertainment, 'coding' can take shape as certain costume choices, linguistic patterns and genres of music becoming aligned with race, gender, ability and sexuality. Despite a history of race and, in some cases, gender-blind casting within *SIX*, the wives are not immune to the pressures of coding, which stems largely from composition choices and casting histories. Of the six queens featured in this musical, each has an assigned character archetype informed by the pop-star Marlow and Moss drew 'queenspiration' from: Catherine of Aragon: Beyoncé, Ann Boleyn: Lilly Allen, Jane Seymour: Adele, Anna of Cleves: Nicki Minaj, Katherine Howard: Ariana Grande, and Catherine Parr: Alicia Keyes.[37] The alignment of each queenspiration with the six characters creates rich and exciting performance opportunities, but when viewed through a colour-blind (rather than colour-conscious) artistic model, the race of the actor, music composition and genre influence within their solos, and archetype of the character contributes to the typecasting unfortunately legible throughout *SIX*'s production histories.

Marlow and Moss made clever and intentional use of popular culture, music genre, costume design, casting and character archetype to create dimensional personalities for the six wives of Henry VIII, successfully subverting their reduction to 'one word in a stupid rhyme'.[38,39] One of their most effective characterizations is that of Jane Seymour, the only woman to bear Henry a legitimate son and the only wife who received a proper queen's funeral in Windsor Castle.[40] In the musical, Seymour delivers the Adele-inspired power ballad 'Heart of Stone', in which she admits her love for Henry, despite his treatment of his former wives, and acknowledges her suspicion of Henry's motives: 'But I know, without my son your love could disappear.'[41] 'Heart of Stone' delivers a complex message to audiences who eagerly await the next quip about Henry's love-life, instead weaving a tale of desperate, ill-fated love and Seymour's reluctant acceptance of her own mortality ('Soon I'll have to go, I'll never see him grow, but I hope my son will know he'll never be alone'[42]). Historically, Seymour has been described as 'silent, subservient and sweet-tempered', a descriptor that Marlow and Moss translated into the stock character of the ingénue, recognized in literature and performance as an innocent and good-natured young woman.[43] By characterizing Seymour as the ingénue, her tragic ballad and admission of genuine love for Henry reads as naïve, pure and tragic, rather than confusing the established narrative of restorative justice for the six women. In *SIX*, Seymour becomes 'the only one he truly loved', positioning her as what her five compatriots aspire to – undeserving of her fate, unblemished by promiscuity and ambition, and, above all, loved.[44]

In the astronomically successful three years between the debut of *SIX* and its arrival on Broadway, more than five casts of ex-wives have graced stages from Edinburgh to North America; however, none of them featured an actor of colour in the role of Jane Seymour. It is worth noting that a Black British actress, Carly Mercedes Dyer, was intended to assume the role in the 2020–1 UK tour, but due to the Covid-19 pandemic, her debut was cancelled indefinitely.[45] Despite the intention to bring a Black actor into the role, the legacy of Seymour as a blonde, able bodied, cis-gendered white woman haunts ideations of her in the minds of fans and publicity images alike. In *The Haunted Stage: The Theatre as Memory Machine* (2001), Marvin Carlson describes the phenomenon of artistic pasts 'haunting' actors, spaces, productions and characters. Put simply, Carlson posits that iconic or controversial performances may eclipse future representations, creating 'ghosts' that occupy the minds of audiences and artists alike. Carson states,

> Very often the actor; who creates a particular role in a popular success or in a major revival that overshadows the original production will create so strong a bond between himself and that role that for a generation or more all productions are haunted by the memory of that interpretation, and all actors performing the role must contend with the cultural ghost of the great originator.[46]

By engaging with 'non-traditional' casting in five out of six roles, *SIX* effectively creates a reputation as a performance of opportunity, one that allows any body to become queenly, yet it does not fold piety and sympathy into non-normativity onstage. *SIX* runs the risk of haunting the role of Seymour with the ghost of a thin, cis-gendered white woman, while allowing audiences to read promiscuity and anger in the faces of non-binary actors and actors of colour. Further, the casting history of characters such as Anna of Cleves, and her pop-diva 'queenspiration', descriptions from the script and compositional allusions reveal a reliance on racial stereotypes to craft characters that fail to break barriers and ultimately reinforce traditional, discriminatory casting decisions. In '"Why the Green Girl Is Never Black?": Racism in Casting', Shannon Gaffney illuminates a similarly troubling casting history in the 2003 hit musical *Wicked*: 'We welcome black people into the arts community when they exist to educate white people about systemic racism – but we slam the door in their face when they ask to belt "Defying Gravity" or be a princess.'[47] Gaffney's statement is urgently relevant to my reading of *SIX* in that it articulates the perceived function of actors of colour as activists and educators first, and artists second. Actors of colour can play the harlot and the mean girl, but never the ingénue. Within Marlow and Moss's world, a Black, Brown or non-binary actor playing Aragon, Boleyn, Cleves, Howard or Parr must convince the audience and each other of their brutal mistreatment, while Seymour's grand tragedy is that she died before she could enjoy happiness with Henry. *SIX* has done a commendable job in welcoming diversity to its casting, but many productions have fallen short of colour consciousness, instead allowing the role of the ingénue to once again become typecast, or ghosted, as an able-bodied, thin, white woman.

In '"Must be Heavyset": Casting Women, Fat Stigma, and Broadway Bodies', Ryan Donovan writes, 'Musicals celebrate performative excess while disciplining other kinds of excess: differences of ability, gender, race, size, and sexuality.'[48] The Tudor-inspired 'excess' of *SIX* is legible in its period-influenced costume silhouettes, clever nods to historical instrumentation and composition, and characters, but contemporary 'excess' is the currency by which Marlow and Moss secured their creation's legacy. By weaving contemporary language, including British slang and African American Vernacular English (AAVE), Marlow and Moss intentionally demarcated the performance with race and class, coding characters such as Anna of Cleves with a decidedly anachronistic – and racialized – identity.

In 'Get Down', Anna of Cleves's sarcastic send-off to her marriage with Henry, Cleves's 'queenspirations', Rihanna and Nicki Minaj, are particularly legible in both the genre of the song and its lyrics. Beginning with a heavy bass thrum and snapping fingers, Cleves's drawl is laden with references to her wealth and independence, a frequent theme within hip-hop. Here, Cleves is imbued not only with the style of hip-hop, but with the unfortunate stereotypes that often plague Black women, such as aggression, oversexualization and the financial manipulation of men. Notably, Cleves uses several linguistic turns which could be credited to various global accents, but placed in the context of her queenspiration, the genre of 'Get Down' and the casting history of Cleves, I interpret these stylistic choices as coding Cleves as Black American. Lines such as 'Fill my goblet up to the brim, sippin' on mead, And I spill it on my dress with the gold lace trim', and 'I'm not fake 'cause I've got acres and acres, Paid for with my own riches, Where my hounds at? Release the bitches' are more reminiscent of Beyoncé and Nicki Minaj's 2014 collaboration 'Flawless (Remix)' than the polyphonic chorales of Cleves's time. Further, several key lyrics serve as signals to Anna of Cleves's racial coding; 'get down', which offers a pun – both asserting Cleves's class status as she commands underlings to submit, and the more popular use of the phrase, which is rooted in Black and African diasporic tradition, meaning a party or dance gathering.[49] Most notable is Cleves's allusion to Beyoncé's lead single from her album *Lemonade* (2016), 'Formation': 'Dance so hard that I'm causin' a sensation, Okay ladies, let's get in reformation'.[50] Like *SIX*, *Lemonade* is a testament to surviving the pain of a broken marriage and the immense labour required to repair oneself after heartbreak. Despite this thematic similarity, race is critical to *Lemonade* in ways that *SIX*'s history of colour-blind casting and racially ambiguous aesthetics rejects. Since its release, 'Formation' has become a rallying cry for fans of all gender identity and races, yet 'Formation' has an unassailable identity as a unifying anthem for Southern Black American women, a facet that is diminished by its sprinkling in 'Get Down'.

Anna of Cleves's characterization relies on more than hip-hop stylings to communicate her roguish independence. Of the various performers cast as Cleves, most have been actors of colour, and in prominent performances, such as the original Arts Theatre production, were Black.[51] Interestingly, the original Anna of Cleves was played by Tilda Wickham, a white non-binary actor, which challenges the historical narrative of Cleves's dissatisfactory appearance (according to Henry) and invites contemporary audiences to consider what exactly makes Marlow and Moss's ideation of Cleves the 'Flander's Mare'.[52] Historian Debbie Kilroy writes, 'Although lacking social skills, she was considered "a ladie of right commendable regards, courteous, gentle, a good housekeeper and verie bountifull to hir servants". It is possible – or even probable – that her "faults" were exaggerated by the whimsical King, who was already lusting after another.'[53] Assuming that many audiences of *SIX*, particularly those outside of the UK, have little knowledge of Cleves's history, Marlow and Moss present Cleves as a probable 'catfish', or someone who deceives a potential partner by providing them with photos that falsify their appearance.

In 'Ex-Wives' Cleves introduces herself: 'When he saw my portrait he was like – "Jaa" – but I didn't look as good as I did in my pic.'[54] Here, *SIX* engages with the politics of attractiveness, which are underscored by the presence of a non-binary or dark-skinned actor of colour, two marginalized groups who have long been considered 'different excesses' by musical theatre. The casting of Cleves is particularly important, for her framing of un/attractive can complicate contemporary notions of beauty or accidentally reinforce them, depending on the direction. However, it is critical to note that this flaw cannot be solved by casting choices alone; one hopes that a future acknowledgement from Marlow and Moss may encourage other hopeful librettists to consider how coding can impact the reception and legacy of their work.

'Free to take our crowning glory': *SIX* resumes performances on the global stage

In a 2021 interview about the return to live performance after Covid-19, Marlow and Moss stated, 'theatre is at a crossroads between accessibility and elitism.'[55] *SIX* is well positioned to lead the way towards accessible theatre, both in regard to representation on stage and in proving that an investment in young artists like Marlow and Moss can result in theatre that holistically captures the sociopolitical moment in which it's made. *SIX* succeeds in creating positive roles for actors of various identities, but reinforces stereotypes surrounding typecasting, which reveals a need for greater representation of diverse voices during the development of a performance and, equally important, during casting. *SIX* challenges notions of historical redemption, gender representation and the porousness of the archive, but future productions of this work must reconsider how casting can support the strong foundations laid by Marlow and Moss.

Recently, the 2022 cast for the Vaudeville Theatre in London's West End announced that Claudia Kariuki, a Black British actress, would assume the role of Jane Seymour, marking the debut of a Black actor in this role. Viewed holistically, *SIX* represents a curious time capsule of popular politics, from the mainstreaming of 'Beyoncé feminism', the rise of social media protest movements such as Black Lives Matter and #MeToo and calls for equitable diverse representation in theatre and film. Toby Marlow and Lucy Moss's work at times engages with anti-Black stereotypes that deserve deeper interrogation by critics and audiences in order to fully move away from the pitfalls of colour-blind writing and casting. *SIX* demonstrates that 'excess', especially that of race and gender, deserves robust exploration within musical theatre, in order to become 'one of a kind, no category'.[56]

Notes

1. Tim Wilcock, 'Six', *Edinburgh Fringe 2017*, 25 August 2017, http://fringereview.co.uk/review/edinburgh-fringe/2017/six/.
2. 'Carly Mercedes Dyer', *Six! The Musical*, https://www.sixthemusical.com/uk-tour/company/carly-mercedes-dyer.
3. Michael Paulson, 'The Making of "Six": How Tudor Queens Turned into Pop Stars', *The New York Times*, 27 February 2020, https://www.nytimes.com/2020/02/27/theater/six-broadway.html.
4. Karen David, 'We Wrote a Musical During Our Finals . . . Now it's on in the West End', *The JC*, 9 June 2018, https://www.thejc.com/culture/theatre/six-the-musical-steps-from-fringe-to-the-west-end-1.469323.
5. Paulson, 'The Making of "Six"'.
6. Sarah Crompton, 'With SIX, Playwrights Lucy Moss and Toby Marlow Dramatize the Tudor Dynasty—One Power Ballad at a Time', *Vogue*, 16 January 2020, https://www.vogue.com/article/six-playwrights-lucy-moss-toby-marlow.
7. Crompton, 'With SIX, Playwrights Lucy Moss'.
8. Crompton, 'With SIX, Playwrights Lucy Moss'.
9. Harriet Cunningham, 'Shiny, Loud, Subversive: Six is the Must-see Show of the Summer', *The Sydney Morning Herald*, 12 January 2020, https://www.smh.com.au/culture/musicals/shiny-loud-subversive-six-is-the-must-see-show-of-the-summer-20200112-p53qr4.html.
10. Paulson, 'The Making of "Six"'.
11. David, 'We Wrote a Musical During Our Finals . . . Now it's on in the West End'.
12. Paulson, 'The Making of "Six"'.
13. 'Olivier Awards 2019: Full Winners List', *The Hollywood Reporter*, 7 April 2019, https://www.hollywoodreporter.com/lists/olivier-awards-2019-full-winners-list-1193956/.
14. Toby Marlow and Lucy Moss, 'Ex-Wives', in *Six!*, Concord Theatricals, 2016.
15. Marlow and Moss, 'Ex-Wives'.
16. Marlow and Moss, 'Ex-Wives'.
17. Marlow and Moss, 'Ex-Wives'.
18. Hedy Weiss, 'In Knockout Musical "Six", King Henry VIII's Wives Have Their #MeToo Moment', *WTTW*, 23 April 2019, https://news.wttw.com/2019/05/23/six-chicago-shakespeare-theater-review.
19. Weiss, 'In Knockout Musical "Six", King Henry VIII's Wives Have Their #MeToo Moment'.

20. '"Six" the Musical Catherine Parrs perform Survivor by Destiny's Child', *Official London Theatre*, 11 March 2020, https://www.youtube.com/watch?v=2K-0cljD9KE.
21. Toby Marlow and Lucy Moss, 'I Don't Need Your Love,' in *Six!,* Concord Theatricals, 2016.
22. 'Transforming the Tudors: An Interview with SIX Co-creator Lucy Moss', *Sydney Opera House*, 8 September 2019, https://www.sydneyoperahouse.com/backstage/theatre/transforming-the-tudors-six-lucy-moss.html.
23. Naila Keleta-Mae, 'A Beyoncé Feminist', *Atlantis* 38, no. 1 (2017), https://core.ac.uk/download/pdf/322498145.pdf.
24. Keleta-Mae, 'A Beyoncé Feminist'.
25. Keleta-Mae, 'A Beyoncé Feminist'.
26. 'Black Lives Matter: Demands', http://blacklivesmatter.com/.
27. 'Black Lives Matter: Demands'.
28. Reggie Ugwu, 'The Hashtag that Changed the Oscars: an Oral History of #OscarsSoWhite', *The New York Times*, 2 June 2020, https://www.nytimes.com/2020/02/06/movies/oscarssowhite-history.html.
29. Juliana Vaccaro, 'Broadway Musicals Support Black Lives Matter During Shutdown', *Glitter*, 6 March 2020, https://glittermagazine.co/2020/06/03/broadway-musicals-support-blacklives-matter-during-shutdown/.
30. 'AAPAC Report Reveals Larger Pattern of Inequities in NY Theatre', *American Theatre Magazine*, 10 January 2020, https://www.americantheatre.org/2020/10/01/aapac-report-reveals-larger-pattern-of-inequities-in-ny-theatre/.
31. 'ALW Diversity Report', 12 January 2016, http://andrewlloydwebberfoundation.com/downloads/2016-12-01-ALW-Diversity-Report.pdf.
32. Wind Dell Woods, '"Bonding Over Phobia": Restaging a Revolution at the Expense of Black Revolt', in *Reframing the Musical: Race, Culture and Identity*, ed. Sarah K. Witfield (London: Springer Nature Limited, 2019), 216.
33. Woods, Woods, '"Bonding Over Phobia"'.
34. Robin Prichard, 'From Color-Blind to Color-Conscious: Advancing Racial Discourse in Dance Education', *Taylor & Francis* 19, no. 4 (25 March 2019), https://www.tandfonline.com/doi/abs/10.1080/15290824.2018.1532570.
35. Prichard, 'From Color-Blind to Color-Conscious'.
36. 'Coded Language', National Education Association, https://neaedjustice.org/social-justice-issues/racial-justice/coded-language/.
37. Paulson, 'The Making of "Six"'.
38. Marlow and Moss, 'Ex-Wives'.
39. The folk-rhyme reads, 'King Henry VIII, To six wives he was wedded.
    One died, one survived,
    Two divorced, two beheaded
    Boleyn and Howard lost their heads,
    Anne of Cleves he would not bed,
    Jane Seymour gave him a son – but died before the week was done,
    Aragon he did Divorce,
    Which just left Catherine Parr, of course!'
40. 'The Six Wives of Henry VIII', *PBS*, https://www.thirteen.org/wnet/sixwives.
41. Toby Marlow and Lucy Moss, 'Heart of Stone', in *Six!,* Concord Theatricals, 2016.

42. Marlow and Moss, 'Heart of Stone'.
43. 'The Six Wives of Henry VIII', *PBS*.
44. Marlow and Moss, 'Heart of Stone'.
45. 'Carly Mercedes Dyer', 'Six! The Musical', https://www.sixthemusical.com/uk-tour/company/carly-mercedes-dyer.
46. Marvin Carlson, *The Haunted Stage: The Theatre as Memory Machine* (Ann Arbor: University of Michigan Press, 2001), 134.
47. Shannon Gaffney, '"Why the Green Girl Is Never Black?": Racism in Casting', *On Stage Blog*, 19 December 2020, https://www.onstageblog.com/editorials/2020/12/19/why-the-green-girl-is-never-black-racism-in-casting.
48. Ryan Donovan, '"Must be Heavyset": Casting Women, Fat Stigma, and Broadway Bodies', *The Journal of American Drama and Theatre* 31, no. 3 (Spring 2019), https://jadtjournal.org/2019/05/13/must-be-heavyset-casting-women-fat-stigma-and-broadway-bodies/.
49. Georgia Hemmings, 'Discovering Africa in Jamaica', *Jamaica Gleaner*, 3 February 2003, http://www.jamaica-gleaner.com/gleaner/20030223/arts/arts2.html.
50. Toby Marlow and Lucy Moss, 'Get Down', in *Six!*, Concord Theatricals, 2016.
51. Beyoncé Knowles, 'Formation', *Lemonade,* Parkwood Entertainment, 2016.
52. Debbie Kilroy, 'Anne of Cleves', *Get History,* 18 November 2015, https://www.gethistory.co.uk/historical-period/early-modern/tudor/anne-of-cleves-stinky-and-ugly.
53. Kilroy, 'Anne of Cleves'.
54. Marlow and Moss, 'Get Down'.
55. Helena Wadia, 'Six the Musical's Toby Marlow and Lucy Moss: "Theatre is at a Crossroads between Accessibility and Elitism"', *Evening Standard*, 23 February 2021, https://www.standard.co.uk/culture/future-theatre-fund/toby-marlow-lucy-moss-six-the-musical-theatre-interview-b920886.html.
56. Marlow and Moss, 'Ex-Wives'.

Bibliography

'AAPAC Report Reveals Larger Pattern of Inequities in NY Theatre' (2020), *American Theatre Magazine*, 1 October, https://www.americantheatre.org/2020/10/01/aapac-report-reveals-larger-pattern-of-inequities-in-ny-theatre/.

'ALW Diversity Report' (2016), 1 December, http://andrewlloydwebberfoundation.com/downloads/2016-12-01-ALW-Diversity-Report.pdf.

'Black Lives Matter: Demands' (2012), http://blacklivesmatter.com/.

Carlson, Marvin (2001), *The Haunted Stage: The Theatre as Memory Machine*. Ann Arbor: University of Michigan Press.

Carly Mercedes Dyer (2019), 'Six! The Musical', https://www.sixthemusical.com/uk-tour/company/carly-mercedes-dyer.

'Coded Language' (2021), National Education Association, https://neaedjustice.org/social-justice-issues/racial-justice/coded-language/.

Crompton, Sarah (2020), 'With SIX, Playwrights Lucy Moss and Toby Marlow Dramatize the Tudor Dynasty – One Power Ballad at a Time', *Vogue*, 16 January, https://www.vogue.com/article/six-playwrights-lucy-moss-toby-marlow.

Donovan, Ryan (2019), '"Must Be Heavyset": Casting Women, Fat Stigma, and Broadway Bodies', *The Journal of American Drama and Theatre*, 31 (3), https://jadtjournal.org/2019/05/13/must-be-heavyset-casting-women-fat-stigma-and-broadway-bodies/.

Gaffney, Shannon (2020), '"Why the Green Girl Is Never Black?": Racism in Casting', *On Stage Blog*, 19 December 2020, https://www.onstageblog.com/editorials/2020/12/19/why-the-green-girl-is-never-black-racism-in-casting.

Hemmings, Georgia (2003), 'Discovering Africa in Jamaica', *Jamaica Gleaner*, 3 February, http://www.jamaica-gleaner.com/gleaner/20030223/arts/arts2.html.

Keleta-Mae, Naila (2017), 'A Beyoncé Feminist', *Atlantis*, 38 (1), https://core.ac.uk/download/pdf/322498145.pdf.

Kilroy, Debbie (2015), 'Anne of Cleves', *Get History*, 18 November, https://www.gethistory.co.uk/historical-period/early-modern/tudor/anne-of-cleves-stinky-and-ugly.

Knowles, Beyoncé (2016), 'Formation', *Lemonade*, Parkwood Entertainment.

'Olivier Awards 2019: Full Winners List' (2019), *The Hollywood Reporter*, 7 April, https://www.hollywoodreporter.com/lists/olivier-awards-2019-full-winners-list-1193956/.

Marlow, Toby and Lucy Moss (2016), *Six!*, Concord Theatricals.

Prichard, Robin (2019), 'From Color-Blind to Color-Conscious: Advancing Racial Discourse in Dance Education', *Taylor & Francis*, 19 (4), https://www.tandfonline.com/doi/abs/10.1080/15290824.2018.1532570.

'"Six!" the Musical Catherine Parrs Perform Survivor by Destiny's Child' (2020), *Official London Theatre*, 11 March, https://www.youtube.com/watch?v=2K-0cljD9KE.

'The Six Wives of Henry VIII' (2003), *PBS*. https://www.thirteen.org/wnet/sixwives.

'Transforming the Tudors: An Interview with SIX Co-creator Lucy Moss' (2019), *Sydney Opera House*, 8 September, https://www.sydneyoperahouse.com/backstage/theatre/transforming-the-tudors-six-lucy-moss.html.

Ugwu, Reggie (2020), 'The Hashtag That Changed the Oscars: An Oral History of #OscarsSoWhite', *The New York Times*, 2 June, https://www.nytimes.com/2020/02/06/movies/oscarssowhite-history.html.

Josh Bird interview

Digital producer *SIX*

What is your favourite British musical?
Billy Elliot

What's your favourite British musical theatre song?
'Consider Yourself' from *Oliver!*

What training did you do for your career?

None really. I studied music at Surrey University but my work on *SIX* involves video editing and graphic design and, apart from making videos with my siblings as a hobby growing up, I've never done any training in that.

I've always wanted to be a musical theatre composer so that's why I studied music. I chose to do the four year course which had a placement year and that's when I found Perfect Pitch. I figured that if I could spend a year interning with them as they developed new musicals that it would inform my writing. I never left after my placement and eight years later I have learnt so much about every aspect of musical theatre. Initially I was working for Perfect Pitch and then more recently they created Global Musicals, as the more commercial arm of the company, and I work for them as well. When I started working for them I did a bit of everything – reading scripts, looking through scores, doing all sorts of production assistant jobs – and then naturally I started doing more of the video editing stuff, and now my official job title is Digital Producer, which covers the wide variety of things that I do.

SIX has had massive success, with multiple international productions. Do you, or indeed did you, see this as a key British musical?

I think it is still too soon to say. I know it was never intended to be what it is. Initially the show was pitched to the Cambridge MT society, as a fun piece for the Edinburgh Fringe. It was meant to be a fairly simple concept that would sell at the fringe and make Marlowe and Moss's mates laugh. That was all that it was intended to be. At Edinburgh a number of producers and industry people, including George Stiles, saw the show and saw the potential in the show and

I would say that their influence and experience has made the show what it is. People love *SIX* for different reasons and the show has layers but at its heart it's an entertaining night out and I'm not sure how much it will influence other shows going forward. There are some musicals currently that you can tell have been inspired by it but time will tell if it continues to have this impact. When I saw *SIX* on the fringe I thought it was pretty good but I didn't think much more of it. It was Andy and Wendy (from Perfect Pitch) who could see the potential.

How would you describe your contribution to *SIX*?

My official title is Digital Producer, and in that capacity I'm responsible for the social media. I took it on when we had about a thousand subscribers and followers, before the show's first small UK tour and West End run. Initially the show's producers had hired a consultant – Genevieve Ampaduh, who had worked with Little Mix and One Direction – and it was her influence that made us treat the Queens in *SIX* as if they are a real girl band. When I took over Genevieve's strategy became my social media bible as we developed the social media. The main thing that I took from the original strategy was to not just be 'sell sell sell' online but to create and nurture this online community of fans. Which has evidently worked as we now have the most followed Instagram account of any West End musical. The strategy was built around themes from the show, and celebration was one of the key themes. Celebration of the Queens, of female empowerment, and of new theatre in general. At the time there were other new shows, like *Everybody's Talking About Jamie,* in the West End so we were messaging them on social media and making it feel like a celebration rather than a competition. The themes really set the tone of what we posted and what we focused on. There was also an awareness of what the best kind of content was for each channel. I was really aware that it wasn't me posting or responding to comments, so I had to think about what Lucy and Toby might say and how they would respond because I wanted it to fit with the feel of the show. Now, there are multiple social media accounts for the multiple runs of the show and I work with them to ensure cohesion.

We have used paid ads to promote the show but the thing that has developed the audience the most is this feeling that, via social media, people are really chatting to the Queens. As a result the majority of the ad spend will go on digital content rather than posters on the underground or adverts in newspapers. The audiences who love the show tend to be people who use social media a lot so it has married up well. A benefit of having me doing this role, rather than a marketing company, was that I've been able to focus on the show for the last five years rather than having a number of projects to oversee. I create the content as well, so we don't hire a freelance graphic designer or video editor. This means that I can create more content and it doesn't incur an additional cost for the producers. Every time there is a new cast we have a long discussion with them about social media where we teach them about the heightened attention they're going to get from fans and how to manage this responsibility alongside their own mental health.

How would you describe the rehearsal/production process for *SIX*?

The directors and writers really want each new cast member to bring their own voice and personality to the roles. At the start of the process a lot of time is spent focusing on what each new cast member is going to bring to the role, coming up with their own riffs and making their Queen their own. I feel like this is much more so than in other shows. Because of the way that the show is written you never have to put on an accent, it's always your own. Even when Hannah Stewart (alternate on West End production) went over to Broadway to cover roles she still had her Essex accent, apart from when she had to sing in harmony and then she had to use an American accent to blend with the rest of the cast! As with most big West End shows the beats are very specific and there is a rhythm to the delivery to get the gags. Even though it seems quite free with the Queens just talking to the audience it is all very scripted. Timing is key because the show runs to a track and there's a lot of choreography.

How do you feel about *SIX* now?

I'm very proud of my small contribution to the show. I've seen it so many times so when I saw it for the first time on Broadway and I cried, I was quite surprised, but it felt like it had been leading up to that moment. Even after five years I still really enjoy the show and know that I'm going to have a great night out when I watch it. It was amazing to see the original cast members come back recently to do the filming. That reminded me of how they'd created the roles and how iconic they were.

How did the experience of working on *SIX* shape your future work?

It has massively impacted me as a writer. I've learnt so much. The main thing being that growing up we spoke about how great composers – like Alan Menken or Stephen Sondheim or Andrew Lloyd Webber – made a great show. What I've realized is that yes you have to have that but that it's everything else that contributes to make the show a great success – the amazing costume design, the lighting, the producers. As a writer that realization is rather humbling because you realize you have to relinquish control and enjoy the process. It's clear why *SIX* is such a success given the style of the music and the length of the show but that the awards the show has accrued aren't the only measures of success. It's also worth noting that Toby and Lucy never intended for the show to be as big as it has been, so every achievement has been a bonus.

Are you still working in musical theatre?

Yes, still working on *SIX* and with Perfect Pitch, who now have resources thanks to the success of *SIX*, and still writing my own work.

What advice would you give aspiring writers?

Learn as much as you can about all aspects of theatre, find people you really want to work for and collaborate with and have a go at everything.

9   My ~~Left~~/Right Foot the Musical

JUDITH DRAKE

Disability has always existed in theatre; however, the stories around disability have usually focused on particular characterizations and narrative archetypes in the form of metaphors. Embodied disability on stage is still a relatively new phenomenon. Disability as metaphor functions as an outward portrayal of inner turmoil or evil, it represents societal ills and the sole purpose of the disabled character is to further the story which would culminate in their death or cure, thus providing a neat resolution and the eradication of disability. These characters have almost always been portrayed by nondisabled actors who are lauded and awarded for their ability to perform the impairment effects of disability, usually mimicking the movements of disabled people.[1]

Disability theatre is about showing the stories of the lived experiences of disability and disabled people on stage. In the past thirty years professional disabled theatre companies, like Graeae (based in London, England) and Birds of Paradise (based in Glasgow, Scotland), have changed how disability is represented on stage. Disability is gradually finding its way onto mainstages throughout the country.[2] While disability theatre is becoming more normalized, musical theatre is still finding a way to include disabled performers and the stories of disabled people as part of its genre.[3] Part of this difficulty pertains to the requirement of musical theatre actors, to be able to sing, dance and act; this does not align with an image of disability, which is perceived as lacking. As Samuel Yates asserts, it is not only a virtuosic performance but almost a superhuman feat is required: 'Today, musicals are predicated on expectations of the performer's bodily congruity with a kind of able-bodied exceptionalism or hypercapacity.'[4] This expected hypercapacity in musicals performers means disability creates discomfort as it is viewed as the opposite, a literal incapacity. This makes disability a difficult topic for writers, producers and audiences to imagine as a primary theme for a musical, or for disabled performers to feature as stars in musical theatre.

Birds of Paradise Theatre Company (BOP) is Scotland's only disability-led professional theatre company that works with disabled and nondisabled artists. In 2018, they joined forces with the National Theatre of Scotland (NTS) to write and produce a new musical comedy about disability for the 2018 Edinburgh Fringe Festival.[5] In six months, they developed the award-winning show *My ~~Left~~/Right Foot* (*MLRF*), which was written by Robert Softley Gale, with music and lyrics by Richard Thomas and additional music and lyrics by Noisemaker (Scott Gilmour and Claire McKenzie).[6] The production was set around an amateur dramatic club's adaptation of the film *My ~~Left~~ Foot* (1989). The film, staring Daniel Day Lewis, was based on the memoir of disabled artist and writer Christy Brown.[7] The Fringe production was developed into a full-length musical that toured in 2019.

While debates around the issues of casting nondisabled actors to play disabled characters – 'cripping up' 'crip face', 'disability drag', 'disability masquerade', 'disability simulation' – have, as Ann M. Fox and Carrie Sandahl suggest, 'become canonical within disability studies and activism as a point of political debate'[8] (and, I would assert, gradually in wider society), the conversation has yet to make it on to stage.[9] *MLRF* as a bawdy, politically incorrect and at times intentionally, highly offensive musical comedy does exactly this. The production explores issues of disabled representation on stage and screen by showing how disabled people and their stories are depicted in the arts. It challenges the notion of diversity and inclusion through examining tropes and stereotypes of disability. It produces a positive example of disability theatre, through its theme and embedded creative access (ECA).[10] The use of musical form in *MLRF* allows for a deeper exploration of disability and highlights how disability disrupts the conventions of musical theatre.[11]

Key concepts and terms for disability theatre

Before focusing on an in-depth discussion of the musical, it is necessary to define four disability concepts and terms. First, there are two main models of disability – the medical model and the social model.[12] The medical model traditionally interprets the body of a person as the source of disablement based on a sensory issue or medical condition. They are lacking in ability and are therefore unable to participate in society. The social model, which takes its roots from the early disability rights movement of the 1970s, views society and its structures as the excluding and disabling factor for a person. A blunt example would be a wheelchair user trying to access a building without a ramp or a lift: the medical model would view that as a problem for the individual as they are unable to move in a normative way. Conversely, the social model would see the design of the building as the disabling issue by not including access for all people; that is, the infrastructures are lacking, not the individual.

Second, the production's main discussion is around 'cripping up', which is loosely defined as nondisabled actors portraying disabled characters. I will use Yates's term 'disability simulation' to provide a deeper understanding of the concept which moves away from racial terms – cripping up versus blacking up – which risk being elided when applied to disability.[13] The term 'disability simulation' explains the failure that occurs when nondisabled actors portray disabled characters. For Yates, the nondisabled actor cannot become disabled themselves; therefore, disability simulation is based on the assumptions about disability made by the actor and wider society, rather than from a lived experience of disability.[14] *MLRF* highlights the active creation of disability simulation, based on stereotypes, and what it entails, rather than focusing on and praising an actor's performance. This uncovering exposes the issues around disability simulation and what it means for disabled representation.

Third, in literary analysis, David Mitchell and Sharon Snyder, coined the term 'narrative prosthesis' to show how disability can function as metaphor in the story and how it is used as a prosthetic device to forward the action or narrative.[15] Sandahl suggests, 'that narrative relies on disability as a metaphor for complex social issues. These social issues are "made flesh" in the disabled character. A "problem" of disability stands in for the social problem it signifies.'[16] Thus, if the character (or what the character symbolizes), is cured, killed, saved or reconsidered as positive, the disabling condition disappears, and the social issues can be neatly resolved.

Finally, my focus will be on the concept of 'diegetic disability', the term coined by Yates, which, unlike 'narrative prosthesis', functions in musicals to make explicit a disabled character in their embodied form as part of the musical.[17] Disability is part of their identity and cannot be glossed over or removed, or the character would no longer function: notably the character is not there for the benefit of the nondisabled characters or their storyline arc.[18] The disabled character within *MLRF*, Chris, functions as the diegesis for disability. His disability is never resolved, and his embodiment, portrayed by a disabled actor, means his disability creates a performative centrality that the production is forced to embrace. The discussion of disability simulation is confronted by an actual disabled body; disability is not resolved thematically or materially and is enacted in its instability, subverting the common musical theatre ending where the majority of the plot has been tied up and all is well in the musical theatre world.

MLRF: A summary

MLRF is set in the rehearsal room of a fictional small Scottish town amateur dramatics club, the Kirktoon Players. The action follows the club's long-standing attempt to win the Scottish Amateur Dramatics Association's (SADA) one-act play festival. One of the younger members, Amy, finds out that SADA will award more points for entries that embrace inclusivity and diversity; she convinces the other members, with the help of her best friend Gillian, who ends up as the haphazard movement director, to let Amy direct a play that covers diversity. After much debate, the club chooses disability as a theme and adapts the 1989 Oscar-winning film *My ~~Left~~ Foot*. Gillian suggests to Amy that they speak to Chris, a crew member, who she desires and who also has lived experience of cerebral palsy (CP), the same condition as Brown, to get help on the show. Chris has a crush on Amy and believes she wants him to star as Brown, even though he has no acting experience. Chris learns Grant, a nondisabled, failed West End actor, who hopes this will be his return to glory, is to play the lead role of Brown. Also present for most of the action is Nat, Amy's friend, who has come to practice her sign language for theatre and is also the British Sign Language Performance Interpreter (BSLPI) for the musical.

The older club members, Sheena who believes she's in charge of the club, and her put-upon sidekick Ian, are concerned that the play is going to go wrong for the club. Gillian becomes jealous of Chris's attention to Amy. Gillian secretly contacts SADA to inform them that Grant is to play the disabled character Brown in the hope that Chris will get the part. SADA threatens they either cast a disabled actor or withdraw their entry. Chris takes on the role. Gillian's plan backfires, and he spends more time with Amy, making a fumbled sexual pass at her which she rejects.

The club keeps going with rehearsals, but the pressure gets to Chris as the club realize that he cannot act, and he believes they do not understand the issues with disability simulation. In retaliation for Chris brushing her off after a one-night stand, Gillian reveals that she told SADA about Grant. Chris quits the show when he realizes that everyone is angrier about the club losing its chance of winning, rather than telling the authentic story of Brown's life. After a humorous dream sequence with Brown, performed over audio and using subtitles, he decides to come back to do the show, as if he does not, the only version out there will be Daniel Day Lewis's performance. The club welcomes him back, and they go ahead with the competition.

In the Fringe version it is not known whether the club wins or loses the SADA festival and the musical ends as they are competing. In the remount, the club loses the competition to the Edinburgh Entertainers, which Grant has joined. He plays the title role in their version of *The Elephant Man*, another disabled character; the audience does not find out how this casting gets past the SADA rules. The club members are somewhat bitter and believe they lost due to Chris's lack of acting ability but promise to make up for it next year by coming back with a musical.

Having contextualized *MLRF* and the wider disability theatre sector, this chapter will now consider how *MLRF* uses the musical theatre form to thematically and structurally explore and understand disability and disability representation in four areas. I will start with disability simulation and the song 'Spasticity', which, through choreography and lyrics, demonstrates the work that nondisabled actors have to do to produce disability simulation. In the next section I will explore authentic casting with the song 'I'm An Actor', which discusses disability representation on stage and screen. I will use the songs 'Maybe' and 'Spastic Finger' in the subsequent section to explore Chris's character. Chris as the only visibly disabled character in the musical functions, along with the theme, as a diegetic disability. In the final section I will analyse how ECA and the finale function metatheatrically as a performative display of structural diegetic disability, showing how a musical about disability can be inclusive while subverting the musical form.

Disability simulation: 'Spasticity'

In scene seven, the big musical number 'Spasticity' performatively demonstrates the work involved in disability simulation by nondisabled actors when the Kirktoon Players try to get to grips with how Brown's impairment affects his physicality. The number occurs after the read-through, during which Chris finds out Grant is going to play Brown. Amy abandons the current version of the script after getting Chris onboard to help her with rewrites; she puts Gillian – who has little experience apart from childhood dance classes – on the spot by asking her to do a movement session. Gillian decides the club should explore their inner 'cripple' so they can understand what it is like to be Brown.[19]

Though humorous, the scene is intentionally offensive and highly parodic. Importantly, it reveals what disability simulation entails. In the opening verse Gillian sings:

> I think to move like Christy Brown
> We should start on the ground
> Cos Christy Brown, he couldn't walk,
> He just sort of flapped around
> Then think about what it means

to be crippled on the floor
Flail your arms and thrash your legs
Like a salmon on the shore[20]

She then directs the club members to roll around on the floor like salmon, which they do with varying degrees of success. Brown is reduced to an animalistic Other that flaps around with a lack of sentience, the implication being his movement is synonymous with him being less than human. The use of the word 'crippled' functions doubly, both as a lack of bodily movement and as a lack of capacity or autonomy of thought due to an impaired body. The choreographed image is a gross parody of the stereotyped disabled body. Seeing actors badly performing spasms, to music, on the floor is shocking and it is meant to be. This is the reality, albeit a dramatized version, of the disability simulation process, one that an audience would prefer not to see.

Rachel Drazek's choreography is intentionally incongruous, demonstrating how the early stages of disability simulation are going to appear jarring and offensive. This is not the award-winning rendition but rather the raw mockery needed in order to begin to force the presumed normative embodiment of a musical theatre actor into the appearance of impairment. The scene has the appearance of caricature as musical theatre actors are the so-called 'triple-threat performer', excelling in being able to sing, dance, and act flawlessly without effort.[21] The start of the number shows the Kirktoon Players as the opposite of this hypercapacity as the dramatized attempts at disability fail. The song segues into a *Flashdance*-style 1980s number with song world lighting and highly stylized choreography, the return to the typical musical number heightening the juxtaposition with exceptionalism. This problematizes the perfect musical theatre actor as it shows them both as able and unable to portray the disabled character (Figure 4).

This performance of disability in *MLRF* calls attention to the pervasive idea that disabled people cannot be part of theatre and musical theatre as they cannot remove their disability. This is due to the idea that body neutrality is essential for an actor, they have to be able to

Figure 4 *My Left/Right Foot the Musical* (2019), National Theatre Scotland. Credit: Tommy Ga-Ken Wan.

remake their own embodiment to create a new character.[22] As Sandahl argues, 'Disabled bodies, though, cannot be cured. They may tremor, wobble, or be asymmetrical. Implicit in the various manifestations of the neutral metaphor is the assumption that a character cannot be built from a position of physical difference.'[23] The disabled actor's body will always be foregrounded and imbued with negativity. However, MLRF demonstrates that disability allows for different styles of movement. The disabled body is one that cannot compete with the expected virtuosity of musical theatre actor, but on stage it can expose the work that is done to disguise the effort and skill of the nondisabled actor to portray a disabled character, while simultaneously revealing that a nondisabled actor can never fully convey a disabled person's lived experience.

Disability humour is imperative in 'Spasticity' as without it the scene is mocking disabled people's embodiment.[24] Alongside the choreography the lyrics are making fun of nondisabled people's awkwardness and assumptions when confronted with disability. Grant reflects the viewpoint that it would be better to be dead than to live with the effects of an impairment, even though he wants to be able to mimic those effects for his own professional gain. Grant dramatically interrupts Chris's explanation of disability in the song, 'And the pain gets so distracting/That you've no choice but to/Cry, and scream, and moan and wish you were dead!'[25] Chris responds, 'No. That's not what I was going to say at all,'[26] which causes a laugh. Susanne Hamscha, discussing the work of disabled comedians, finds, 'Crip humor plays with these contradictory impulses – the desire to stare and refusal to see – through its blunt use of misconceptions and stereotypes about disability that invite members of the audience to take a good look, only to make them cringe at the crudeness of what they see and thus become conscious of their voyeuristic behavior'.[27] 'Spasticity' forces this dichotomy as a practical presentation of Hamscha's findings without didacticism. The humour, albeit cringing, relieves discomfort and enables the audience to laugh at views that position disabled people as inferior. 'Spasticity' lyrics highlight that while the impairment effects of disability can be difficult the most disabling factor is how society treats disabled people.[28] The song's humorously offensive lyrics juxtaposed with a big dance number is difficult to watch, but it also gets to the heart of disability simulation; the mimicry of an impairment's effects will never lead to understanding the lived experience, the negative societal perceptions and discrimination that disabled people face.

Authentic casting: 'I'm an Actor'

Grant's number, 'I'm an Actor', explores authentic casting and disabled representation.[29] The lyrics and musical style are over the top, which adds to the dissonance between the meaning of the lyrics and the hilarity of how it's being presented. Due to Grant's camp and egotistical characterization the song is simultaneously funny and purposefully offensive. He believes, as a nondisabled actor playing Brown, he is now the target of SADA's discrimination. The song argues that to be an actor is to portray a different lived experience. 'Do I have to be a real Tory/To act a Tory in a story?/To be a gay in a play/Do I have to be a/Cock-sucking gay gay gay!'[30] This is the heart of the argument against authentic casting, that acting is make believe, so it should go to the person best suited to the part irrespective of embodiment. This allows the status quo to continue and does not ask what different lived experiences can bring to a role. As Yates suggests, 'To say "that's what acting is" allows artistic inequities favoring able-bodied actors and stereotypes about what disabled bodies do, or what disabilities are, to continue in film, television, stage, and other performance arts.'[31] By excluding disabled actors and creatives from being part of the conversation about and the making of drama, nondisabled people's understanding of disability will continue to be the norm.

Nondisabled actors performing disability simulation draw attention to their nondisabled status. Disability scholar Tobin Siebers highlights that disability simulation is a failure of drama as the audience are no longer engrossed in the story but are in awe of the actor mimicking the bodily movements of a disabled person.[32] For the audience, doubling is occurring, whereby they must hold both versions of the actor simultaneously: there is safety in this knowledge as the audience can enjoy being entertained knowing the actor will return to 'normal', for example, nondisabled, at the end of the show.[33]

This simulated performance of disability then becomes the norm. This can be seen in act one, scene eleven of the 2019 production in the song 'Super Human Feat',[34] in which Grant has perfected his portrayal of Brown. Amy's lyric describes Grant's successful performance of Brown: 'It is so authentic/The funny thing is this/Grant's CP looks more real/Than the real CP in Chris – no offense.'[35] The 'authenticity' of Grant's performance is seen as real as it is depicted on stage and screen which is where the majority of people are exposed to disability. Ironically, this perceived reality allows the audience to feel safe in its falsity. In contrast Chris's actual disability is negated as it fails to be disabled enough. This is further erasure of the lived experience of disability where the messy realities of actual disabled bodies are considered simultaneously as being not enough and too much. *MLRF* discusses disability simulation without reducing the argument that authentic casting will fix the situation; it needs to also be about the stories of Brown and Chris and how they fit, or do not, into the society around them and where those stories are seen.

Diegetic disability: 'Maybe' and 'Spastic Finger'

As a character, Chris can be read as an instance of diegetic disability. In other words, his disability cannot be removed from the production without disrupting the logic of the play's narrative. In narrative studies, 'diegesis' refers to the narrator's telling of the story. In this instance, Chris explores disability as part of his character narration, which makes his disability an essential element of the story's world. In performance, disability becomes material in the body of the actor. And this means that it is Chris's disability that is visibly narrating the story through the actor's embodiment of the character. As Yates argues, 'A diegetic disability is preferential precisely because of its discoverability. If a disability is central to a character's onstage presence it cannot be covered over, ignored, or translated into a shorthand for an able-bodied character's experience.'[36] In other words, if the experience and presentation of a specific disability is essential to the story itself and cannot be omitted or changed without altering that story, then it functions as a 'diegetic disability' within the play.

Chris's rounded characterization is flawed and also empathetic; he is not portrayed as either the classic demon or angel disabled stereotype. Chris joins the club because he wants to be with Amy and uses Gillian when he is rejected by Amy. He is not overtly political in engaging with disability rights and activism, but he understands and identifies with the negative treatment of Brown. Chris is seeking accurate representation and spends most of the musical trying to communicate why Grant's disability simulation does not allow for a nuanced understanding of the lived experience of disability as Grant has not faced daily discrimination. Chris, as a character, is not a narrative prosthesis device; he shows how disability functions in society in the way he is treated by the club members and demonstrates that his disability is not his defining feature.

Chris's 'I wish' songs ('Maybe', 'Chris' Revelation' 2018 and 'I Hate Other People', 'What Was I Thinking' 2019) show Yates's idea of discoverability as diegetic disability.[37] In both productions these songs highlight how Chris is Othered by the club and wider society because of his disability. The club is his attempt at trying to find his place and define himself, rather than through the perception of others. The song 'Maybe',[38] in scene five, provides the backstory for Chris's scepticism in joining the Kirktoon Players but at the same time his hope for a different outcome. An example of his desire for change can be found in the chorus of 'Maybe' – Chris sings of what he usually does, 'And normally I'd walk away/Normally I'd hide'.[39] His desire for Amy boosts his confidence, allows him to think that he might be able to get more from life and change how people perceive him. In the final verse of the song, Chris sings,'Maybe I am changing/The story people know/Maybe Amy will want me/Once I'm starring in her show/Maybe Mum could be right/Maybe I've found my place/Maybe Amy will want me/When she's sitting on my . . . knee'.[40] The song shows that it has not been easy for Chris, but that does not mean he does not have hope for a different future. Chris does not function as a narrative prosthetic device; he does not want to alter his disability, nor does disability become a positive element by the end of the production. While the song is earnest in Chris's desire for Amy, the club and hopeful acceptance, it is underscored by humour; at the end of the song the choreography implies that he would like her to be sitting on his face rather than his knee. This crass choice is intentional as the reality is that Chris has sexual desires and does not conform to the asexual stereotype of disabled people.

Act One's 'Spastic Finger'[41] – which featured in the 2019 revised production – is an in-depth exploration of disabled sexuality as diegetic disability.[42] In 'Spastic Finger' Chris, Gillian and Amy's love triangle presents a double mode of diegetic disability: first, Chris as the disabled character enacts disability throughout the play; but, second, the foregrounding of disabled sexuality makes explicit another set of prejudices about differing embodiment by making spasticity appear sexually positive. As Yates, suggests, 'diegetic disabilities open space for nonnormative embodiments to be considered as having equal if not greater value to the conveyance of a story and characters' experience . . . Encountering disabilities onstage challenge able-bodied notions of what bodies are livable, marketable, healthy or well, capable, and desirable.'[43] 'Spastic Finger' is a direct challenge as to what constitutes desirability. Amy, Gillian and Chris sing the lyrics while at home in their bedrooms. Chris's lyrics convey the stereotyped lustful desire of an early twenties male, Gillian focuses on ways she could get Chris to have sex with her and Amy explores how she could help Chris to make his life 'easier'.

While ludicrously sexually graphic and obscene, the intention of the song was to demonstrate humorously that depictions of an overt disabled sexuality are still uncommon. As Roxanna N. Pebdani and Amanda Tashjian's systematic literature review on attitudes towards disabled sexuality suggests, 'sexuality is not viewed for individuals with disabilities as it is for the general public and in fact the notion of a person with a disability being a sexual person remains outside of the norm.'[44] Having such a sexually graphic, camp song disabuses the audience that this is the case and furthermore shows disabled sexuality as positive and normal. The song highlights Chris's perceived sexual prowess because of his impairment – his spastic fingers provide digital sexual gratification to women. This belief of impairment improving sex lives from both a psychological and a physical aspect is backed by research. Michael A. Rembis suggests:

> Some disabled people claim that disability has made them a better lover or partner. Since sexual pleasure seems to be associated with psychosocial rather than strictly physical factors, some disabled people see disability as a vehicle for learning about and exploring their own sexuality, as well as that of their lover or partner, which they claim makes them a more sensitive and responsive, or in some cases, creative and courageous lover.[45]

By Chris being able to use his impairment creatively to sexually gratify a woman he is positioning himself as a better lover, which increases his confidence. Chris believes he can provide an orgasm that would be unachievable for a nondisabled person, 'I got precious skills/That will give you special chills/Whatever a normal dude does/He'll never give you the same buzz/As a guy with CP does.'[46] Chris's view still positions his sexuality outside the 'norm', as Pebdani and Tashjian suggest; however, it is one of superiority. This different portrayal of disabled sexuality alters the perception of Chris being inferior.

Gillian's character is unusually depicted as openly desiring and also objectifying a disabled sexual partner, 'I think he's sexy I find him hot/Something about this cheeky bugger hits my spot/He's very quiet but he's not shy/There's more to him than a regular guy.'[47] Gillian fetishises Chris singing, 'I find your spasms kinky',[48] suggesting she does not view him as a 'regular guy'. This view of nondisabled people as sexually deviant if attracted to disabled people is part of how disability is understood as a negative. Disabled embodiment is imbued as abnormal, ergo those who are attracted to disabled people are also aberrant in their desire. Over the course of the musical, we see Gillian's desire for Chris change as she wants to pursue a relationship with him. There are few examples on mainstream stage and screen where disabled people are sex-positive and have an active sex life. This song explores provocatively how a person's disability can unapologetically benefit their sexual expression.

Chris is not perfect and is shown to make foolish mistakes but at the same time he cares deeply for how Brown was treated and the right way to depict his life. Chris cannot make all the club members truly understand disability oppression, but by him being part of the club they can see that he brings something different to the club. The actors portraying Chris, Matthew Duckett and Christopher Imbrosciano, both have CP, which was a requirement of the casting call. This casting decision added a fourth layer to the production; the musical is about disability, featuring a disabled character, played by a disabled actor and a play within a play about a real disabled person.

Structural diegetic disability: Embedded Creative Access and finale

MLRF uses disability metatheatrically, first, by incorporating ECA in its design as part of the musical form; and second, using disability narratively to subvert a resolved ending of the finale. Thus, functioning as a structural diegetic disability, the production is not reliant on Chris; rather, he is part of an overall disabled form that includes character, story, design, music, casting, choreography and ECA.[49] *MLRF* asks why actual disabled people are not represented on stage and in film. It presents the idea that it is too difficult to stage a play about disability, which is then exactly what the musical does. Moreover, incorporating ECA performatively creates access for a wider audience, demonstrating it is not enough to have disability inclusion on stage; disabled audiences have to be able to access the theatre as well. *MLRF does* not disguise ECA; rather, it is placed front and centre to be part of the action performatively, thereby enacting inclusion as a structural diegetic disability.

In the opening of the original 2018 production, the performance set up the use of audio description (AD), BSLPI and surtitles in the opening scene. Nat explains, orally and in BSL, to Gav Whitworth (2018)/Alex Parker (2019) (who were the musical directors, a near-constant presence on stage providing live music and AD) that she was there to 'practice her sign language for theatre'.[50] I will return to her role in the production later. Gav's response to Nat uses humour, and specifically disability humour, to provide the AD of the set:

Gav   Cool – sounds like a well thought out, integrated idea. If only we also had someone to describe our surroundings for people with visual impairments. This coral and brown rehearsal hall from the 70s, with small high windows, double doors on the back wall and a cupboard in the left hand corner really needs describing for people who can't see it. Oh, and the colour of this floor is what I believe you Scottish folk call 'Pish'.[51]

Gav describes the set but also gives a knowing nod to some disabled audience members, and their allies, that many productions do not provide embedded AD. This line also subverts the traditional formal AD language by humorously describing the floor colour as 'pish'. These lines were delivered straight, which added more humour to the scene. Surtitles were also part of the design and projected with animation onto the set and are referenced later in the show as part of a dialogue between Chris and Brown.[52]

To return to the integral role of Nat in the story line of *MLRF*. She functions as a confidante to the other characters as she is on stage for nearly all of the musical as well as being the BSLPI. Without her character the story would not make sense. Nat's presence disabuses the notion that musical theatre is not for a deaf or BSL using audiences.[53] As a soft start opening (as described earlier), its humour and highlighting of ECA sets up the production as inclusive. The AD, BSLPI, surtitles, being part of the script and production design, allowed for humorous, self-reflexive and metatheatrical moments that highlighted, to both a disabled and a nondisabled audience, an awareness of what *MLRF* was attempting to convey, while also making fun of theatre's difficulties in integrating access into productions. As a form of structural diegetic disability ECA forces audiences to be aware of disability: it is part of the production that is at once both inside and outside the performance; this duality is integral to the success of an inclusive production.

In traditional musical theatre, the finale tends to be a happily ever after ending, with the main plot and most of the subplots resolved, the audience leaves on a high knowing all is well. For *MLRF*, the endings were problematic. The two main options available were: the Kirktoon Players won the festival, everyone had learned from the process and now truly understood diversity and inclusion, or they lost the competition because Chris was not a good actor and realistic stories about disabled people's lives remain uncommon and are not celebrated. In the 2018 production, an open ending let the audience decide whether the club won or lost. In the 2019 version, the ending was more realistic; the club lost the competition as Chris was a bad actor, losing out to Grant's new club, the Edinburgh Entertainers. The finale showed the Kirktoon Players had returned to believing they were being robbed of the prize and nothing had really changed.

The endings narratively reinforced a structural diegetic disability, Chris has not been cured or killed off; the club is no further forward in understanding the lived experience of disability. In *MLRF* disability subverts the musical convention of resolution, albeit in a humorous way, but it also perpetuates the disability narrative of chaos and immutability. The circle cannot be squared because of disability, and the production makes clear that this is acceptable and a welcome change. By not 'fixing' the 'problem' of disability the production is closer to the lived experience of disability, while simultaneously showing that disability is a welcome and entertaining subject for musical theatre. As a metatheatrical moment the ending states that inclusivity has not really moved on as much as it should have. However, this production has been created, written, directed and performed by disabled people, featuring disability as one of the major themes and was co-produced by the NTS. Thus, demonstrating while there is a long way to go in terms of representation of disability on stage, it is possible.

Future of inclusive musical theatre

MLRF does not tell the audience that disability simulation is wrong; rather, it introduces them to what it means and how it impacts on disabled people and their representation in society. The story, when stripped back, is about Chris trying to find himself and his place in the world. The other club members are being asked to be truly inclusive, which means altering what they thought they knew about disability, their behaviour and practice. *MLRF* also purposely uses offensive material to shock the audience into questioning how inclusive they really are. Mixing this discomfort with humour softens the blow but still exposes inclusivity as a facade. I have discussed how disability simulation, the debate around authentic casting, disability humour, diegetic disability, disabled sexuality, ECA and the finale of *MLRF* highlight how disability functions in the production. I have described how they simultaneously disrupt the musical theatre framework, when embodied on stage and how they also call attention to who is on stage, which stories are being represented and what those stories mean. Given the ubiquity of disability in theatre, *MLRF* should not be classed as groundbreaking in its storyline or form, but it is and it will pave the way for future musicals that can represent the lived experience of disability in a funny and entertaining way.

Notes

1. I use the term 'disabled people' instead of 'people with disabilities' to identify people with sensory, physical, learning and mental health conditions or impairments prioritizing the disabling societal aspect rather than the impairment of the individual. I use 'nondisabled' to describe those without a disability, avoiding positioning them as the normative identity.

2. See Birds of Paradise, https://www.boptheatre.co.uk/ and Graeae, https://graeae.org/. See also DaDa Fest, https://www.dadafest.co.uk/, Disability Arts Online, https://disabilityarts.online/, Lung Ha, https://www.lungha.com/, Mind the Gap, https://www.mind-the-gap.org.uk/, National Disability Arts Archive, https://the-ndaca.org/, Ramps on the Moon, https://www.rampsonthemoon.co.uk/, Solar Bear, https://solarbear.org.uk/, Unlimited, https://weareunlimited.org.uk/.

   Traditional theatre companies have started to include disabled actors in their productions, including Arthur Hughes, *Richard III* (2022) Royal Shakespeare Company, Liz Carr, *The Normal Heart* (2021) National Theatre and Fictionhouse.
3. Most recently the National Theatre of Scotland produced, to critical acclaim, the musical *Orphans* (music and lyrics by Roddy Hart and Tommy Reilly, book by Douglas Maxwell, directed by Cora Bissett) 2022 based on the 1997 film by Peter Mullan, featuring disabled actor Amy Conachan.
4. Samuel R. Yates, *Cripping Broadway: Neoliberal Performances of Disability in the American Musical* (The George Washington University, 2019), 31, accessed 2 June 2022, https://scholarspace.library.gwu.edu/concern/gw_etds/cn69m481p?locale=en.
5. I was part of the creative team on *MLRF* as an Academic Theatre Consultant and used the productions in my PhD research.
6. The critical and audience reception was overwhelmingly positive, with the run selling out early on. The Fringe production won a Fringe First award, a Herald Angel award, Broadway Musical – Best New Musical, nominated for a Carol Tambor Best of Edingburgh Award and later received six nominations for the Critic's Awards for Theatre in Scotland winning best Music and Sound. The production was featured as a 'must see show' in a variety of mainstream media outlets.
7. Daniel Day Lewis presents as nondisabled.
8. Ann M. Fox and Carrie Sandahl, 'Beyond "Cripping Up": An Introduction', *Journal of Literary & Cultural Disability Studies* 12, no. 2 (2018): 121–7, accessed 20 November 2021, http://dx.doi.org.ezproxy.is.ed.ac.uk/10.3828/jlcds.2018.10.
9. Caroline Casey, 'It's Time for the Disabled Community to Take Center Stage', *Fortune* (2022), accessed 3 September 2022, https://fortune.com/2022/08/02/time-disabled-community-stage-screen-disability-diversity-hollywood-bbc-media-caroline-casey/. D. Evans, 'Please Stop Comparing Disabled Mimicry to Blackface', *Dominick Evans* (2017), accessed 31 July 2021, https://www.dominickevans.com/2017/07/18/please-stop-comparing-cripping-up-to-blackface/. A. Leary, 'Sia, Stories About Autism Should Centre Autistic People. Period', *Refinery 29* (2020), accessed 29 June 2021, https://www.refinery29.com/en-gb/2020/11/10184250/sia-music-trailer-maddie-ziegler-autism-speaks-controversy. A. Sutherland, 'Why We Need More Disability Inclusiveness in the Entertainment Industry', *Hollywood Insider* (2021), accessed 15 August 2021, https://www.hollywoodinsider.com/disability-inclusiveness-entertainment/.
10. Embedded creative access includes British Sign Language Performance Interpreters, audio descriptions, surtitles and relaxed performances integrated as part of the production usually from the preproduction stage.
11. For more information on the cast, creative team and crew please see: https://www.boptheatre.co.uk/left-right-foot-musical/.
12. Colin Cameron, *Disability Studies: A Student's Guide* (London: SAGE, 2014) and J. L. Davis, *The Disability Studies Reader*, 5th edn (New York: Routledge, 2017).

13. Yates, *Cripping Broadway*, 55–7.
14. Yates, *Cripping Broadway*, 57.
15. For more information on 'narrative prosthesis' see David T. Mitchell and Sharon L. Snyder, *Narrative Prosthesis: Disability and the Dependencies of Discourse* (Ann Arbor; Great Britain: University of Michigan Press, 2014).
16. Carrie Sandahl, 'Using Our Words: Exploring Representational Conundrums in Disability Drama and Performance', *Journal of Literary & Cultural Disability Studies* 12, no. 2 (2018): 129–44 (134), accessed 14 April 2022, https://link.gale.com/apps/doc/A541401198/LitRC?u=ed_itw&sid=bookmarkLitRC&xid=62880a30.
17. Samuel Yates, 'Disability and the American Stage Musical', in *The Routledge Companion to Literature and Disability*, ed. A. Hall (Abingdon, Oxon and New York: Taylor & Francis, 2020), accessed 1 May 2022, https://bookshelf.vitalsource.com/books/9781351699679.
18. Yates, 'Disability and the American Stage Musical'.
19. Spasticity is a common symptom of neurological conditions in which muscles all over the body can experience stiffness or muscle tone issues. It can cause pain and spasms throughout the body and lead to jerky movements.
20. Claire McKenzie and Scott Gilmour, 'Spasticity', in *My Left/Right Foot*, ed. Robert Softley Gale (2018), 14 [unrecorded song].
21. Yates, *Cripping Broadway*, 31.
22. Carrie Sandahl, 'The Tyranny of Neutral Disability & Actor Training', in *Bodies in Commotion: Disability and Performance* (Ann Arbor: University of Michigan Press, 2005), 255–67 (262), accessed 21 September 2021, https://ebookcentral.proquest.com/lib/ed/detail.action?docID=3414573.
23. Sandahl, 'The Tyranny of Neutral Disability & Actor Training', 255–67 (262).
24. There is a distinction between disability humour and disabling humour. Disabling humour denigrates disability or the disabled person. See Kim D. Reid, Edy Hammond Stoughton and Robin M. Smith, 'The Humorous Construction Of Disability: "Stand-Up" Comedians in the United States', *Disability & Society* 21, no. 6 (2006): 629–43, accessed 17 June 2022, https://doi.org/10.1080/09687590600918354.
25. McKenzie and Gilmour, 'Spasticity', 16.
26. Robert Softley Gale, *My Left/Right Foot* (2018), 16 [unpublished play manuscript].
27. Susanne Hamscha, 'Crip Humor', in *Gender: Laughter*, Macmillan Interdisciplinary Handbooks, ed. B. Papenburg (Farmington Hills, MI: Macmillan Reference USA, 2017), 349–62 (356) [online facsimile], accessed 17 June 2022, https://link.gale.com/apps/doc/CX3648400036/GVRL?u=ed_itw&sid=bookmark-GVRL&xid=ae1b41c1.
28. McKenzie and Gilmour, 'Spasticity', 14–17.
29. In the 2018 production the original title was 'How Very Dare You?' which was expanded on for the 2019 production.
30. Richard Thomas, 'I'm An Actor', in *My Left/Right Foot*, ed. Robert Softley Gale (2019), 30 [unrecorded song].
31. Yates, 'Disability and the American Stage Musical'.
32. Tobin Siebers, 'In/Visible: Disability on the Stage', in *Body Aesthetics*, ed. S. Irvin (Oxford: Oxford University Press, 2016), accessed 2 June 2021, https://doi.org/10.1093/acprof:oso/9780198716778.003.0009.

33. Siebers, 'In/Visible'. Due to the continued perceived dearth of disabled actors in the UK, unless a disabled actor is well known, there is the assumption that disabled characters will be portrayed by nondisabled actors. Neither disability simulation nor Siebers' thoughts on doubling acknowledge actors with hidden disabilities, an area which requires separate discussion and scholarship.
34. Richard Thomas, 'Super Human Feat', in *My Left/Right Foot*, ed. Robert Softley Gale (2019) [unrecorded song].
35. Thomas, 'Super Human Feat', 27.
36. Yates, *Cripping Broadway*, 271.
37. 'I wish' or 'I am' songs explicate a character's hopes and desires and usually are the impetus for action, see J. Woolford, *How Musicals Work and How to Write Your Own* (London: Nick Hern Books Limited, 2012), 150–3.
38. Claire McKenzie and S. Gilmour, 'Maybe', in *My Left/Right Foot*, ed. Robert Softley Gale (2018) [unrecorded song].
39. McKenzie and Gilmour, 'Maybe', 10.
40. McKenzie and Gilmour, 'Maybe', 11.
41. Richard Thomas and Robert Softley Gale, 'Spastic Finger', in *My Left/Right Foot*, ed. Robert Softley Gale (2019) [unrecorded song].
42. The song was written and composed in 2018 but did not fit in with the original storyline due to the time constraints of the Fringe show.
43. Yates, *Cripping Broadway*, 43–4.
44. Roxanna N. Pebdani and Amanda Tashjian, 'An Analysis of the Attitudes of the General Public Towards the Sexuality of Individuals with Disabilities Through a Systematic Literature Review', *Sexuality and Disability* 40 (2022): 21–55 (51), accessed 26 June 2022, https://doi.org/10.1007/s11195-021-09700-4.
45. Michael A. Rembis, 'Beyond the Binary: Rethinking the Social Model of Disabled Sexuality', *Sexuality and Disability* 28, no. 1 (2010): 51–60 (54), accessed 24 June 2022, https://doi.org/10.1007/s11195-009-9133-0.
46. Thomas and Softley Gale, 'Spastic Finger', 36.
47. Thomas and Softley Gale, 'Spastic Finger', 36.
48. Thomas and Softley Gale, 'Spastic Finger', 37.
49. ECA also included relaxed performances to accommodate neurodivergent audience members and provided packs that described the performance, narrative and characters to audience members with learning disabilities.
50. Softley Gale, *My Left/Right Foot* [unpublished play manuscript], 1.
51. Softley Gale, *My Left/Right Foot* [unpublished play manuscript], 1.
52. Softley Gale, *My Left/Right Foot* [unpublished play manuscript], 40.
53. There is an argument around whether a hearing BSLPI is the best person to interpret for a D/deaf audience about whether it is reinscribing ablism, but for this production the club's discriminatory attitude towards Chris would mean the story dynamics would have been altered if the club welcomed a deaf person but not him.

References

Cameron, Colin (2014), *Disability Studies: A Student's Guide*. London: SAGE.
Davis, Leonard J. (2017), *The Disability Studies Reader*, 5th edn. New York: Routledge.

Fox, Ann M. and Carrie Sandahl (2018), 'Beyond "Cripping Up": An Introduction', *Journal of Literary & Cultural Disability Studies*, 12 (2): 121–7, http://dx.doi.org.ezproxy.is.ed.ac.uk/10.3828/jlcds.2018.10 (accessed 20 November 2021).

Hamscha, Susanne (2017), 'Crip Humor', in B. Papenburg (ed.), *Gender: Laughter*, 349–62, Macmillan Interdisciplinary Handbooks. Farmington Hills: Macmillan Reference USA, [online facsimile], https://link.gale.com/apps/doc/CX3648400036/GVRL?u=ed_itw&sid=bookmark-GVRL&xid=ae1b41c1 (accessed 17 June 2022).

McKenzie, Claire and Scott Gilmour (2018), 'Maybe', in Robert Softley Gale, *My Left Right Foot*, [unrecorded song].

McKenzie, Claire and Scott Gilmour (2018), 'Spasticity', in Robert Softley Gale, *My Left Right Foot*, [unrecorded song].

Pebdani, Roxanna N. and Amanda Tashjian (2022), 'An Analysis of the Attitudes of the General Public Towards the Sexuality of Individuals with Disabilities Through a Systematic Literature Review', *Sexuality and Disability*, 40: 21–55, https://doi.org/10.1007/s11195-021-09700-4 (accessed 26 June 2022).

Rembis, Michael A. (2010), 'Beyond the Binary: Rethinking the Social Model of Disabled Sexuality', *Sexuality and Disability*, 28 (1): 51–60, https://doi.org/10.1007/s11195-009-9133-0 (accessed 24 June 2022).

Sandahl, Carrie (2005), 'The Tyranny of Neutral Disability & Actor Training', in C. Sandahl and P. Auslander (eds), *Bodies in Commotion: Disability and Performance*, 255–67. Ann Arbor: University of Michigan Press, https://ebookcentral.proquest.com/lib/ed/detail.action?docID=3414573 (accessed 21 September 2021).

Sandahl, Carrie (2018), 'Using Our Words: Exploring Representational Conundrums in Disability Drama and Performance', *Journal of Literary & Cultural Disability Studies*, 12 (2): 129–44, https://link.gale.com/apps/doc/A541401198/LitRC?u=ed_itw&sid=bookmark-LitRC&xid=62880a30 (accessed 14 April 2022).

Siebers, Tobin (2016), 'In/Visible: Disability on the Stage', in S. Irvin (ed.), *Body Aesthetics*. Oxford: Oxford University Press, https://doi.org/10.1093/acprof:oso/9780198716778.003.0009 (accessed 2 June 2021).

Softley Gale, Robert (2018), *My Left Right Foot* [unpublished play manuscript].

Softley Gale, Robert (2019), *My Left Right Foot* [unpublished play manuscript].

Thomas, Richard (2019), 'I'm An Actor', in Robert Softley Gale, *My Left Right Foot*, [unrecorded song].

Thomas, Richard (2019), 'Super Human Feat', in Robert Softley Gale, *My Left Right Foot*, [unrecorded song].

Thomas, Richard and Robert Softley Gale (2019), 'Spastic Finger', in Robert Softley Gale, *My Left Right Foot*, [unrecorded song].

Yates, Samuel R. (2019), *Cripping Broadway: Neoliberal Performances of Disability in the American Musical*. The George Washington University, https://scholarspace.library.gwu.edu/concern/gw_etds/cn69m481p?locale=en (accessed 2 June 2022).

Yates, Samuel R. (2020), 'Disability and the American Stage Musical', in A. Hall (ed.), *The Routledge Companion to Literature and Disability*. Abingdon, Oxon and New York: Taylor & Francis, https://bookshelf.vitalsource.com/books/9781351699679 (accessed 1 May 2022).

Noisemaker interview

Claire McKenzie (Music) Scott Gilmour (Lyrics) *My ~~Left~~/Right Foot*

What is your favourite British musical?

Scott One of the most enjoyable experiences I've had in the theatre was when I saw *SIX* for the first time. It has such great songs and it's not trying to be anything other than what it is. It meets the audience where they are and just gives them a good time – I loved it!

Claire *London Road* for me. It was really inspiring, a unique way of storytelling and really great writing. And it was inspiring to see the National Theatre make something like that as well.

What's your favourite British musical theatre song?

Scott 'Where Is Love?' from *Oliver!*

Claire I'm going to shout out to our fellow Scottish musical theatre writer and say 'Same But Different' from *Islander* by Finn Anderson.

What training did you do for your career?

Scott Claire and I met whilst studying at the Royal Conservatoire of Scotland. I was doing a BA in musical theatre and Claire was doing composition.

Claire I was Scott's MD for a couple projects. Without me knowing Scott had submitted us to write a musical at a festival at the Arches in Glasgow, so it was a bit of a surprise when we got that. It hadn't really been something I had thought about.

Scott That's a good piece of advice for people starting out with writing partnerships, don't tell them you're applying for stuff and see what happens

[*both laugh*]

Claire We got the commission, had to write the show in two weeks, and we've been together ever since.

Do you see *My Left/Right Foot* as a key British (Scottish) musical?

Scott At the time we were writing it, absolutely not. We were so preoccupied with how the show would even work as a story that I don't think we had time to acknowledge its place in the grander scheme of things and what it was trying to do.

I think it ended up being more significant than we realized purely because of the subject matter and how it handled that. I think, certainly within the realm of Scottish theatre but probably more broadly, that it allowed the form of the musical to tackle something that is quite a serious subject; how we approach and present disability on stage. Doing it in a way that was quite close to the edge and funny.

Musically, it was poppy, it was really accessible music, and it was hooky. I think that put a bit more of a stamp on what an original musical – certainly from Scotland – could sound and feel like because prior to that there had been successes with things like *Sunshine on Leith* and *Our Ladies of Perpetual Succour*

Claire And they were both jukebox musicals

Scott Exactly, and I think this was just putting a bit more confidence in the natural wit that's really present (more in Glasgow than anywhere else), allowing that to be the language that the show was told in.

Claire I think we knew it was a brave and risky idea. And we didn't know which way it was going to go. It's probably the riskiest thing we've attached ourselves to, but because it was such a fast paced rehearsal, production and writing period, we didn't really have time to think about that.

Scott Being able to write in an accent, without it being pastiche or 'here comes a funny Scottish character' or 'here's the evil cockney', was key I think. *My Left/Right Foot* is a significant show because it used regional accents, and that affected rhyme and word setting. What's happened a lot in the last sort of 5–10 years is that we're leaning more into dialect and stuff being a way that doesn't just shape how a show feels, but how songs sound.

You wrote additional music and lyrics for *My Left/Right Foot*, can you talk a little bit about the process?

Scott Up to that point all of our work had been just the two of us. We would come up with a story and concept together. I would write the book and the lyrics, Claire would do the music, and then together we would turn it into a show. *My Left/Right Foot* was the first time we'd been brought in exclusively as songwriters.

The process was super fast. Robert Softley Gale (the writer and director) knew he wanted the show to be about an amateur theatre company that attempts to do a production of

My Left Foot. He didn't have a structure or anything like that. He just had the bones of the idea and was really open about making it with us. He brought us on as a songwriting team and we structured this story with him, coming up with characters and stuff together.

It was our first experience of working with a book writer like that. He was really open to us bringing as much to the table as we wanted and it allowed us to think a bit more about what song needed to go where. The songs were allowed to take centre stage in that way, which I think we've maybe struggled to do a little bit in our own writing, because you're so busy being like 'oh my god its such a good scene'. So being there explicitly as songwriters was a new and important thing for us.

Claire It was a really fluid and quite organic writing process. I remember that Robert would use Google Docs and the script would be up on a big screen, and it would be changing in real time. The whole cast were there, so we were all basically around a table responding to the script and songs changing very quickly, which is the only time we've written like that. Writing at that speed is exciting. The actors were bringing so much to that process which really helped us write songs around them, knowing exactly what they could do and really playing to their strengths.

This was also a collaboration with Richard Thomas as well wasn't it?

Scott Yeah, it was. We had a couple of conversations with him about the structure and feel of the show. Then we just identified a moment in the show that he would come in and do his thing with. So there was one particular actor in the show that he ended up writing the music for, and it was very much in that sort of a classic Richard style that was really kind of like *Jerry Springer*. I think we brought a lot of daft rhymes and play with the lyric but Richard is much closer to the bone in terms of the subject matter.

Claire He helped us be more brave. I think that whenever you've got multiple songwriters on one project – that's the only time that we've had that happen – but whenever you've got that it's about trying to get a score that feels like one voice, even if it isn't. If the audience is sitting there, distracted by whether a song is by a different writer, then you haven't really collaborated in the best way. We wanted to make sure that the tone and the energy felt like one score. Which I think in the end it did, and that was because we were listening to each other's work, even though we were writing very separately.

Scott A really nice part of working with Richard is that he leaned into the accent and dialect of the piece and let that affect his writing, which helped us as well.

Claire I think if we'd had two years to think about it, I think we would all have taken less risks, thought too much about it, and maybe backed off. But because we had to write and react in real time it really helped the show. So you're really getting a first instinctive response from all the writers and actors in the room.

We had, I think, some of the best actors in Scotland in that first cast, and they really helped shape the show and we were just reacting to them, and it was quite a special way of making something.

How do you feel about *My Left/Right Foot* now?

Scott It's weird because it's coming up to five years ago. I think whenever you have that distance away from something you look back and go 'oh I wish we'd done that'. For me, it really did hit how successful and clear it can be to access and to talk about 'issue' based theatre without it feeling overly sincere, or worthy, or preachy. And that accessing it through humour, and being a bit close to the bone with the topic, and poking fun at the things that people poke fun at, that's the way that you allow a mirror to be held up to an audience as opposed to being something that is scolding or castigating people. When I think about how I feel about it now, I feel like the aim of the show was successful because of the discussion that happened after it.

Claire I'm really proud that we took a risk as writers because I felt very out of my comfort zone. I struggled to make music funny, certainly the pieces we were writing before were kind of filmic, they were not funny. Sometimes the jobs where you start out thinking you can't do it are the best, because you always find a way and you learn while doing it. And with this one it was a really big learning curve, for me in particular, but for both of us because we've never written in that bold, funny and approachable style.

How did the experience working on *My Left/Right Foot* shape your future work?

Scott We've gained a bit more confidence knowing that maybe a producer doesn't always know best in terms of what has to happen, or the structuring or the actual sound and feel of a story.

Claire We had no choice but to be bold with this show or else it just wouldn't have worked. And we learned a lot. I don't think we take ourselves as seriously now with our writing.

Scott For us it was chilling out a little bit. If a song has a hook or a catchy chorus that can be a good thing and it doesn't make the work feel any less valuable. And actually sometimes being a bit poppier with the writing can help the storytelling in a way that I don't think we were really acknowledging up to that point.

Are you both still working in musical theatre?

Scott This is our tenth year being a writing partnership. The kind of work that we make and where we make it has changed.

Claire We've done a lot of work in Scotland, but we're also working more and more in the States now. What's lovely about that is in both places it's about being really proud of who you are and staying authentic as writers.

What advice would you give to aspiring writers?

Scott I would always say, be eclectic in your ideas. Have more than one idea, write in more than one style. It's not just about developing your craft, it's what's asked of you now more than ever.

Claire Be yourself. Be authentic to you. Try and find your own voice. Think about what the audience is going to want in ten years, rather than now, and write that thing.

Sheffield
    audiences   5, 139
    city   2, 5–6, 101, 129, 139
    representations of   125, 126, 138
    'Sheffieldness'   138
    theatres in (see Theatre, UK regional)
Signal (new musicals concert)   195
SIX (musical)
    Aragon, Catherine of, as character in   141, 146
    Boleyn, Anne, as character in   141
    choreography in   155
    Cleves, Anna of, as character in   141, 146–9
    Howard, Katherine, as character in   141, 146
    Parr, Catherine, as character in   141, 144, 146
    racial coding in (see racism, coding)
    Seymour, Jane, as character in   141, 146, 147, 150
social media
    as digital platform   89
    as fandom space   89, 103
    as faux verbatim   178
    as means of promotion   xii, 155
    as sight of protest   150
    as vehicle for hate   180, 192
Softley Gale, Robert (director)   157, 173
Sondheim, Stephen (composer lyricist)   xiv, 32, 53, 156
South Asian communities   8, 69
    Aunty   7, 130–1
SpitLip (musical theatre company)   197
Standing at the Sky's Edge (musical)   1, 6, 139
Starlight Express (musical)   63
Stiles, George (composer)   142, 143, 154, 196
Stop Asian Hate (Campaign)   13
Stratford-upon-Avon   2, 34, 50, see also Royal Shakespeare Company
Sunset Boulevard (musical)   99
Sunshine on Leith (musical)   173
Sylvia (musical)   1

Taylor, Diana   70, 76
Taylor, Millie   1, 55, 67
Taylor, Richard (composer)   87, 92, 93, 196
temporality   53–4, 57, 90
theatre
    Donmar Warehouse   137
    Japanese   125
    London, West End
        Apollo Theatre   125
        Theatre Royal, Drury Lane   190
        Vaudeville Theatre   150
    London
        Arts Theatre   30, 143, 149, 184
        Royal Court, the   100
        Trafalgar Studios   103, 122
        Tricycle Theatre   181
        Turbine Theatre   180
        National Theatre (Royal National Theatre)   6, 88, 121, 172, 179
        Open Air Theatre, Regent's Park   124
    Seoul   125
    Soho Theatre, the   89, 100
    Swedish   191
    UK, Scottish
        National Theatre Scotland   8, 157, 161 (see also awards (theatrical), Edinburgh Fringe Awards; Edinburgh Fringe Festival)
    UK, Welsh
        Theatre Clwyd   180
    UK, regional
        Birmingham Hippodrome   197
        Bolton Octagon   196
        Bristol Old Vic Theatre   2, 103, 115, 121–3
        Chichester Festival Theatre   87, 88, 93, 137
        Sheffield Theatres   87, 137
        Storyhouse Chester   196
        York Theatre Royal (YTR)   197
    US, regional
        Alliance Theatre   196
        Las Vegas   125
theatre director
    collaboration   31, 34, 100, 190–1
    discussion of process   52, 64, 69, 155
    role   3, 91, 101, 122
    training   137
theatrical training
    Guildhall   121
    Motley Theatre Design   190
    Royal Central School of Speech and Drama   121
    Royal Scottish Conservatoire   172
    Sylvia Young Theatre School   83
Thomas, Richard (musical writer)   157, 174
Trump, Donald (President)   17, 42

University of Cambridge   100, 142, 154

verbatim
   faux-verbatim   178–82, 184, 185
   theatre   177–9, 181–2, 184, 185
   verbatim musicals   xiv, 8, 121, 177–85
   Welsh language   179
video editing   154

Wagstaff, Rachel (playwright)   87, 91, 93, 99–101
Warchus, Matthew (director)   33, 34, 51
Wax, Kenny (producer)   xiv, 143
West End (London)
   Broadway-West End binary   3, 55, 60
   casting practices in   145–5, 150
   finances of   1, 196
   musicals from regional theatres moved to   128, 129
   musicals having limited runs in   196
   musicals in the   4, 5, 33, 142, 143
   producers   142
   representation of British South Asian community in   67, 69–70, 78, 84
   small workshop venues in   103
   social media and the   155–6
   as a stand-in for all British musical theatre   2–3
Whitfield, Sarah K.   2, 4, 7, 53, 87, 126
Wicked (musical)   xiii, 99, 107, 148
Williams, Robbie (singer-songwriter)   19
Wolf, Stacy   19, 41, 54, 75
women
   Black women   145, 148
   characters   7, 36, 42, 43, 73
   experiences   89, 90, 144
   Women of Colour   89, 145

Yates, Samuel   110, 111, 158, 159, 163, 164
YouTube   29, 88, 93, 177, 179

Zavros, Demetris   177, 185

10 'As if gathered in a verbatim fashion'

The (mis)use of documentary markers in Chris Bush and Matt Winkworth's *The Assassination of Katie Hopkins* (2018)[1]

CYRIELLE GARSON

'Perhaps *London Road*, as a unique "line of flight" of the verbatim musical, is only a point of departure in experimenting with form and content [. . .] thereby re-inventing the musical in the 21st century'.[2]

'If you know the quote you want you can literally put the words in people's mouths'.[3]

Perhaps the most characteristic aspect of so-called verbatim musicals in Britain is their explicit reliance on the exact words of real people that have been previously gathered during a more or less prolonged R&D phase. Such a reliance or 'constraint'[4] can be said to have radically transformed what is typically understood as the contemporary British musical,[5] be it in terms of aesthetics,[6] politics,[7] music,[8] acting,[9] dramaturgy or even spectatorship. George Rodosthenous even goes as far as calling this phenomenon 'structural revolutions'[10] in his *Twenty-First Century Musicals: From Stage to Screen*. A good example of this radical transformation is most certainly found in Alecky Blythe and Adam Cork's 2011 pioneering verbatim musical *London Road* that has often been considered as a de facto paradigm shift for both the musical and verbatim theatre landscapes. Indeed, *London Road* is openly infused with strangeness as its music follows the pace and rhythm of recorded spontaneous speech, rather than the more conventional methodology of rhythmicizing text to fit musical metrics, and the generic distinctions between spoken and sung voice are almost completely dissolved.

Against expectations (even) within this context of relentless innovation, then, Chris Bush and Matt Winkworth's daringly titled musical theatre piece *The Assassination of Katie Hopkins* begins by telling its readers in the 'Notes' prior to the play itself that '[w]hile the events of the play are pure fiction, they are presented *as if gathered in a verbatim fashion*'.[11] In other words, even though the piece has the appearance of verbatim theatre – a type of performance based on actual words spoken by 'real people' – with 'interviews [. . .] audience address, [. . .] clips from television or radio broadcasts, Youtube videos, news bulletins, vlogs, minutes from meetings, voicemail messages',[12] the verbatim material does not in fact refer to any tangible external reality and is therefore no more than an aesthetic component in the musical, as is the immense sliding wall of lights designed by Lucy Osborne to look like the back of smartphones on stage and the multi-layered video design by Nina Dunn.

Similarly, the spectators in attendance are greeted by an apparently familiar disclaimer in the context of verbatim (musical) theatre:

> The following performance is constructed from interviews, audio recordings, CCTV footage, television and radio broadcasts and social media communications gathered following the tragic events of June 2018. While this material has been edited, no words have been changed, or meaning altered.

Except for the fact that the audience is well aware that the performance describes an imaginary future – the performance indeed premiered in April 2018 – and that Katie Hopkins was, of course, never assassinated in the world outside the performance. Quite clearly, we are no longer in the realm of verbatim musical theatre proper, but of *faux*-verbatim, and yet something from verbatim theatre remains intact, beyond the fact that the lyrics of the songs are all derived from real tweets.[13]

In light of this preliminary observation, it will be argued throughout this chapter that the *faux*-verbatim format chosen by Chris Bush and Matt Winkworth has profound implications for what will be called here 'pact of performance' – the theoretical contract between theatremakers and audiences that always frames reception – as well as for both the aesthetics and politics of an 'explicitly political 21st-century theatre'[14] piece. It will therefore be necessary to thoroughly question the role of hybridity within the general and specific stated aims of the authors. Indeed, does it serve a mere role of parody and critique of the verbatim genre itself, as once did Dennis Kelly's *Taking Care of Baby* (2007), and James Fritz's *Lines* (2011) to some extent? Or does the verbatim discourse invoked here self-reflexively serve to destabilize any definite meaning (following Jacques Derrida's seminal call for a practice that never ceases to interrogate its own premises), in keeping with the subject matter of the piece, namely – as projected on the wall of lights at the very start of the performance – 'free speech, public outrage, anonymity, fame, fact, opinions, lies, truth, social media mob'. Put another way, a fake, or rather *faux*-verbatim multimedia musical piece may appear particularly appropriate to address the post-truth era of fake news, spin, mistruths, half-lies and conspiracy theories in which we live in today. Next, in which ways are Bush and Winkworth using and misusing verbatim/documentary markers, and to what effect?[15] Last, but not least, how to account for this new aesthetic trajectory in the context of the ever-expanding practice field of the contemporary British musical?

The boom of the verbatim musical in Britain

'Verbatim and musical theatre make improbable bedfellows'.[16]
'I could do these [verbatim] plays AND have an exciting vehicle for my songs'.[17]

As Adam Lenson persuasively demonstrates throughout his *Breaking into Song*, musicals are by essence 'an intersected form'.[18] Indeed, the musical is neither a static genre, nor is it a conservative form per se. It is inherently hybrid and complex, and harbours a wide variety of practices and phenomena involving text, music and songs. Arguably, the contemporary musical in its 'integrated', 'dis-integrated'[19] and even 'post-integrated'[20] formats is increasingly flexible and interdisciplinary. Not surprisingly, the renaissance of verbatim theatre in Britain since the mid-1990s has also intersected with the musical theatre genre, despite their apparent contradictions signalled by Stuart Young above.

In recent years, the verbatim musical – to be understood here as 'a verbatim performance which prominently displays its musical and sung material'[21] – has in effect become a recognizable experimental field within the contemporary British musical theatre ecology, with its own terminologies, practices and boundaries.[22] This led to entirely new styles of writing musicals in Britain and further afield beyond the aforementioned groundbreaking *London Road*: Leeds-based company 203 Theatre's verbatim musical *Untold Wars* (2015) condensed 100 years of Britain at war in about sixty minutes, Bethan Marlow created *Nyrsys*, a Welsh-language verbatim musical on nurses' real-life experience in 2018, and, more recently, Francesca Forristal and Jordan Paul Clarke's *Public Domain* (2021) – a verbatim musical parody about the internet entirely created from tweets, Instagram posts and YouTube videos – featured actors lip-synching to actual footage of Mark Zuckerberg. The verbatim musical realm also had its own version of the tribunal play in 2017, *Committee*, about the collapse of UK charity Kids Company.[23]

Similar to the verbatim play, the verbatim musical in Britain also started to embrace the massaged-verbatim format, that is to say, following Australian verbatim playwright Alana Valentine's coinage of the term (2009), either the use of verbatim techniques to create fiction or the shaping of the verbatim material around a fictional narrative structure. A good example of this practice is undoubtedly Bryony Kimmings and Brian Lobel's *A Pacifist's Guide to the War on Cancer* (2016), an experimental, hybrid documentary musical piece made in collaboration with Complicité Associates and the National Theatre with its own experimental sonic universe and an intermittently onstage band.[24] *A Pacifist's Guide* initially presents itself as a musical about illness and death, specifically examining life with a cancer diagnosis and containing 'adult themes and strong language', rather than as a documentary piece based on interviews. The characters are all, we later discover, based on thirty real-life cases of cancer patients (the show was also made in collaboration with them), but this is a fictional musical piece, until we reach the third part, 'getting real', that is.[25] In this final part, '[t]he verbatim scene plays. Slowly throughout it Emma listens. She is being surrounded by real people with cancer. As each voiceover plays, the corresponding ACTOR mouths along'.[26] Even more poignantly, in the final minutes of the show, the audience is introduced to a real cancer survivor – Lara Veitch, a non-actor who has had six bouts of cancer in her lifetime due to a rare inherited genetic condition: '*A CANCER PATIENT comes onstage, introduces themself and talks about their diagnosis. They read out their hopes*'.[27]

One of the questions that musical performances mixing verbatim and non-verbatim material such as *A Pacifist's Guide to the War on Cancer* raise is whether or not the proportion of documentary/verbatim material in the final production drastically affects the reception of a given audience. Interestingly, a piece like Look Left Look Right's *See Me Now* (2017) about the life of sex workers takes the exact opposite approach. Within the massaged-verbatim musical field of practice, this is a verbatim show with movement and musical sequences. As a particular arrangement of facts, fiction, songs and music, such hybrid verbatim musicals put fact and fiction into such close proximity that the line dividing and demarcating them is entirely blurred. Yet, another subversion is at play when it comes to the mock/*faux*-verbatim musical that constitutes the main focus of this chapter. However, in what follows, I suggest that these hybrid verbatim musicals are best viewed not as merging two different dramatic and theatrical modes, but as generating a new form that stimulates a vigorous and fruitful debate regarding what constitutes facts and fiction within and beyond the frame of the musical performance.

Patterns of spectatorship and generic instability in the *faux-*verbatim musical

The Assassination of Katie Hopkins premiered at Theatre Clwyd, Mold, in North Wales, in April 2018, in a production directed by James Grieve that went on to win Best Musical Production at the 2018 UK Theatre Awards. It was also briefly revised and updated to reflect recent shifts in politics for the MTFest at the Turbine Theatre, London, in February 2020. The musical piece revolves around two asymmetrical tragic events in the complex digital (mis)information age we live in today: the contentious imagined death of the eponymous 'character' Katie Hopkins, one of Britain's most controversial and outspoken alt-right commentators, at the fictional BME (British Media and Entertainment) Awards, and that of twelve ordinary people who mysteriously died in a caravan fire on a fruit-picking farm in Kent. Despite the contentious media and social media reaction back in 2017 when the musical was first publicly announced, Katie Hopkins is never represented on stage, and the real focus of the piece is on the aftermath of the event and how it completely overshadowed the low-profile tragic event that happened on the same day, rather than the event itself.[28] The story is mainly told through two young female protagonists: human rights' charity worker Kayleigh Harris and trainee solicitor Shayma Hussaini whose stories never quite meet, apart from one instance in the antepenultimate number 'Your Official Update' when they both sing the same chorus 'empathy exhaustion' together. The musical is in many respects a post-Brexit piece that accurately captures the divisions within British society, as well as the polarization around matters of free speech in the digital age. The characters on stage, portrayed by a cast of eight who multirole and play both sides of the arguments, spend most of their time – within two acts and a total of thirty-nine numbers – interacting with media.

One of the most striking features of the production concerns its deployment beyond documentary and verbatim musical theatre *stricto sensu* of documentary markers, which are the generic elements enabling an audience to understand that the performance they are watching is made out of either found documents in the public realm or interviews with real people conducted by the creative team. These 'authenticity' markers are indeed everywhere to be seen on stage, not least with the omnipresence of the Dictaphone or 'recording apparatus',[29] which typically serves to remind an audience of the verbatim origin of the piece. In fact, their multiplicity and accumulation may paradoxically entail the opposite effect: rather than creating documentary realism on stage, they produce an effect of strangeness, of an acceleration beyond reason that is more a reflection of one's perception of our media-saturated age, than the empirical reality of it. Alternatively, as Tom Cantrell has convincingly argued on a related subject in his *Acting in Documentary Theatre*, we may extrapolate that, ironically, despite the countless and constant influx of documentary markers featured in the performance, the audience eventually becomes desensitized and may simply accept these markers as a new convention in the pact of performance without them 'necessarily interrupt[ing] the narrative flow or the audience's identification with the characters'.[30]

This is even more true in the case of *faux*-verbatim, as the audience is well aware from the very beginning that these documentary markers are part of the fable. Indeed, contrary to Dennis Kelly's 2007 *faux*-verbatim piece *Taking Care of Baby* that attempted to mislead the audience with the following disclaimer – 'The following has been taken word for word from interviews and correspondence. Nothing has been added and everything is in the subject's own words, though some editing has taken place. Names have not been changed'[31] – *The Assassination of Katie Hopkins* employs a different strategy with full-frontal and early acknowledgement of its fictional status and a more creative use of documentary markers. This immediately raises the question of its generic belonging along the 'continuum of reality theatre practices',[32] especially if these documentary markers are more likely to slip in and out of the margins of attention. If we temporarily posit that the *faux*-verbatim musical exemplified by *The Assassination of Katie Hopkins* has a different relationship to both reality and verbatim theatre, and that the documentary markers have only an intermittent effect, or perhaps even no 'reality' effect at all, we can conclude that the *faux*-verbatim musical is also different from a *faux*-tribunal play such as the Tricycle Theatre's 2007 *Called to Account: The Indictment of Anthony Charles Lynton Blair for the Crime of Aggression Against Iraq—A Hearing* which showed to an audience what a trial of then prime minister Tony Blair for war crimes might look like. In both *Taking Care of Baby* and *Called to Account*, the 'reality' effect is turned on, and both pieces attempt to sustain the unsustainable, that is to say documentary realism, while *Taking Care of Baby* is pure fiction and *Called to Account* is actual verbatim, but at the time of the production, the trial of Tony Blair had not yet taken place. Arguably, in this context, the *faux*-verbatim musical represents a deliberate generic confusion of sorts.

With its easily identified lineage to *London Road*, *The Assassination of Katie Hopkins* was first considered by theatre reviewer Natasha Tripney as 'a kind of Twitter-literate London Road'.[33] Like *London Road*, the language appears unpolished, with the familiar repetitions, hesitations, glottal stops, interruptions reproduced in the *faux*-verbatim speech and songs: 'We call it empathy exhaustion. Um. Yeah, Empathy Exhaustion. Cos it's a battle – a real battle, y'know'.[34] Likewise, in the fifth number of Act Two, 'One in a Million', Shayma Hussaini performs a typical 'false start' in the middle of her presentation at work: 'And the cot bed – camp bed – There was a camp bed',[35] giving the impression of spontaneous speech.

However, it is also clear that Bush and Winkworth's piece significantly departs from *London Road*. For Clare Chandler, *The Assassination of Katie Hopkins* can be considered as 'a post-dramatic, post-integrated, post-truth verbatim musical' (2019), which seems to indicate that another subversion of the genre may be at stake in this performance. To these compelling labels, one could also add 'post-verbatim' (musical), a term used by British company Breach Theatre to describe 'using verbatim techniques but in a way that acknowledges their failure to tell a full version of the truth'.[36] Strikingly, the Bloomsbury database 'Drama Online' classifies the piece as belonging to no less than three different categories: musical theatre, verbatim theatre and postmodern theatre.[37] The label 'postmodern theatre' – which is not used on the site to describe *London Road* – seems to connote the presence of transgressive elements in the piece that go well beyond a verbatim musical such as *London Road*. While dissent may arise in respect of some of these categorizations, it is clear that the plurality of these labels signals a musical resisting and exceeding (easy) categorization.

For the purposes of this chapter, I will consider here two main ways in which these documentary markers are (mis)used in this *faux*-verbatim musical performance. First, these documentary markers perpetuate the idea of authenticity, as if we were in a 'conventional' verbatim musical. In the antepenultimate number of Act One, 'Interview with Beyoncé Knowles', for instance, we encounter a typical documentary marker. The audience first sees projected on the screen the actual MP3 file being played with people singing 'England til I die', before seeing the actors singing the same song afterwards. Actors appear in that instance to be replaying an original verbatim recording, similar to the AGM at the very start of *London Road*: 'The original audio recording of Ron's speech is heard over the PA in the auditorium. It fades out as Ron starts to sing'.[38] Crucially, some of these documentary markers are not concerned in the slightest with advancing the plot. A good example of this can be found in the second number of Act Two, 'Empathy Exhaustion', when Fazil – the dentist who was mistakenly confused with Katie Hopkins' murderer – is seen adjusting his mic and testing the sound, and later '*unclip[ing] his microphone*',[39] replicating a verbatim interview in direct address to the audience. There is also an unmistakably comic side to this reproduction in the context of a *faux*-verbatim piece. One cannot help but see the underlying comedy in songs created from everyday banality, such as this one sung by Shayma in Act Two, '**I just lost signal on my phone**'.[40]

Second, some of the documentary markers are tainted with strangeness, just enough strangeness to make us question the whole process, or perhaps the process of verbatim theatre itself. In the fourth number of Act One, 'Where were you when?' for example, Kayleigh Harris and Shayma Hussaini's interviews are heard alongside some music that make them sound slightly odd, out of kilter with the otherwise impression of authenticity. These strategies create ambiguity and a critical distance from the documentary markers used in the piece. Throughout the performance, one notices a gradual progression, ranging from subtle to progressively more direct and intrusive interventions, serving to undermine the pretence of documentary and verbatim material. In the eleventh number of Act Two, we thus see '*an auto-tuned remix of the interview*'[41] we have seen before. There is even more distortion when later on '*OLLIE and the BAND perform a lounge/swing version of the remixed song*'.[42] Quite plainly, several characters address the inauthenticity in using interview material throughout the piece. Towards the end of Act Two, Stuart, the host of a late-night comedy show, further highlights this juxtaposition when he says the following: 'Now remember, these are all the exact words you said, Miss Harris – we might've just had a little fun with the order of them'.[43] Here, Stuart is by extension also highlighting the inauthenticity of verbatim theatre as a whole, and perhaps even serving as a mouthpiece for Bush and Winkworth.

Importantly, there is also the presence of musical markers that seemingly clash entirely with what some of the documentary markers were attempting to construct. These moments in the piece, such as the end of the ninth number of Act Two, 'Allahu Akbar, Motherfucker',[44] do not seek to recreate a feel of verbatim theatre. Towards the end of this number – after the racial harassment of Shayma in a tube carriage by (drunk) MAN 1 – MAN 1 addresses Shayma in these terms 'So what d'you say'[45] when all of a sudden '*[a]ll apart from SHAYMA are frozen, as we cut to an interview. She sings to us*'.[46] Shayma's song in that moment freezes time and takes us away from any semblance of verbatim theatre.

Part of what makes this musical so powerful, though, is its sustained use and adaptation of verbatim (musical) theatre techniques. If the aesthetics of the piece are undeniably complex, as we have just seen, so too are its politics.

Political theatre

As to be expected, the satirical *The Assassination of Katie Hopkins* provoked strong reactions, and even ironically political recuperation, long before its actual premiere on 20 April 2018, but this section will steer away from these to address the politics of the piece, rather than the complex and contradictory discourse that surrounded it at the time.[47]

Despite what may be assumed from the title, one of the show's co-writers, Chris Bush, explained in an interview that 'she hoped the production would challenge audiences' preconceptions about Hopkins'.[48] In other words, the stated intention of the creative team was to offer a sympathetic portrayal of Hopkins, or at least a more nuanced one. It is to be conceded at this point that there is a greater degree of freedom in *The Assassination of Katie Hopkins* (in comparison to actual verbatim musicals) that inevitably affects the politics of the piece, even if one must keep in mind the need to refrain from assuming, following Liz Tomlin's cautionary argument in *Acts and Apparitions* (2013), that a given theatre form is automatically and uniquely invested in certain politics.

One of the things that the format allowed, though, was more fluidity in the characters' trajectories throughout the performance. Not being tied to a necessarily limited and static picture of the characters (due to an exclusive reliance on verbatim material) allowed the audience to witness the transformation of characters. One such transformation spectacularly occurs in the character of Kayleigh who progressively relates to Katie Hopkins, to the point that she ends up founding the Justice 4 Katie movement. However, rather than conceiving of middle-ground positions with sympathy for Katie Hopkins without the need to adhere to alt-right ideologies threatening democracy itself, the musical shows Kayleigh going all in. Although she arguably never surpasses her new role-model, Kayleigh eventually expresses her wish to change fundamental human rights in the UK in favour of complete freedom over hate speech. The reverse, that is the opposite trajectory for a character, is not, however, represented in the piece, and the two main characters are self-identified as left-leaning. From this perspective, the musical cannot be accused of 'preaching [. . .] to the converted'.[49]

Instead, the musical addresses the political hypocrisy of a subdivision of the left, what Kayleigh calls 'liberal, all-welcoming utopia' or 'lovely little left-wing bubble',[50] while astutely camouflaging its own position in the same manner as Grace Harwood, *The Guardian* journalist in Act Two, attempts to camouflage her political affiliation from the radio show presenter Joey and his producer Mark. For James Hudson, this is somewhat pernicious, as the musical implicitly authorizes a 'moderate centre position, one that is not only no less ideological than the positions they critique, but to some degree arguably works to legitimize the nationalistic, racist and socially reactionary perspectives they examine'.[51] Arguably, the attempt to painstakingly create a 'moderate' centre position was dictated by the need to mitigate the boldness of the act of creating a musical titled *The Assassination of Katie Hopkins*. This being said, there also seems to be an awareness of these caveats within the piece itself, most clearly visible in the character of Pippa Goldstein, one of the guests in a late-night comedy show towards the end of Act Two who is aware of one of the fault lines with a society 'so obsessed with the idea of everyone's opinion being valid that we hear lunatics calling for a race war and rather than calling the police we book them in for *Newsnight*'.[52] To pursue the point even further, the scenography laying bare multiple perspectives for each action can be said to offer a tacit invitation to constantly question one's own political certainties. This is made especially clear through the presence of the COMPANY – a modernized chorus figure who constantly shifts perspectives – in several numbers throughout the performance. In the eighth number of Act Two, 'Have You Seen This? (Part 1)', for instance, the 'COMPANY come forward as various online commenters, talking about the interview we've just seen'.

Another target of the political intervention showcased by the piece is verbatim theatre itself, as Clare Chandler has astutely demonstrated in her 2019 paper, but not to the level of deconstruction proposed by Dennis Kelly's *Taking Care of Baby*. In the penultimate number, 'England 'Til I Die', the reporter talks in direct address to the audience 'as if being interviewed'[53] to reveal some unethical journalistic and editing practices, pointing to verbatim theatre by extension and the need to remain critical:

> So I–I can say to someone like–(*Turning to a protestor*) 'Katie Hopkins was an icon, wasn't she?' and they go: PROTESTOR. Yeah Katie Hopkins was an icon. REPORTER (*to audience*). I cut the 'yeah' and: PROTESTOR. Bingo. That's the line I needed, right there on tape.[54]

But there is no apparent critique of the critique of verbatim theatre, or of *faux*-verbatim theatre to be found in the performance. What is clear, though, is that the piece problematizes boundaries, what is deemed acceptable, that is to say the 'Overton Window'.[55] The whole musical constantly asks this through its title, through its choice of a *faux*-verbatim format, through the choices made by the two protagonists and more openly in the third number of Act Two, 'Zombie Hopkins',[56] where the radio presenter Joey asks in response to Grace Harwood's article: 'is that acceptable?',[57] which can be perceived as an almost self-reflexive gesture alluding to this musical's own controversial status.

Unlike *London Road*, there is no real closure for both plots, as the 'investigation into the death of twelve fruit-pickers in Kent has found no evidence of wrongdoing'[58] and 'the Metropolitan Police [has] issued a statement [. . .] saying they were suspending their investigation into the murder of media personality Katie Hopkins'.[59] And in the final number, even the hopeful creation of 'British Justice' by Shayma Hussaini – a new not-for-profit organization to make justice more accessible to those in less privileged positions – is undercut by the (social) media machine: '*She is interrupted by a bleeping message [. . .] More bleeps and messages*'.[60] Shayma is seen here frenetically competing for people's attention until '*she's totally lost them*',[61] and they have inexorably moved on to the next algorithmically produced media instant, a potent image that feels like a repetition (of the opening number) with a difference, now that the audience has critically and emotionally engaged with the musical for more than two hours.

Conclusion

As this chapter has shown, verbatim theatre and, in particular here, verbatim musical theatre have become an actual stylistic device in twenty-first-century Britain. If for verbatim pioneer Peter Cheeseman, music was in effect considered as a 'bloodstream that pulses through [documentary]',[62] could it be now that we have come full circle, and that verbatim has become, to some extent, a bloodstream that pulses through musical theatre itself, with all the creative possibilities that this presents for the contemporary British musical? As Demetris Zavros suggests in the epigraph that precedes this chapter, it may be the case that the mainstream success of London Road opened the gates for new and bold experiments, markedly putting an end to some erroneous claims according to which the prolonged use of verbatim methodologies were to deprive theatre of its precious vitality and playfulness.[63]

From a startling approach to dramatic language and musical composition to the (mis)use of documentary markers in the *faux*-verbatim musical, the adaptation of verbatim techniques in the contemporary British musical cannot be reduced to the sole purpose of creating documentary realism on stage, as the close study of The Assassination of Katie Hopkins in this chapter has demonstrated.[64] Quite the contrary, this case study revealed that the *faux*-verbatim musical mediates a productive tension between facts and fiction, and usefully complicates conventional understandings of both the musical and verbatim theatre. More important, The Assassination of Katie Hopkins in the context of the continuous developments of the verbatim musical in Britain should not be considered as an outlier, but as typical of the ever-growing body of the twenty-first-century musical, and especially the contemporary British musical that 'interrogates, parodies and subverts its own status'.[65]

There have also been some recent and notable developments in the digital theatre realm that have interesting potential for verbatim musical theatre, as we move into the future of a post-COVID-19 world a whole decade after London Road first opened in the Cottesloe Theatre. For one, machine learning (ML) and artificial intelligence (AI) have already impacted the world of musical theatre. There is even a new breed of verbatim musicals, not based on the exact words of real people, but on compiling raw data from hundreds of past musicals (scores, scripts, structure, music, etc.) to generate new melodies, lyrics and the actual script thanks to a computer programme. In 2016, the first ever computer-generated musical, *Beyond the Fence*, was thus produced at the Arts Theatre in London, and we can certainly expect to see far more verbatim musical experiments of this kind in the not-too-distant future.

Notes

1. Heartfelt thanks to Matt Winkworth and Gus Gowland for helping me access a copy of the 2018 production of the *Assassination of Katie Hopkins*. This quotation is from the 'notes on text and production' in the published playtext of *The Assassination of Katie Hopkins*.
2. D. Zavros, 'Encounters with "The Same" (But Different): *London Road* and the Politics of Territories and Repetitions in Verbatim Musical Theatre', *Studies in Musical Theatre* 15 (2021): 219–35.
3. Chris Bush and Matt Winkworth, *The Assassination of Katie Hopkins* (London: Nick Hern, 2018). Kindle Edition.
4. Élisabeth Angel-Perez, 'La contrainte comme artifice sur la scène anglaise contemporaine: Tom Stoppard, Martin Crimp, et Caryl Churchill', *Études Britanniques Contemporaines* 10 (2009), https://journals.openedition.org/sillagescritiques/1877.
5. David Roesner, 'Genre Counterpoints: Challenges to the Mainstream Musical', in *The Oxford Handbook of the British Musical*, ed. Robert Gordon and Olaf Jubin (Oxford: Oxford University Press, 2017), 651–72; Charles Spencer, 'London Road', *Telegraph*, 15 April 2011, https://www.telegraph.co.uk/culture/theatre/theatre-reviews/8453051/London-Road-National-Theatre-review.html.

6. Cyrielle Garson, *Beyond Documentary Realism: Aesthetic Transgressions in British Verbatim Theatre* (Berlin: De Gruyter, 2021).
7. Zavros, 'Encounters with "The Same" (But Different)'.
8. Tom Parkinson, *Music and Contemporary Theatre*. Unpublished PhD thesis (Royal Holloway, University of London, 2019).
9. Tom Cantrell, *Acting in Documentary Theatre* (Basingstoke: Palgrave Macmillan, 2013).
10. George Rodosthenous, *Twenty-First Century Musicals: From Stage to Screen* (London: Routledge, 2018), 2.
11. Bush and Winkworth, *The Assassination of Katie Hopkins*, my emphasis.
12. Bush and Winkworth, *The Assassination of Katie Hopkins*.
13. *Faux* verbatim designates theatre works that are not based on the exact words of real people, but adopt a specific language and strategies that make the audience think it is verbatim. As for the *faux*/mock verbatim musical itself, its main activity is not the musical treatment of verbatim material but the appearance of verbatim within a musical.
14. James Hudson, 'Right from the Centre: The Dramaturgy of Right-Wing Politics in Chris Hannan's *What Shadows*, Chris Bush's *The Assassination of Katie Hopkins*, and Rob Drummond's *The Majority*', *Studies in Theatre and Performance* 41, no. 3 (2021): 2.
15. In this chapter, documentary markers are understood as the opposite of 'markers of theatricality' indicating that we are in the world of fiction and musical theatre. In other words, they are markers of authenticity, the use of the 'real' within the frame of the performance.
16. Stuart Young, '*London Road* (review)', *Theater Journal* 64, no. 1 (2012): 101.
17. Mark Wheeler, *Verbatim: The Fun of Making Theatre Seriously* (Glasgow: Salamander Street, 2021), 40.
18. Adam Lenson, *Breaking into Song: Why You Shouldn't Hate Musicals* (Glasgow: Salamander Street, 2021), 30.
19. Dominic Symonds and Dan Rebellato, 'Editorial', *Contemporary Theatre Review* 19, no. 1 (2009): 6.
20. Millie Taylor, *The Routledge Companion to The Contemporary Musical*, ed. Jessica Sternfeld and Elizabeth L. Wollman (New York: Routledge, 2020), 18.
21. Garson, *Beyond Documentary Realism*, 260.
22. More surprisingly, perhaps, the verbatim musical was even used in the context of dementia care Stuart Wood, 'Beyond Messiaen's Birds: The Post-verbal World of Dementia', *Medical Humanities* 46 (2019): 73–83.
23. The piece's full title is *The Public Administration and Constitutional Affairs Committee Takes Oral Evidence on Whitehall's Relationship with Kids Company*. Tribunal plays are verbatim reconstructions of public inquiries which typically give a different perspective on current affairs (i.e. the ones done by the then-named Tricycle Theatre under the directorship of Nicolas Kent in North London on the invasion of Iraq, human rights abuses and torture, racism in the police force, etc.).
24. Complicité Associates is a new programme whereby Complicité commissions and produces new work from other theatremakers. *A Pacifist's Guide to the War on Cancer* was their first project. In 2018, a new version of the piece with a smaller cast featured Bryony Kimmings telling the story of the making of the original 2016 show. This section focuses on the original version only.
25. Bryony Kimmings and Brian Lobel, *A Pacifist's Guide to the War on Cancer* (London: Oberon, 2016), 49.

26. Kimmings and Lobel, *A Pacifist's Guide to the War on Cancer*, 49.
27. Kimmings and Lobel, *A Pacifist's Guide to the War on Cancer*, 55.
28. The character of Hopkins is never on stage, but her name appears in numerous numbers. Her face is also projected on the screen during the opening number, 'Have You Seen This'.
29. Bush and Winkworth, *The Assassination of Katie Hopkins*.
30. Cantrell, *Acting in Documentary Theatre*, 168.
31. Dennis Kelly, *Taking Care of Baby* (London: Oberon, 2007), 15.
32. Caroline Wake, 'Verbatim Theatre within a Spectrum of Practices', in *Verbatim: Staging Memory & Community*, ed. Paul. Brown (Strawberry Hills: Currency Press. 2010), 6.
33. Natasha Tripney, 'The Assassination of Katie Hopkins', *The Stage*, 27 April 2018b.
34. Bush and Winkworth, *The Assassination of Katie Hopkins*.
35. Bush and Winkworth, *The Assassination of Katie Hopkins*.
36. Jen Harvie, Billy Barrett and Ellice Stevens (2019), 'Episode 9: Breach Theatre: It's True, it's True, it's True', *Stage Left with Jen Harvie* [podcast], https://soundcloud.com/stage_left/episode-9-breachtheatre-its-true-its-true-its-true.
37. *London Road* is classified in the Drama Online database as musical theatre, verbatim theatre and also as a history play but not as an example of postmodern theatre.
38. Alecky Blythe and Adam Cork, *London Road* (London: Nick Hern, 2011), 5.
39. Bush and Winkworth, *The Assassination of Katie Hopkins*.
40. Bush and Winkworth, *The Assassination of Katie Hopkins*.
41. Bush and Winkworth, *The Assassination of Katie Hopkins*.
42. Bush and Winkworth, *The Assassination of Katie Hopkins*.
43. Bush and Winkworth, *The Assassination of Katie Hopkins*.
44. Bush and Winkworth, *The Assassination of Katie Hopkins*.
45. Bush and Winkworth, *The Assassination of Katie Hopkins*.
46. Bush and Winkworth, *The Assassination of Katie Hopkins*.
47. The musical was turned into a political argument by Katie Hopkins herself, claiming that the performance incited hate crime.
48. Mark Brown, 'Theatre to Stage Musical Based on Imaginary Death of Katie Hopkins', *The Guardian*, 11 October 2017.
49. Tiffany Jenkins, 'Political Theatre's Final Curtain', *Independent*, 28 December 2011.
50. Bush and Winkworth, *The Assassination of Katie Hopkins*.
51. Hudson, 'Right from the Centre', 2.
52. Bush and Winkworth, *The Assassination of Katie Hopkins*.
53. Bush and Winkworth, *The Assassination of Katie Hopkins*.
54. Bush and Winkworth, *The Assassination of Katie Hopkins*.
55. Named after Joseph P. Overton, a vice president of the Mackinac Center for Public Policy who developed the concept in the 1990s, the Overton window refers to the range of ideas that are considered to be politically acceptable at a particular time within a given society. In short, the Overton window is not a static concept, as it shifts over time following the change in the public's views and attitudes. The Overton window can be influenced by a variety of factors, including media coverage and social media (i.e. amplification, echo chambers, fake news, etc.).
56. Bush and Winkworth, *The Assassination of Katie Hopkins*.
57. Bush and Winkworth, *The Assassination of Katie Hopkins*.
58. Bush and Winkworth, *The Assassination of Katie Hopkins*.

59. Bush and Winkworth, *The Assassination of Katie Hopkins*.
60. Bush and Winkworth, *The Assassination of Katie Hopkins*.
61. Bush and Winkworth, *The Assassination of Katie Hopkins*.
62. Roy Nevitt, 'Peter Cheeseman', *Documentary Arts Reports* 2 (1986): 7–10.
63. Aleks Sierz, *The Theatre of Martin Crimp* (London: Methuen Drama, 2006), 155–6.
64. As I have argued elsewhere (Cyrielle Garson and Madelena Gonzalez, '"What a Carve up!": The Eclectic Aesthetics of Postmodernism and the Politics of Diversity in Some Examples of Contemporary British Verbatim Theatre', *Études Britanniques Contemporaines* 49 (2015), https://ebc.revues.org/2685.), documentary realism is to be understood as a historical aesthetic exponent that unproblematically draws the audience into the reality of a particular situation, topic, event or narrative being dramatized and authenticated through verbatim sources.
65. Roesner, 'Genre Counterpoints: Challenges to the Mainstream Musical', 652.

References

Angel-Perez, Élisabeth (2009), 'La contrainte comme artifice sur la scène anglaise contemporaine: Tom Stoppard, Martin Crimp, et Caryl Churchill', *Études Britanniques Contemporaines*, 10, https://journals.openedition.org/sillagescritiques/1877.
Blythe, Alecky and Adam Cork (2011), *London Road*. London: Nick Hern.
Brown, Mark (2017), 'Theatre to Stage Musical Based on Imaginary Death of Katie Hopkins', *The Guardian*, 11 October.
Bush, Chris and Matt Winkworth (2018), *The Assassination of Katie Hopkins*. London: Nick Hern. Kindle Edition.
Cantrell, Tom (2013), *Acting in Documentary Theatre*. Basingstoke: Palgrave Macmillan.
Chandler, Clare (2019) '"Have You Seen This?" Notions of Authenticity in Post-Truth Verbatim Musical Theatre', unpublished paper given at the 14th Song, Stage and Screen Conference held at the University of Leeds on 26-29 June.
Garson, Cyrielle (2021), *Beyond Documentary Realism: Aesthetic Transgressions in British Verbatim Theatre*. Berlin: De Gruyter.
Garson, Cyrielle and Madelena Gonzalez (2015), '"What a Carve up!": The Eclectic Aesthetics of Postmodernism and the Politics of Diversity in Some Examples of Contemporary British Verbatim Theatre', *Études Britanniques Contemporaines*, 49, https://ebc.revues.org/2685.
Harvie, Jen, Billy Barrett and Ellice Stevens (2019), 'Episode 9: Breach Theatre: *It's True, it's True, it's True*', *Stage Left with Jen Harvie* [podcast], https://soundcloud.com/stage_left/episode-9-breachtheatre-its-true-its-true-its-true.
Hudson, James (2021), 'Right from the Centre: The Dramaturgy of Right-Wing Politics in Chris Hannan's *What Shadows*, Chris Bush's *The Assassination of Katie Hopkins*, and Rob Drummond's *The Majority*', *Studies in Theatre and Performance*, 41 (3): 321–38.
Jenkins, Tiffany (2011), 'Political Theatre's Final Curtain', *Independent*, 28 December.
Kelly, Dennis (2007), *Taking Care of Baby*. London: Oberon.
Kimmings, Bryony and Brian Lobel (2016), *A Pacifist's Guide to the War on Cancer*. London: Oberon.
Klein, Bernhard (2013), '"*Stuff Happens*": David Hare and Verbatim Theatre', in Marie Hologa, Christian Lenz, Cyprian Piskurek and Stefan Schlensag (eds), *Cases of Intervention: The Great Variety of British Cultural Studies*, 207–22. Newcastle upon Tyne: Cambridge Scholars.
Lenson, Adam (2021), *Breaking into Song: Why You Shouldn't Hate Musicals*. Glasgow: Salamander Street.

Nevitt, Roy (1986), 'Peter Cheeseman', *Documentary Arts Reports*, 2: 7–10.

Norton-Taylor, Richard and Nicolas Kent (2007), *Called to Account: The Indictment of Anthony Charles Lynton Blair for the Crime of Aggression against Iraq – A Hearing*. London: Oberon.

Parkinson, Tom (2019), *Music and Contemporary Theatre*. Unpublished PhD thesis, Royal Holloway, University of London.

Rodosthenous, George (2018), *Twenty-First Century Musicals: From Stage to Screen*. London: Routledge.

Roesner, David (2017), 'Genre Counterpoints: Challenges to the Mainstream Musical', in Robert Gordon and Olaf Jubin (eds), *The Oxford Handbook of the British Musical*, 651–72. Oxford: Oxford University Press.

Sierz, Aleks (2006), *The Theatre of Martin Crimp*. London: Methuen Drama.

Spencer, Charles (2011), 'London Road', *Telegraph*, 15 April, https://www.telegraph.co.uk/culture/theatre/theatre-reviews/8453051/London-Road-National-Theatre-review.html.

Symonds, Dominic and Dan Rebellato (2009), 'Editorial', *Contemporary Theatre Review*, 19 (1): 3–7.

Taylor, Millie (2020), *The Routledge Companion to The Contemporary Musical*, edited by Jessica Sternfeld and Elizabeth L. Wollman, 17–25. New York: Routledge.

Tomlin, Liz (2013), *Acts and Apparitions: Discourses on the Real in Performance Practice and Theory, 1990–2010*. Manchester: Manchester University Press.

Tripney, Natasha (2018a), 'Playwright Chris Bush: "With Social Media, it's Like we're Learning a New Language"', *The Stage*, 20 April.

Tripney, Natasha (2018b), 'The Assassination of Katie Hopkins', *The Stage*, 27 April.

Valentine, Alana (2009), 'Captivated by Reality: The Alex Buzo Lecture 2009', https://performing.artshub.com.au/news-article/news/performing-arts/media-release/-captivated-by-reality-the-alex-buzo-lecture-2009-by-alana-valentine--179013.

Wake, Caroline (2010), 'Verbatim Theatre Within a Spectrum of Practices', in Paul Brown (ed.), *Verbatim: Staging Memory & Community*, 6–8. Strawberry Hills: Currency Press.

Wheeler, Mark (2021), *Verbatim: The Fun of Making Theatre Seriously*, Glasgow: Salamander Street.

Wood, Stuart (2019), 'Beyond Messiaen's Birds: The Post-verbal World of Dementia', *Medical Humanities*, 46: 73–83.

Young, Stuart (2012), '*London Road* (review)' *Theater Journal*, 64 (1): 101–2.

Zavros, Demetris (2021), 'Encounters with "The Same" (But Different): *London Road* and the Politics of Territories and Repetitions in Verbatim Musical Theatre', *Studies in Musical Theatre*, 15: 219–35.

Lucy Osborne interview

Designer *The Assassination of Katie Hopkins*

What is your favourite British musical?

Matilda – I saw the show when it was first on in the RSC's Christmas season, and it was fantastic because there was no hype.

What training did you do for your career?

For me formal training and 'training' training run parallel. While I was at Newcastle University, studying Fine Art, I was working as a follow-spot operator at the Theatre Royal. I also worked at the National Student Drama Festival. Initially, on the technical team, but I worked my way up to being a venue designer. So by the end of my degree, I was designing the spaces that all of the shows happened in and I was on the selection panel.

When I finished my degree, I did the year long Motley Theatre Design course which, sadly, doesn't exist anymore. We basically lived for a year in the back of the Theatre Royal Drury Lane. We weren't taught by anybody who wasn't a practising theatre maker. So when a director came in, it was a current director who was making work, and over the course of the year we completed six theoretical design projects.

So that's my training, as it goes. When I left Motley I just started working. And I was quite lucky because when I was at Motley I met Josie Rourke (the director) and we hit it off. A few years later she came and found me and asked me to do a show with her. So Motley became a real springboard for me straight into the industry. I didn't really assist so much – lots of designers assist and I never ended up doing that. I was more of a sort of making shows in fringe venues kind of early, early career designer.

Do you see *The Assassination of Katie Hopkins* as a key British musical?

I think it was a really important moment. I feel like there were a few things that did come together to make it feel like quite a unique show. The idea of using verbatim in musical theatre is obviously not a new one, but the idea of using it to explore such a contemporary hot, hot topic – a bit of a cliche way to put it perhaps.

For me it was, personally, an incredibly important show because we as a creative team, we'd been to Sweden and we had done our first musical, we had all worked together. So

James Grieve as the director, me as the designer and the lighting designer, we all went to Sweden and we made a new production of *Les Misérables*. It's a beautiful chocolate box theatre in the north of Sweden. And that was the first musical theatre we'd ever done. I've worked with James for years and years now, since my late twenties, so fifteen, eighteen years, something like that. And we'd never done a musical before, and I don't think we particularly wanted to. Then we got this opportunity to do *Les Misérables*. We created *Les Misérables* and we just absolutely got the bug as a team, and thought this is really interesting. And I think because until *Les Misérables* all we'd done was work on new plays – that was what I loved most was new plays and I was an associate at the Bush for many years and that was kind of the thing that always got me out of bed in the morning excited; new writing and working with writers directly. And then we made *Les Misérables*, and we went oh my goodness musicals are brilliant and we sort of fell in love with the genre. And then *Katie Hopkins* was an opportunity to bring those two things together. I think we suddenly went 'Oh, my goodness, we've been refining all of these skills, making new plays and now we get to do it with music!' And I think for us, it kind of exploded our idea of what we could be as artists and the work that we could make together as a team. So it was very, very important from that point of view, I would say for me, certainly.

How would you describe your contribution to *The Assassination of Katie Hopkins*?

I think that particularly on that project, because it was constrained in terms of time and money and we're making it in quite a scratchy way in a way – we hadn't got a massive budget, we were doing the best we could with the resources that we'd got. It was all very holistic. So there were very few boundaries between departments or disciplines. We were all working on it the whole time. I think because Chris and Matt were literally writing it during the rehearsal process. I mean, whole sections didn't exist and the script was changing weekly. So I think partly because of that as well. We were very much kind of in each other's lanes all the time and just constantly sort of looking at what each other was doing and trying to feed it round to make it into a circle.

So my husband David was the orchestrator and musical supervisor, so we worked on it together. The closeness of that relationship meant that, from the very beginning, my visual ideas were all about the sonic landscape of it and how it sounded. And I had this idea that it would be great if the set was completely reactive, so that the music and the words created the visual landscape. I was interested in the idea of the orchestration being run through Ableton (the music software) and then that Ableton itself would control the lighting. So we would give that system parameters and then when you said a word repetitively, for example, then the lighting would go with that and we would kind of be completely created by what they were saying and how they were saying it. And we got close to that. But it was this idea that you put something into the internet, and it gets looped and repeated, and repeated and it comes out a bit different at the other end. And so we wanted to do something sonically and visually that did the same thing that you fed in a word or even a sound and then it looped and looped and looped and created a colour and what might that look like, or feel like for the audience. So that was kind of where we ended up.

How would you describe the production process?

I think in some ways, it was quite a conventional process. I've worked for Theatr Clwyd before so I knew I had a good relationship with the building. The main thing was that the script was being written the whole way through, which obviously brought its own set of challenges. That's so common that there is a kind of mode you go into as a designer, the 'there is no script' mode. And so then it just becomes about enabling possibility, so that everything you design is going to support the piece of work as it exists, but nothing is going to get in the way of any other ideas or anything new that happens. So I think that *Katie Hopkins* is definitely a version of that. We knew we wanted the different levels. We knew we wanted it to feel like it was about the macro and the micro so that the individual phones became the micro and then having so many of them became the macro and became a nice metaphor for the population and the internet and all of those things. We knew we wanted it to be really, really simple. So in a weird way, the design process was quite conventional, I guess. And it was trying to work with the resources we'd got. Theatr Clwyd, because they have such an amazing community, found us twenty or thirty volunteers who came and helped make the phones. So that was really great, because otherwise there was no way we could have afforded to have done what we were trying to do. I think it was a really ambitious show on a tight resource. So the rehearsal process reflected that really because it was quite, it was quite busy.

How do you feel about *The Assassination of Katie Hopkins* now?

Do you know, it's an interesting one. If I was to be really honest, it was a really, really hard show. It was a really tough show to make, as often all the best things are. It was really, really challenging, but it was also incredibly enjoyable. We were all absolutely working together. I would be lying if I didn't say that at the time it wasn't really stressful and quite hard work. And we did have so much outside pressure. We were all getting messages on social media, we were getting threats, and that didn't help. It was fine but it doesn't help when you feel like you're under that kind of external pressure when you're making a piece of work. It did make me really alive to the idea of making musicals and actually since then I've hardly done anything else. For me, career wise, it was completely transformative.

How did the experience working on *The Assassination of Katie Hopkins* shape your future work?

For me personally, it absolutely turned a switch in my head, and since then I've mainly worked on new musicals. It's so funny for me because I was in my late thirties when I made *Katie Hopkins*, you wouldn't think there would be a change of option to you at that point. You sort of think 'I'm a designer, I love what I do, here I am'. Since then, the same team, we've gone on to do a few projects together. So we've just worked on a new musical; *Fisherman's Friends*, and that's been three or four years in development. We have also opened a new production of *Cabaret* in Gothenburg. And we're also about to do *Berlusconi the Musical* at the Southark Playhouse which is gonna be super fun.

What advice would you give to aspiring designers?

Make your own projects. You've got to create your own opportunities. If you wanna make a show, go and make a show. You can't just be a designer anymore. You've got to kind of do a bit of everything and you've got to prepare to really hustle to be able to make the work that you want to make. So I think that'd be my number one thing. Create your own parameters and then start your own stuff from scratch. Don't be afraid of that.

Conclusion

This book began as a riposte to the so-called lack of new, good, musical theatre writing in the UK. Anecdotally, we knew that there was a huge wealth of exciting and innovative work being made here, but the general consensus still put us lower on the ladder than, in particular, the United States. As Andy Barnes says, 'I'm pretty confident I would already have $1 million if I were given a buck for every time someone in our industry asked me where the "British Hamilton" is'.[1] Throughout the course of this edited collection, we have shown a snapshot of the diversity and skill of musical theatre storytelling that exists in the UK. In doing so, we've shone a light on just some of the shows that have made a mark since 2010. We are conscious that there are some shows you will likely have heard of, and others that perhaps you are being introduced to here. The discourse suggests that if a show hasn't had a long run, or won major awards, it isn't worth evaluating, and this book has hopefully proven that to be false. Each of the shows selected for this collection has something unique to bring to the musical theatre landscape and deserves to be acknowledged and explored, regardless of their financial or commercial success.

A high proportion of the shows examined in this collection have emerged from the many development organizations that have sprung up to support new musicals and their writers over the past decade or so. Initiatives such as *From Page to Stage*, *Signal*, *BML*, *MT Fest*, *BEAM* and *MT Darkroom* have all helped discover new works and provide opportunities for creatives. It feels that we have now begun to look further afield than the megamusicals of the 1980s and 1990s to find value in the smaller shows. What links all of these shows is that they didn't set out to become the next mammoth hit; none of them had any claims to be the British *Hamilton*. Their success seems to have taken everyone involved somewhat by surprise. Perhaps this is because the people making the show, from the writers to the producers, were simply focused on telling the story in the best way they could, rather than aiming for a commercial goal. Crucially, these shows, and their writers, were invested in, and given the chance to find their way in front of an audience. The many routes to musical theatre development in this country have resulted in a plethora of workshops of new shows – this is both exciting and frustrating. Exciting, because it demonstrates the sheer size of skill and interesting musical voices we have to offer. Frustrating, because a musical lives and dies on how it works in front of an audience and too many shows get lost in the land of development, having workshop after workshop without ever reaching a full production. Every single one of the shows discussed in this book not only made it to the stage but also made an impact on the cultural landscape when it got there.

Current landscape

Recently, we've seen a hybrid model emerge, with US writers working with UK production houses – *The Time Traveler's Wife* premiered at Storyhouse, Chester, with a score by British Joss Stone and Dave Stewart, but a book by American Lauren Gunderson (with additional lyrics by Kait Kerrigan). *The Book Thief* was produced at the Octagon Theatre, Bolton, directed by Lottie Wakeham but has an all-American writing team (Jodi Picoult for the book and Samsel & Anderson for the score). Despite all of the success in developing and nurturing new musical theatre voices in the UK, it could be seen as concerning that theatres and producers are looking across the pond to find the talent to create new musicals, rather than those much closer to home. Of course, this cultural exchange can provide dividends (as the excellent reviews of *The Book Thief* attest), but is it also hampering the development of writers in the UK? There is an argument to be made for this international cross-pollination of creatives, and recently Noisemaker have been commissioned by Goodspeed Musicals, Stiles and Drewe have presented *Becoming Nancy* at the Alliance Theatre, and *A Mother's Song* by Finn Anderson and Director Tania Azevedo was commissioned as part of an exchange between the RCS in Glasgow and American Musical Theatre Project at Northwestern in Chicago, so the traffic is not one-way. And there are British success stories closer to home as well. *Operation Mincemeat* has transferred to the West End, following two hugely successful runs on London's Fringe. Similarly, *The Great British Bake Off Musical* had a limited run in the West End after premiering in Cheltenham in 2022. What is striking about both of these shows is that they feel distinctly British. They tell British stories (whether that be a true one, as in *Mincemeat*, or a fabricated one based on a global phenomenon, as with *Bake Off*), and somehow feel as though they could only have been made here. And of course, there are the anomalies – *SIX* continues to be a juggernaut that sweeps across the globe, no doubt prompting producers everywhere to ask where the new *SIX* is. I wonder if in the United States they are asking when they will find the American *SIX*!

Where next?

We asked each of our interviewees what they believed was necessary for British musical theatre to thrive in the coming years, and there was one resounding answer: funding. The financial support for creatives to make new work and be allowed to fail. Choreographer Ellen Kane suggests that 'in order to encourage people to fail, the risk has to be low'[2], and the finances of a musical can be prohibitive to the learning and growth required for new writers. Most of our conversations acknowledged that, put simply, musicals cost more than other shows. This can be challenging to producers and commissioning theatres. As Richard Taylor notes, 'it costs so much to put on a musical. It costs more to commission a musical, if there's more than one writer involved. And it costs lots to put them on and audiences are squeezed of what they can spend their money on.'[3] Taylor's collaborator Rachel Wagstaff echoes this sentiment, highlighting the challenge of earning a living as a writer: 'every time I teach writing, I've always said "have another job". And that's not failure. And just keep writing and find a job that doesn't take up your creative energy'.[4] Musical theatre writers often aren't paid adequately, with West End productions being used as a collateral for writers to waive their royalties. As Dougal Irvine notes, 'that kind of thing should never happen, but it does all the time'.[5] It may be that the relationship between funding bodies and the commercial sector needs to be addressed, as noted by Andy Barnes and echoed by Josh Bird, so that the successful shows are able to provide financial support for the development of others. Noisemaker add that 'Americans just take it very seriously. It really, really matters as an art form'[6]. They go further to link the seriousness with which the form is approached as being 'because it is a commercial business. And that is even on a regional level. Smaller regional theatres could develop a show that could go to Broadway'[7].

One of the things that has emerged in recent years is the musical theatre collective. A number of companies who write and perform their own shows have arrived on the scene and had considerable success: Sheep Soup are associate artists at Leicester Curve, while Fat Rascal have toured extensively with their origin story of Ursula, the Sea Witch in *Unfortunate*. SpitLip have seen their madcap musical *Operation Mincemeat* grow from playing small fringe venues, with multiple sold-out runs, to running in the West End. These companies blend comedy and musical theatre and as such, their shows thus far have had a somewhat anarchic and chaotic playfulness to them. What they demonstrate, particularly *Operation Mincemeat*, is that the audience's appetite for new British works is there.

It's undeniable that the pandemic has had a seismic effect on the theatrical landscape in the UK. We are currently in a period of recovery with no certainty of when we will emerge completely, or what we will end up with when we get there. Despite this, there is hope. Audiences are slowly returning to live theatre. More and more new musicals are being produced each year. It's clear that there is an appetite, from producers, writers and audiences alike, for new British musical work. Indeed, there was an announcement from Birmingham Hippodrome that they were intending to become the 'UK's national theatre of new musicals'[8] by creating a department that is solely dedicated to developing and producing new shows. This is exciting news for all of us who write, and love, new musicals. But while we greet this with enthusiasm we also tread carefully. For there have been a number of schemes (as discussed previously) created to further the lot of British musical theatre – how will this be different? The major challenge for makers of musicals in this country is not development but production. It seems that this scheme, with its studio space readily available to try things out publicly, intends to take development a step further than previous attempts by ensuring shows reach the stage. I recently had a new musical of my own, *Mayflies* (2023), commissioned and produced by York Theatre Royal (YTR) for their main house (Figure 5). The show went from idea to stage in less than a year, an unheard-of pace in musical theatre. YTR were inexperienced in musical theatre and so produced the show like they might any other non-musical piece, hence the speed. Granted, *Mayflies* is a one-set, two-hander show so relatively simple in the grand scheme of things, but still, it was incredibly brave of them. In other hands, *Mayflies* might have been in workshop after workshop for years without being seen by a paying audience. I can assure you, sitting in the theatre with people who have paid good money for a ticket tells you more about the success (and failures) of a show than any workshop ever will. When discussing the new initiative at Birmingham Hippodrome, editor of *The Stage*, Alistair Smith, hopes that 'it does not become an endless hub for short development runs of new musicals – which has often been the downfall of similar schemes in the past'.[9] I share this hope. We don't want to see

Figure 5 *Mayflies*. Credit: Sam Taylor.

new work always relegated to the studio spaces either, but able to take on the main houses of our theatres. I'm optimistic. I hope, after reading this collection, that you are too.

Gus Gowland, July 2023

Notes

1. Andy Barnes, 'Six-Producer-Andy-Barnes-Where-Is-the-British-Hamilton-Let-Me-Tell-You', *The Stage*, 11 July 2019, sec. Opinion, https://www.thestage.co.uk/opinion/six-producer-andy-barnes-where-is-the-british-hamilton-let-me-tell-you.
2. Ellen Kane, interview with the authors, 26 July 2022.
3. Richard Taylor, interview with the authors, 6 October 2022.
4. Rachel Wagstaff, interview with the authors, 6 October 2022.
5. Dougal Irvine, interview with the authors, 22 July 2022.
6. Scott Gilmour, interview with the authors, 8 September 2022.
7. Scott Gilmour, interview with the authors, 8 September 2022.
8. Matthew Hemley, 'Exclusive: Birmingham Hippodrome Launches UK's Firstin-House Musicals Department', *The Stage*, 27 April 2023, sec. News, accessed 8 May 2023, https://www.the-stage.co.uk/news/exclusive-birmingham-hippodrome-launches-uks-first-in-house-musicals-department?Preview=1.
9. Alistair Smith, 'Can Hippodrome Help Musicals Hit a New High Note?', *The Stage*, 27 April 2023, sec. Opinion, https://www.thestage.co.uk/opinion/can-hippodrome-help-musicals-hit-a-new-high-note.

Index

#MeToo, see Me Too movement
#OscarsSoWhite, see Oscars So White movement
#StopAsianHate, see Stop Asian Hate

actors, see also casting
   actor musicians   123
   actors of colour   23, 147–50
   directors working as   137
   disabled actors   105, 159–63, 165
   gender identity of   7, 39–40
   in musical theatre   113, 174, 175
   non-actor   179
   non-binary   147–9
   nondisabled actors   107, 158, 161–3
   thoughts on musicals   93
   writers working as   14, 29
Adams, Craig (composer lyricist)   29, 53, 89, see also Lift (musical)
adaptation from novel
   depictions of in musicals   157–8
   from film   67, 70, 124
   from musical   125–7, 129, 133
   performer experience of   84
   process of   101, 124
Adele (singer-songwriter)   146, 147
Andrew Lloyd Webber Foundation, see Lloyd Webber, Andrew
Arts Council England   1, 5, 63, 88, 110, 116
Arts Theatre, see theatre, London
Asian American Performers Action Coalition (AAPAC)   145
Assassination of Katie Hopkins, The
   characters in   181
   faux-verbatim in   177, 179, 181, 185
   Katie Hopkins in   178, 180, 184
   plot of   180
   reactions to   183, 184
audiences
   as co-creators   116, 121
   of colour   7, 133
   contemporary   149
   digital (see audiences, virtual)
   disabled   94, 166
   discomfort of   21, 104, 161, 162, 180
   feedback   30, 31, 195
   global   2, 88
   identification   103, 114, 115, 133, 144, 180
   lessons for   33, 34
   live   90
   modern (see audiences, contemporary)
   new   xii, 20, 24, 90
   queer   125
   regional   5, 139
   virtual   88–90, 94, 155
Australia   17, 34, 35, 141
awards (theatrical)
   Critics' Circle Awards   70
   Edinburgh Fringe Awards   142, 157
   musicals winning awards   13, 142–3, 156, 195
   Olivier Awards   33, 50, 85, 143
   performances of musicals at   100
   Tony Awards (US theatre award)   3, 110
   UK Theatre Awards   180

Barlow, Gary (singer-songwriter)   15, 19
Barnes, Andy (producer)   30, 63–6, 143, 155, 195, 197
Barnes, Wendy (producer)   30, 63–6, 143, 155, 195, 197
BEAM (new musical showcase)   195
Beckham, David, see *Bend It Like Beckham: The Musical*
Bend It Like Beckham (film)   67, 69, 96
Bend It Like Beckham: The Musical
   choreography in   71, 73–4, 76–7
   David Beckham as referenced in   67, 68, 71, 72, 77
   discussion of racism in (see racism)
   opening sequence of   67
   parents in   67, 68, 76

Beyoncé (singer-songwriter) 144, 148, 182
Beyoncé feminism, *see* feminism
Billy Elliot (the musical)
    ballet in 71
    as beloved musical 99, 154
    comparing personal experiences to 49
    intergenerational tension in 71
    male identities in 56, 70
    production of 49, 51
Bird, Josh (composer and digital producer) 1, 154–6, 197
Birds of Paradise (Scottish theatre company) 8, 157
Black Lives Matter 13, 142, 145, 150
Blood Brothers (musical) 83, 99
Blythe, Alecky (playwright) 177
BML (book, music and lyrics, writing course) 195
body
    choreographed 73, 105, 111
    disabled (*see* disability)
    equity 145, 147
    politics 141, 143, 146, 149
    positivity 141
Boublil, Alain (lyricist) 1
Brexit 2, 20, 77, 180
Britain
    class antagonism in 20, 23
    class structure in 14, 17
    middle-class men in 22
    upper-class identities in 17
    working-class identities in 18, 56, 90, 91, 126
    working-class towns in 70–1
British
    boybands (*see* musical styles, Boyband)
    cultural memory 71
    culture 72
    holidaymakers 14, 23
    identity 2, 67, 77
    male identity 14
    media 125, 130
    pantomime 38, 39
    pop (*see* musical styles, pop)
    Prime Minister 87
    slang (*see* English language, slang)
    social history 14
    television 127
Broadway
    'British invasion' of 3
    casting practices on 145–7
    conventions of 75
    LGBTQ+ characters on xii, 55, 60

musicals (as a type) 1–4, 34
musicals about women 92
as neoliberal institution 33
West End transfers to 5, 156, 197
Broadway Cares 88
Burke, Tarana (activist) 144
Burt, Clare (actress) 87
Bush, Chris (playwright) 177, 183
Butterell, Jonathan (director) 138

Cambridge (town) 143
Carlson, Marvin 147
casting
    'authentic' casting 160, 162, 163, 167
    'colour blind' 145, 146, 149, 150
    colour conscious 141
    cross-gender 33, 38, 39
    'gender-blind' 146
    inclusive 131, 133, 141
Chadha, Gurinder (director) 67, 69, 73, 77, 84
Chandler, Clare 4, 181, 184
Christian Dior (fashion house), *see Flowers for Mrs Harris* (musical)
Christy Brown (artist) 158, 160
class
    structures, 146, 148 (*see also* Britain, class structure in)
    working-class identities 18, 56, 90, 91, 126
    working-class women 92–3
Connell, Raewyn 14, 17
Conservatives, the (UK political party) 20, 132
Cork, Adam (composer) 177
Covid-19
    impact on the arts 93, 94
    impact on theatre 139, 143, 144, 149, 185
    lockdowns during 88–9, 125, 144
    pandemic in Britain 20, 87–9
    UK disabled community's experience of 94, 110
Crucible Theatre, *see* theatre, UK regional, Sheffield Theatres

Dahl, Roald
    anti-Semitism 36
    author 33–5
    nostalgia 35
dance
    styles
        ballet 56, 71
        bhangra 68, 70, 72–4, 76–7
        contemporary 49, 52
        hip-hop 73, 74

dancers
    in musical theatre
        advice for 52
        stereotypes around 56
Darling, Peter (choreographer) 34, 49
Departure Lounge (musical)
    depictions of British holidaymakers in 14
    depictions of homophobia in 20–2
    feminist arguments in 18
    music in 19
    overviews of 7, 13, 15
    relationship to whiteness 23
    representations of masculinity in 14, 17, 20
    representations of women in 16
digital producer 154
director, *see* theatre director
disability
    artists 110, 157, 158
    community 116
    diegetic 159, 160, 163–7
    'disability simulation' concept of 110–11, 158, 160, 163
    discrimination 162, 164
    lived experience of 87, 94, 103, 115, 157, 165
    models of 107, 158
    as narrative prosthesis 109–10, 115, 158–9, 164
    politics of 92, 107, 110
    representation of 107–10, 114, 160–2, 165–7
    and sexuality 164–5, 167
disability drag, *see* disability, 'disability simulation' concept of
drag 40–1, 125–35
drama schools, *see* theatrical training
Drazek, Rachel (choreographer) 161
dream ballet 91
Drewe, Anthony (lyricist) 193
Durham, Christian (director) 31

Edinburgh Fringe Festival 141, 142, 154, 157
English language
    African American Vernacular English (AAVE) 148
    Multicultural London English (MLE) 23
    Newcastle accent 56
    slang 42, 148
equity 13, 142, 144, 145
Equity (acting union) 55
Evans, Daniel
    artistic director Sheffield Theatres 5, 137, 138
    director of *Flowers for Mrs Harris* 88, 90, 93, 101
Everybody's Talking About Jamie (film) 125, 126, 132–4
Everybody's Talking About Jamie (musical)
    choreography in 126
    discussion of 5, 7, 125–40, 155
    drag (*see* drag)
    Ray as Aunty 130–1, 133
    source material 125

fat, *see* body, politics
female characters, *see* women
feminism
    academics 54
    anti-feminist 16
    arguments 18
    attitudes towards 33
    'Beyoncé feminism' 8, 144, 150
    as capital 144
    contemporary 143
    empowerment 144
    feminist possibility 7, 90
    glitch feminism 56
    in musicals 40, 41, 42, 93, 142
    queer feminism 41
    undertones 36
    waves 16
Flowers for Mrs Harris (musical)
    Battersea (*see* London, Battersea)
    Christian Dior fashion house in 91–2
    Cinderella trope 92–3
    disability (*see* disability, lived experience)
    feminism in 93
    live streaming of (*see* theatre, live streaming)
    mothers' experiences of (*see* parents, mothers' experiences of musical theatre)
    women musicians (*see* musicians, women)
    women's experiences of Covid-19 (*see* Covid-19)
    working-class identities (*see* Britain, working-class identities in; class)
football
    English national team 67
    football hooliganism 23
    performance of 68, 70–1, 72, 74, 76, 77 (*see also Bend It Like Beckham: The Musical*)
    women's football 68
Foster, Nikolai (director) 52
fringe, *see* Edinburgh Fringe Festival

From Page To Stage (new musicals festival)   195
Full Monty, The (film), *see* Sheffield, representations of
Fun Home (musical)   xiii, 134

gender
   binaries   16, 22, 41, 55–9
   categories   39
   cisgender   14, 54, 60, 129, 131, 141, 147
   construction of   57
   definition of   53
   divergent   125
   expansive   7
   fluidity   53–6, 59
   ideologies   40
   in language   58–9
   misgendering   55
   non-binary
      definitions and vocabulary   53–4
      growing up as   58
      legal rights of non-binary people   125
      readings   7, 53, 57, 59–60
      representation of   53–6, 58–60
   performance   39
   politics   7, 21, 33–4, 59, 110
   politics of attractiveness   141–50
   queer   54, 56, 131
   relations   17
   representations of   23, 126–9, 132
   roles   39, 55
   scholars of   55
   stereotypes   31, 36, 70
   traditional expectations of   56, 71
   transgender   53, 55, 125, 131
   transphobia   23, 126
Gillespie Sells, Dan (composer)   125
Gilmour, Scott (lyricist)   2, 6
Global Musicals (company)   154
Goodall, Howard (composer)   67
Gowland, Gus (writer and composer)   89
Graeae, *see* Graeae Theatre Company
Graeae Theatre Company   110, 157
Graham, Vicky (producer)   101
Great British Bake-Off Musical, The (musical)   1, 196
Grinning Man, The (musical)
   disability in (*see* disability)
   'disability simulation' (*see* disability, 'disability simulation' concept of)
   fandom (*see* musicals, fans and fan communities)
   freak show representation   103, 111–16
   lived experience (*see* disability, lived experience)
   models of disability (*see* disability, models of)
   narrative prosthesis (*see* disability, narrative prosthesis)
   parents in   112
   representation of disability (*see* disability, representation of)
Guardian, The (British newspaper)   42, 94, 101, 183
Guys and Dolls (musical)   75, 140
Gyre and Gimble (puppetry company)   121

Hadestown (musical)   xiii, 110
Hairspray (musical)   xiii, 40
Hamilton (musical)   xiii, 101, 141, 145, 146, 195
Hammerstein, Oscar (lyricist)   32
Hart, Charles (lyricist)   67
Hastie, Rob (director)   5, 137–40
homophobia, *see* homosexuality, homophobia
homosociality   7, 14, 16, 19, 20
Hopkins, Katie (media personality)   178, 180, 182–4

immigration
   campaigns against   77
   family history of   23
   Islamophobia   23, 130
   Pathan Muslims   23
   policies   69
Irvine, Dougal (musical writer)
   commentary on theatre practices   5, 197
   composition   18, 23
   depictions of masculinity   13–14, 16–17, 24
   depictions of women characters   16
   interview with   29–32
   maturity as a writer   24
   writing *Departure Lounge*   7, 20–1, 29–30

Jamie Drag Queen at 16 (documentary), *see* Everybody's Talking About Jamie (musical)
Japanese Bunraku puppetry   106
Jerry Springer the Musical (musical)   174

Kane, Ellen (choreographer)   3, 49–52, 196
Kelly, Dennis (playwright)   34, 178, 181, 184
Knapp, Raymond   107, 110

Leicester (city)   23, 24
Lenson, Adam (director)   xiv, 178
Les Misérables (musical)   5, 75, 191

LGBTQ+
  acceptance 20
  community 54, 55, 131
  identities 53–5, 57–60
  protest 132
  queer kinship 126
  representation 53, 127
Lift (musical)
  Ballet Dancer as character in 7, 53–60
  French Teacher as character in 7, 53–60
  gender discussion of (*see* gender)
  sexuality discussion of (*see* sexuality)
  temporality (*see* temporality)
Light in the Piazza, The (musical) 107, 110
Lipson, Katie (producer) xiv
live streaming, *see* theatre, live streaming
Lloyd Webber, Andrew (composer) xiii, 3, 5, 145, 156
London
  Battersea 91
  Hounslow 70
  Southall 70
  West End (*see* West End (London))
London Road, (musical) 121, 172, 177, 179, 181–2, 184–5
Lovelock, James 55, 126
Lundskaer-Nielsen, Miranda 1

McKenzie, Claire (composer) 6, 157
Mackintosh, Cameron (producer) xiii, 5
MacRae, Tom (playwright) 125, 134
male gaze 144
Marlais, Kate (composer) xi–xii
Marlow, Toby (composer) 141–3, 150
masculinity
  hegemonic 14, 16–23
  hypermasculinity (in women) 37, 39–41
  inclusive masculinity 22
  lad culture 13, 14, 17
  toxic masculinity 14, 16, 17
  white English masculinity 14
Matilda the Musical (musical)
  choreography in 50
  feminism (*see* feminism, in musicals)
  gender politics 33
  Matilda as character in 36–8, 41–3
  Miss Honey as character in 37, 41–2
  Miss Trunchbull as character in 37, 39–42
  Mrs Phelps as character in 38
  Mrs Wormwood as character in 38
  Mr Wormwood as character in 38, 40–1
  original novel 34–6
  parents in 34, 37, 38

queer feminism (*see* feminism, queer feminism)
rehearsal process 51
Mayeda Berges, Paul (writer) 67
Mayflies (musical) 197
Memoirs of an Asian Football Casual (play) 14, 23–4
Menken, Alan (composer) 156
mental health 92, 155
Mercury Musical Developments xiv, 1
  Minchin, Tim (composer lyricist) xiv, 34, 35, 38, 41, 42
Me Too movement 13, 23, 141, 144, 150
Miranda, Lin-Manuel (musical writer) 19, 89, 145
Miss Saigon (musical) 14, 63, 83, 140
Mold (town in Wales) 2, 180
Morris, Tom (director) 103, 121
Moss, Lucy (musical writer) 141–3, 150
MT Darkroom (new musicals scheme) 195
MT Fest (new musicals festival) 195
musical instruments
  double bass 94
  french horn 93
  guitar 14, 19, 30, 32
  piano 30, 75
musicals
  albums 31, 64, 66, 89, 93, 140
  British contrasted with Broadway xii, 1–6
  definition of xi
  development of xiv, 1–6, 64, 84, 122–3, 192
  fans and fan communities 89, 100–4, 122–3, 134, 142–9, 155
  'I wish' songs in 22, 164
  jukebox 173
  in public discourse xiii–xiv
  sports musicals 68
musical styles
  boybands 19
  British Bhangra 73
  'Britpop' 31
  classical Indian 83
  grime 73
  hip-hop xiv, 148, 149
  Indian 83
  polyphony 148
  pop 14, 18, 19
  pop-rock 141
  Punjabi music 73, 74, 83
  Reggae 73
  rock 19
  soul 73

Musical Theatre Network (organisation)   1
Music Director (MD)   172
musicians
   actor-musicians (see actor, actor musicians)
   composers   xiv, 100, 121, 156
   women   93–4
My Left/Right Foot the Musical (musical)
   amateur dramatics   159–60
   choreography in   159, 161–2, 164, 166
   disability in (see disability)

Newcastle   56, 190
New York Times, The (American newspaper)   1, 33, 142
New Zealand   34, 141, 143
Nicki Minaj   146, 148
Noisemaker (musical theatre writing partnership)   157, 172–6, 196, 197

Oklahoma! (musical)   19, 75, 110
Oliver! (musical)   154
Olivier Awards, see awards
Operation Mincemeat (musical)   1, 196, 197
Osborne, Lucy (designer)   3, 178, 190–3
Oscars So White movement   145
Our Ladies of Perpetual Succour (musical)   173

Pacifist's Guide to the War on Cancer, A (musical)   179
parents   24, 34, 37–8, 67
   mother-daughter relationship   70, 71, 74–6
   mothers' experience of musical theatre   87, 93
Pascoe, C. J. (American sociologist)   20, 22
Pasek, Benj (composer lyricist)   34
patriarchy   17–19, 59, 144
Paul, Justin (composer lyricist)   34
Pearse, Susannah (musical writer)   xiii
Perfect Pitch (musical theatre company)   30
Phantom of the Opera, The (musical)   13, 104, 107, 112
Pieces of String (musical)   89
politics
   disability (see disability, politics)
   gender   7, 33
   millennial   141, 143
   populist   173
   progressive   141

popular culture   127, 138, 141, 145, 147
producer
   collaboration   63–6, 100, 137, 175, 195
   commercial success   5, 142–3
   musical development   xiv, 6, 101, 122, 154–5, 196
   responsibility   157, 197

queer, see LGTBQ+

racism
   anti-Black racism   132, 148
   coding   141, 145, 146, 148, 149
   colourism   141, 145, 147, 148
   in contemporary society   23
   depiction in films   69
   depiction in musicals   69, 71, 128
   political organizations   24
Rahman, A. R. (composer)   84
Really Useful Group (RUG)   88
religion
   Hindu   129
   Muslim   23, 24, 128–30
   Sikh   70, 72, 76
Rihanna (singer-songwriter)   148
Rourke, Josie (director)   137, 190
Royal Shakespeare Company (RSC)   5, 34
Russell, Legacy   55, 56

Schönberg, Claude-Michel (composer)   1
Sedgwick, Eve   14, 16, 19
sexuality
   heteronormative
     beyond   131
     characters who resist the   55
     dramaturgy   57, 60
     family   34, 39
     narrative   19
     productivity   53
     society   55, 129, 141
     structure   53
     time   53, 54, 57
   heterosexual
     masculinity   14
     men   22, 132
     patriarchy (see patriarchy)
     presence   131
     relationships   19–20
     romance   54, 75
   homosexuality   7, 14, 21–3
     homophobia   20–3, 128
   lesbian   41, 53, 54, 59, 74
Sheep Soup (musical theatre company)   197